TWENTIETH CENTURY VIEWS

The aim of this series is to present the best
in contemporary critical opinion on major
authors, providing a twentieth century perspective on their changing status in an era
of profound revaluation.

Maynard Mack, *Series Editor*
Yale University

CERVANTES

CERVANTES

A COLLECTION OF CRITICAL ESSAYS

Series antny (20 views

Edited by
Lowry Nelson, Jr.

Prentice-Hall, Inc. A SPECTRUM BOOK *Englewood Cliffs, N. J.*

Current printing (last number):
10 9 8 7 6 5 4 3 2 1

PRENTICE-HALL INTERNATIONAL, INC. (*London*)
PRENTICE-HALL OF AUSTRALIA, PTY. LTD. (*Sydney*)
PRENTICE-HALL OF CANADA, LTD. (*Toronto*)
PRENTICE-HALL OF INDIA PRIVATE LTD. (*New Delhi*)
PRENTICE-HALL OF JAPAN, INC. (*Tokyo*)

Contents

CERVANTES

Introduction

by Lowry Nelson, Jr.

The number of readers of Cervantes may actually have been diminished by the quirks of his reputation. In those myriad couplings of the names of the great so dear to celebrants and surveyors of literature, Cervantes appears ritually linked to Homer, Dante, Shakespeare, and Goethe: his is the *Spanish* niche in an official literary hall of fame. Then, too, many people with a literary bent have read him (that is, the first part of *Don Quijote*) only in childhood and remain quite content ever after to draw upon their recollections of windmills and inns, fat peasants and village slatterns. This is not to say that such recollections are not valid evidence of an authentic literary experience, but they do run the risk of fragmenting or trivializing or obstructing a mature reading of the work. Both ceremonial lip service and immature recollection tend to blunt the otherwise astonishing impact of the work itself.

For some who in the past have read Cervantes in English translation the effect may also have been a betrayal. The earliest and most famous English translation, Thomas Shelton's, published in 1612 (part one) and 1620 (part two), manages to make do in the narrative but ruins the dialogue with a shallow heartiness and gusty exuberance foreign to Cervantes. Defenders of that archaic translation argue that it is contemporaneous with the original. But the fact remains that English style has greatly changed since that time while Spanish style has remained remarkably stable. To the ordinary English-speaking reader Shelton's version is archaic; to the ordinary Spanish-speaking reader Cervantes' text is idiomatically quite modern. Fortunately, the recent translations of Samuel Putnam, Walter Starkie, and J. M. Cohen, the last in particular, honor both accuracy and idiom. A contemporary reader without Spanish has now worthy versions of *Don Quijote* in English.

Outside of Spain readers are likely to escape a further source of obfuscation: distorting absorption with the life of Cervantes as somehow containing the explanation of his work. Like Shake-spearians of the last generation, Spanish Cervanists are especially likely to be caught up in this, building large edifices out of insubstantial speculation. It is, however, true that many more documents and hard facts concerning Cervantes' life survive than concerning Shakespeare's. Besides, Cervantes, in his several prefaces and his *Journey to Parnassus,* wrote directly about himself, expressing in his ingratiating way the modest circumstances and intentions of his literary efforts. Simply because of the difference between narrative and dramatic discourse we hear the personal voice of Cervantes, however stylized, whereas we can only arbitrarily imagine that of Shakespeare unless we wish to found our notions of it on the stilted and ceremonial dedications he offered to his two long poems, *Venus and Adonis* and *The Rape of Lucrece.* One thing that Cervantes and Shakespeare do have in common, apart perhaps from dying on the same calendar day, April 23, 1616, is that nothing in the surviving facts of their earlier lives could lead us to conjecture or predict their works of genius. Yet in practical terms, the contrast between their lives is stark. Shakespeare encompassed a successful career as playwright, actor, and manager, and retired at the age of forty-eight to spend his last three or four years in retirement in his own native town. Cervantes veered from military vagabondage to itinerant bureaucratic meniality, while persistently failing at the popular literary genres of the time, only to end up in sordid family circumstances as the author, at the ages of fifty-eight and sixty-eight, of the first and second parts of his great novel. Parallels as well as contrasts can be made (both, for instance turned to romance at the end of their careers); still, there is reason to beware of assigning portentous significance to the biographical facts that capriciously come down to us. We do, blessedly, have the works themselves which seem to us far better, and differently better, than they seemed to their creators.

Among those not professionally concerned with Spanish literature, it is a rare reader who explores the lesser works of Cervantes. Many of them are hardly worthy of their author; indeed, if Cervantes had died in his early fifties before writing the first part of *Don Quijote* only extensive histories of Spanish literature would mention him. His early occasional verse and his pastoral novel *Galatea* are the work of an accomplished tyro, hardly above average among the many mediocrely gifted competitors of the time. The market was so glutted with specimens of both genres that it is no wonder Cervantes failed to win public recognition or patronage. His dogged attempts at making a name in the theater, though more commendable, were unlucky in their old-fashioned and awkward verse and also in the brilliantly facile competition they received from Lope de Vega. Only in the *Interludes,* following the well-established Spanish tradition of the short comedy, did Cervantes gain an artistic if not a contemporary success. One could go on cataloguing a succession of failures. It would indeed be difficult to think of a great writer as persistently and barrenly unsuccessful as Cervantes. By way of attenuation it might be said that his strange tragedy *La Numancia* and his episodic comedy *Pedro de Urdemalas* show some degree of power and deftness.

Nothing, however, prepares us for the sudden revelation of the first part of *Don Quijote* (1605): it appeared and prose fiction was transformed. It was the most Spanish thing Cervantes, a quintessential Spaniard, could have done. The suddenness, the seeming finality and yet the infinite consequences of its publication recall the astonishing and unpredictable appearance of *La Celestina* (1499), *Lazarillo de Tormes* (1554), and *El Burlador de Sevilla* (1630). Each of those works created an imperfect though deeply original *type* in modern literature: in the first, the first fully rounded realistic character (Celestina herself); in the second, the first picaroon in the sense, later modified, of a resourceful rogue in a consistently cruel world unredeemed by any notion of social justice; in the third, the first sudden creation of a Don Juan figure from two purely Iberian ballad traditions. For all the greatness of Spanish literature, even its fondest favorers must grant that for the most part it has to be appreciated within the language and the tradition. So often it happens that the splendidly original idea is imperfectly embodied: one may well be dismayed at the learned baggage and stilted bathos occasional in *La Celestina,* at the inconclusive narrative sequence of *Lazarillo,* and at the dramatic crudities of *El Burlador de Sevilla.* While Cervantes' novel also has its imperfections, much more than the other three works it realizes its originality in consistently sustained art. For reasons that will never be entirely explicable, Cervantes managed to create the central formula of the modern realistic novel in terms of a vast range of style accommodating illusion and reality, aspiration and actuality, the dogmatic and the problematical. Chronologically, one must look ahead for so complex a synthesis to the great nineteenth-century novelists, though partial exception might be made for Mme. de La Fayette's *Princesse de Clèves* (1674) and Fielding's *Tom Jones* (1749).

What that formula is in *Don Quijote* cannot be stated without great risk of either oversimplifying or overcomplicating it. Cervantes' immediate readership seems mainly to have perceived crude farce in the situation of the deluded hidalgo brutally treated by crass reality in the company of an earthy fool; while in utter contrast latter-day commentators, such as José Ortega y Gasset and Miguel de Unamuno, have in their several ways taken the novel as a point of departure for their own deep pronouncements on the mysteries of existence. There are, of course, obvious elements of farce: highfalutin names, palpable delusion, mistaken identities, slapstick disasters. But instead of being finally and ignominiously ejected by normal society the protagonist, Don Quijote, creates for himself a whole way of life so consistent and resilient that normal society finds itself variously involved in conforming to its terms, now knowingly indulgent and affectionate, now partisan and even converted. Mysteries also abound in the quixotic cosmos, whose teasing implications tempt the commentator to profundities beyond his depth or, just as often, beyond the scope of the novel. Most of human knowledge could be monstrously subsumed in footnotes and commentary to, say, the plays of Sophocles, the *Divine Comedy,* or *Don Quijote:* universal issues are raised and the deep thinker is lured into their limitless domain. Not that this domain lies outside the province of great art. Yet we are controlled at the same time by the claims of an art that is selective and integral: our grasp of existential implications requires the discipline of a constant surrender and return to the particular shaping of the fictional narrative. The formula of *Don Quijote* may be abstracted as an attar and diluted in still potent solutions, but the very particularity in the elaboration of the original preserves its uniqueness, indeed its quintessence.

In crudest terms, the formula may be expressed as the pairing of a tall thin idealist with a short fat realist and setting them off on a series of hazards. In previous fiction pairs of characters had almost always been young friends or lovers, at least normal, but most often exemplary: Daphnis and Chloe, Cupid and Psyche, Abindarráez and Jarifa, Euphues and Lucio. This new, however simple, arrangement, together with the motif of bad literature influencing life, constitutes a primal and influential glory for Cervantes.

But to take things in proper order, the motif of bad literature determining life comes, of course, first. Cervantes claims actually to have set out to discredit and destroy the novels of chivalry, whose latter-day proliferation had in fact declined both in numbers and in quality since the archetypal *Amadís de Gaula* ("Amadís of

Wales," 1508). Throughout the sixteenth century, however, their vogue had been enormous, claiming for a time the passionate interest of St. Teresa and St. Ignatius, sailing contraband in cargoes to the New World, and providing the existent world, out of their fanciful geographic nomenclature, with an actual California and an actual Patagonia. That Cervantes' original intent seems to become more discriminating or tolerant in the course of a few chapters can be judged from the book burning episode (I, 6). Here the priest and the barber undertake to pronounce sentence on the novels of chivalry in Don Quijote's library, judging them one by one and handing the culpable ones over to the "secular arm" of the housekeeper to be burned. In such a way they hope to strike at the root cause of Don Quijote's mania by destroying his peccant books. Yet their inquisition even at the beginning leads them to conclude that *Amadís de Gaula* should be spared, since, the barber argues, "as it is unequalled in its accomplishment so it ought to be pardoned." Not only novels of chivalry but also pastoral novels come under sentence. The priest inclines to spare them, whereupon the niece exclaims:

> Oh, sir, your worship should order them burned like the rest. For once my uncle is cured of his disease of chivalry, he might very likely read these books and take it into his head to turn shepherd and roam about the woods and meadows, singing and playing and, even worse, turn poet, for that disease is incurable and catching, so they say.

Her foresight is confirmed toward the end of the novel (II, 73) when Don Quijote, in his last mad fantasy, hopes to become the shepherd Quijotiz. Even Cervantes' own pastoral novel *Galatea* barely escapes burning. "His book has something good and ingenious about it," says the barber. "It sets forth something and concludes nothing. We must wait for the second part he promises; perhaps with amendment he will win the full clemency we now deny him. In the meantime, until we see, keep him as a recluse in your room." When their attention turns to vernacular epic (still another mode for Don Quijote's madness?) they begin to become involved in a favorable discussion that is suddenly broken off by Don Quijote's shouts from upstairs. The line between good and bad literature remains ironically provisional and the author has implicated himself.

With open perspectives, like reality itself, Cervantes, in his fiction, allows his reader to surmise the possibility of another novel playing with the pastoral and still another with the epic. To return to the immediate and fruitful example of "bad" literature, short of reading the nearly half million words of *Amadís* or *Tirant lo Blanch,* we

may gain a fair notion of what the novels of chivalry were about by
noting Don Quijote's own version of what befalls a knight errant
(I, 21). This is an account, beginning in the future tense, of what
must authentically take place in the case of such a knight (he becomes, oddly, a *particular* knight); then, as narrative passion and
certainty seize hold of Don Quijote, the account shifts to the vivid
present, as if the line between fiction and reality had been crossed.
For Sancho it *has* been crossed. At the vast vision of a successful
and noble future, he surrenders altogether to his fantasy. In his
narrative Don Quijote describes his knight's adventures and the
qualifications for his renown. When the knight reaches court he is
discovered to be the son of a king; he marries the daughter of the
king he serves; and, at the king's death, he becomes king himself.
As Don Quijote succinctly puts it, "the father dies, the princess in-
herits, the knight in a word becomes king." Immediately following
he continues: "Here then comes the granting of favors to his squire
and to all those who helped him to rise to so high an estate:
he marries his squire to one of this princess's ladies, no doubt
the one privy to his love, the daughter of a most eminent duke."
With the mention of the squire's deserts Sancho chimes in: "That's
just what I ask, a fair field and no favor . . . That's just what I
expect, for things are bound to turn out for you exactly so, since
you are the Knight of the Sad Countenance." Don Quijote tells him
to have no fear. Yet he will have to look the part and trim his beard.
So Sancho must have a barber. "Leave this matter of the barber to
me," says Sancho, "and let your job be to try and become king and
make me a count." "So it shall be," replies Don Quijote and with
that he raises his eyes and sees the next "real" adventure approaching in the form of the galley slaves. In this episode, then, we not
only learn what a novel of chivalry is like, but also at the same time
we see it work its fascination upon Sancho Panza and find its
correspondence in the "reality" of a new adventure.

Sancho, in his simplicity and shrewdness, completes Cervantes'
narrative formula. That Don Quijote had gone out on his first sally
alone may well have constituted a journey of discovery for Cervantes. All by himself Don Quijote, in a long series of misadven-
tures, could easily have become either tiresomely dense or hopelessly
pathetic. His humanity and dignity and even wisdom in the midst
of his real madness depend for their effect upon the intimacy between him and Sancho. Indeed, in the course of the whole novel we
witness in both that sort of gradual, subtle, and complex transformation of character—perhaps for the first time in Western fiction—

which Salvador de Madariaga has conveniently called the quixotification of Sancho and the sanchification of Quixote. Both elements, then, of what we have called the formula, undergo a continuous modification that eventually constitutes transformation. In previous fiction most characters simply elaborate their pre-established essence or experience some sort of conversion. It is true that Don Quijote's relatively sudden and artistically necessary return to sanity may at a distance from the text seem equally a conversion. But both he and Sancho have already gone through a gradual process of formation and transformation. In narrative there is nothing like this before, with the great exception of Chaucer's *Troilus and Criseyde* and, among works contemporary with Cervantes, Shakespeare's plays.

The success of Don Quijote depends greatly on Cervantes' range and ease of style. His syntax is that of a vivid narrator whose colloquial freedom has been disciplined by a fine though unpedantic regard for neatness and accuracy. His normal diction is free of affectation, willful archaism, and superfluity. The several levels of discourse are skillfully modulated. Most of the time, for instance, Don Quijote speaks in the urbane manner of an unaffected but cultivated gentleman. When the noble occasion arises, however, he addresses his adversary or his beloved in the formulaic and archaizing language of the novels of chivalry, for which there is no direct analogy in English. As for Sancho, his language is more like the authentic speech of a true Vermonter or Irishman than that of the crudely and condescendingly presented provincial stereotypes of fiction: our amusement is sustained by novelty and inventiveness rather than by smug or contemptuous superiority. Most crucial in the success of the narrative is, so to say, the narrator's tone of voice. It might be described, negatively, as the absence of aggressive heartiness, crude mockery, and knowing manipulation of puppet characters. Not that such means are not proper and effective in the right hands and in the right context. Cervantes' tone is, however, much more delicately muted, compassionately and sparingly ironic, susceptible to innumerable modulations. The absurdities of Don Quijote's caprices and escapades are granted a certain plausibility in a narration which allows an easy transition to the aftermath of rueful resignation, rationalization, or mere embarrassment. Some sense of superiority and manipulation in the narrative is evident in the device of purportedly translating from the Arabic manuscript of Cide Hamete Benengeli; yet that general procedure, borrowed from the novels of chivalry themselves, serves fictional purposes of authentication and distancing, while simultaneously eliciting appreciation of the earnestness and good will of the "translator." When Don Quijote and Sancho Panza confront Avellaneda's false *Quijote* (II, 59), Cervantes, sublimely consistent, has his fictional characters recoil before the falsity of that imposture and claim the authenticity of their *true* fictionality—all within the fictional world of the novel and without the crudity of sly digs or savage improprieties. It is a triumph of art using "false" fiction to enhance "real" fiction. It is comparable to the play within the play in *Hamlet*.

Regarding the structure of *Don Quijote,* many readers seem to have assumed that the novel proceeds merely by a sequence of exemplifications of the formula, interrupted by intercalated stories which mostly have little to do with the "plot" and, in the case of "Improper Curiosity," practically nothing. At the very least, however, and by the roughest simplification, we may claim that the main narrative proceeds by incremental repetition, that in each episode some new possibility or actuality is revealed and added to our knowledge of the characters in Cervantes' fiction world. To cite some instances: after the adventure of the windmills, Don Quijote insists to a doubting Sancho that the enchanter Fristón has changed the giants he saw at first into windmills to deprive him of glory; after the adventure of the fulling mill Don Quijote, angered by Sancho's mocking laughter, sets about attacking him, but then in contrition, though with bad grace, acknowledges his error; after the adventure of the barber's basin which Don Quijote mistakes for the helmet of Mambrino, he and Sancho reach a linguistic compromise in calling it a "basin-helmet" (*baciyelmo*). Perhaps the richest modulation of this simpler sort is the adjustment they make with each other's convictions in the matter of what Don Quijote saw in his descent into the Cave of Montesinos and what blindfolded Sancho thought he saw, many chapters later, in the ascent of Clavileño. Don Quijote whispers in his ear, "Sancho, since you want me to believe what you saw in the sky, I want you to believe me in what I saw in the Cave of Montesinos. I say no more." Beyond incremental repetition, the novel proceeds by complex echoes and juxtapositions, by a gradual process of deepening revelation, by an intricate elaboration of a fictional world. Even the intercalated stories, which have bothered some modern readers, can be argued to have organic relevance to the narrative structure and technique. They are not only a repertory of types of stories traditional at the time—adventure, Moorish, pastoral, exemplary—they are all concerned with the complexities and practicalities of the direct pursuit of love. Whether the love they present is unreciprocated, thwarted, or fulfilled, they artistically complement the self-willed ideal love of Don Quijote for Dulcinea and, one may even add, the unself-conscious crude love of Sancho for his wife. Not that Cervantes was wholly successful in integrating these stories. One may suspect that he was partly placating a current, somewhat antiquated, taste for the episodic and variegated. In any case, it is fair to say that in the process of inventing the modern novel he made skillful use of everything he had inherited in the narrative tradition. *Don Quijote* as a work of literary art is, in fact, supremely self-aware: it is the first modern novel, and it is about, among other things, the writing of the first modern novel. Its self-awareness is most evident in the elaboration of its structure— in the vital process of choosing, enhancing, and transcending, while preserving consistency and creating wholeness. That Don Quijote at the end recovers his wits before dying has disturbed many readers who, like Sancho, would have him sally forth again; but endings as well as beginnings and middles are necessary to artistic wholeness. Besides, endings may be transformations: Don Quijote becomes again Don Alonso Quijano the Good, as he was before the beginning.

Transformation is, in one way or other, a condition of fiction in relation to reality: a shape is somehow reshaped and yet still recognizable. Even within a particular fiction there is a fictional "reality" which can be mistaken, evaded, transcended, or faced. Since *Don Quijote* deals with multiple levels and kinds of appearance and reality, it inevitably and rightly induces speculation on the ideal and the real, illusion and disillusion, within the fiction itself. At the same time it has encouraged commentators, notably Ortega and Unamuno in their different ways, to use its particular fiction as a source of reflection on the real world, sometimes at the risk of violating its fictional integrity. Indeed, so many ideological problems and paradoxical profundities have been elicited from the pages of *Don Quijote* that an innocent peruser of some of them might even succumb to a quixotic madness. Not that problems and profundities do not exist or that they are not suggested by the novel: the point is that, within the novel, they are modulated and proportioned in their fictional context.

Another point where discrimination is called for in dealing with the vast suggestiveness of *Don Quijote* has to do with the degree and quality of its reflection of the historical times in which it was written. Must there be a kind of sectarian ideological allegiance in the novel? Must it be determined by crypto-humanism or the Counter-Reformation or the endless rise of the bourgeoisie? Many a writer of Cervantes' time can be ideologically typed without gross inaccuracy. But Cervantes, along with Shakespeare, resists simplified "explanation," however indefatigable the "explainers." What is remarkable in the work of both men is the relative absence of overt doctrinal insistence one way or the other, except in tolerance and humanity: Protestants are not vilified in Cervantes nor are Catholics in Shakespeare; some sort of common Christian humanism pervades their work to the confusion of those who would condemn *Don Quijote* as heretical in "doctrine" and Shakespeare's plays as doctrinaire in religion.

As depictors of the human condition both Shakespeare and Cervantes belong to the select company of those I would call universal ironists as distinct from tendentious ironists. Universal ironists contemplate the world with a kind of gentle resignation and compassion in full knowledge of both the grandeurs and miseries of human life: among them I would number Chaucer, Chekhov, Kafka, and Svevo. Tendentious ironists view the world from a programmatic stance connoting accusation, bitter protest, and meliorist reformation of human ills: among them I would include Flaubert, Ibsen, Hardy, and Mann. The distinction is only approximate but nonetheless significant. Neither attitude is qualitatively superior or justifiable, though it is perhaps the universal ironist who can view mankind with greater tolerance and understanding; it is he who can encompass a broader span of human types and human experiences; it is he who can best present the inviolability and unique essence of the particular and the individual. It is precisely this ability in Shakespeare and Cervantes to create particularized essence that leads us, their readers, to draw the general conclusion, to see the individual as representative. Hence the seeming plentitude of humanity we find in such odd and peculiar figures as Don Quijote and Sancho Panza, not to mention Sansón Carrasco, the Curate, Marcela, Ginés de Pasamonte, and others.

Elsewhere in his work Cervantes hardly ever achieved so three-dimensional a fusion. At the beginning and at the end of his literary career, in *La Galatea* (1585) and in *Los Trabajos de Persiles y Sigismunda* ("The Travails of Persiles and Sigismunda," 1617), he seems disastrously to have hobbled himself in the mechanical and outmoded conventions of a pastoral novel and a Heliodoran novel of episodic adventure. His powers as narrator remain evident: the reader finds himself skillfully inducted into the artificial world of those genres and at first disarmed by the fluent description of exotic landscapes and the busy business of seemingly significant action.

But soon, despite the seductive style and the frantic attempts at speed and variety of incident, he realizes that he is being shunted about to no great purpose. The flowers of rhetoric turn out to be imitation and the frenetic fictional characters turn out to be gaudy puppets.

Yet the lover of *Don Quijote* need not wholly despair of finding elsewhere in Cervantes inventive and congenial fictional worlds. Fortunately we inherit the *Exemplary Novels* (1612), among which three or four stand out as truly exemplary, in a purely creative sense, of the early art of the realistic short story. Here we encounter not types but individuals in settings that are fashioned from the grit of recognizable experience in the everyday world and conveyed to us with terse irony and particularity. In any gallery of Cervantine characters we would include the two young adventurers of *Rinconete and Cortadillo* and the one-legged Fagin appropriately called Monipodio; the ill-starred Tomás Rodaja, the graduate who thought he was made of glass; old Felipe Carrizales, the jealous and sadly tricked Extremaduran; and Cipión and Berganza, the two voluble canine interlocutors whose noctural deliberations are over-heard and recorded in the form of a prose mock eclogue by the Ensign in another "containing" novel, *The Deceitful Marriage*. Most of the other characters in the *Exemplary Novels* are familiar types from the stock of storytelling of Cervantes' day: their creator is content to provide them with a happy issue and often a newly found wellborn identity. But in those three or four "novels" we find Cervantes at his near best, an innovator and exemplar in writing the best short fiction of an age or more.

As author of one of the great masterpieces of fiction Cervantes has been an elemental force in determining the nature of the modern novel. His reputation and influence are therefore of the highest importance in the history of fiction. Yet the true depth of his influence is to be gauged not so much in critical mention and interpretation as in the imitation and adaptation of his fictional discoveries. A census of the vast number of translations would be indicative, as would a chronicle of direct imitations beginning with the infamous Avellaneda. But it would be more to the artistic point to plot the trajectory of great fiction indebted to Cervantes from, let us say, Henry Fielding's *Tom Jones* to Stendhal's *The Red and the Black*, Gustave Flaubert's *Madame Bovary*, Herman Melville's *Moby-Dick*, and Mark Twain's *Huckleberry Finn*, to mention only a few notable instances. Of less aesthetic interest, though of considerable cultural moment, would be to trace the shaping and reshaping of the image of Don Quijote himself across the centuries. Such a chronicle would begin with a rather crude conception of a comically mad laughingstock, who becomes for Romantics such as Byron, Ludwig Tieck, and Jean Paul a mournful sufferer and scapegoat, an inwardly heroic Knight of the Sad Countenance. Later in the nineteenth century, Cervantes' novel received the ministrations of textual critics and philologists. These, while keeping bright the letter, went far toward encumbering and embalming the text with misplaced notes and irrelevant references, thus compounding the tendency to see the novel either as a children's story or simply as a scholar's example of seventeenth-century Spanish prose. A more recent aberration of "criticism" has been the use of *Don Quijote* as a textual ground for expansive speculation on large philosophical and existential issues not necessarily unrelated to Cervantes' text though certainly uncontrolled by it. Only in our own time has a body of true literary criticism begun slowly to accumulate. We should be grateful for it as represented in this sampling of essays. If criticism of *Don Quijote* in the past seems rather thin, scattered, and unimpressive, we may still find some excellence and profundity in twentieth-century views.

Cervantes

by Gerald Brenan

A curious thing about Spanish literature is that it travels badly. Whatever the reason may be, few Spanish books have gained general currency beyond their language frontiers. The one exception to this is Cervantes, who has been translated into more than fifty different languages and into English alone some eight or nine times. So well known is his great book in this country that I shall take a certain familiarity for granted and confine myself to aspects that seem less obvious than others. Otherwise I should merely be repeating what other writers with far greater authority than myself have already said.

Let us begin by seeing what sort of a man Miguel de Cervantes was. Born in 1547 near Madrid, the son of an apothecary surgeon with seven children, he had an early introduction to poverty with its harsh routine of pawnshop, money-lender and prison. In spite of this, however, he was able to obtain a fair education—first, it is thought, at Seville and then at the city school of Madrid. Here his master was one of the last of the old humanists and followers of Erasmus; we hear of the young man, just twenty-one, writing a poem which this master singled out for praise and have reason for thinking that his influence was an important one.

A desire to see the world now took him to Italy. At Naples he joined a Spanish regiment as a private soldier and fought in the great sea battle of Lepanto, where he lost the use of his left hand. Other engagements followed. Then, on his way back to Spain with letters recommending his promotion, he was captured by the Moors and taken to Algiers. Here he spent five years as a slave. When at length he was ransomed, his daring in planning escapes and in taking the blame for them when they failed had given him the sort of reputation reserved in our day for the heroes of the Resistance.

Back in Spain at the age of thirty-three, he suffered the common experience of soldiers in peace time: his war services had been forgotten and no one was interested in his Moorish exploits. He decided to take up literature. With his usual energy he began at once to write a pastoral novel, a number of comedies for the Madrid stage and a quantity of verses. Let us consider these for a moment. Cervantes thought of literature as most great writers have done at the commencement of their careers—as something that expresses ideal states and desires rather than experiences. Moreover, this was the general opinion of that time in literary circles: the current was running strongly against realism. Writing a pastoral novel was the obvious and natural thing for a young man to do, especially if he was in love, and though we cannot read *La Galatea* today, we can see that he learned some of the balance and mellowness of his later style from it. His poetry is another matter. To the end of his life Cervantes wished more than anything else in the world to be recognized as a poet. He never was, and his steady output of fluent verses did little to help his literary reputation.

There was then the drama. This belonged to a category that had less prestige, because it was popular. But Cervantes had been deeply interested in it since he had watched the primitive performances of Lope de Rueda as a boy. Here again, however, "literature" interfered. The Spanish drama was a new art waiting to be born: it needed a man who should combine a quick responsiveness to popular taste with a romantic imagination and some faculty for poetry to set it on its proper course. But Cervantes brought only a little Senecan rhetoric and a novelist's tempo: if his comedies held the stage, that was merely because, until Lope de Vega came along a few years later, there was nothing better to choose from.[1] The real trouble, however, about all these literary ventures was that they brought in no money. The reign of Philip II was a reign in which writers starved. Cervantes therefore gave up authorship towards 1585 and took a job at Seville, first as a commissary for requisitioning corn and oil for the Government and then as a tax collector. This move was the easier because his private life had just taken a new turn: a love affair which had given him an illegitimate daughter had been succeeded by a marriage to a girl of nineteen, who

[1] Cervantes' *Entremeses,* or interludes, continuing the tradition of Lope de Rueda's *pasos,* are, however, brilliant. He wrote them late in life, after 1600.

owned a house and a few acres of land not far from Madrid. But the marriage proved to be a failure and after a few months the couple separated. To all intents and purposes Cervantes, who seems to have had little power of pleasing women, was once more a bachelor.

The next twenty years find him leading a roving, harassed, impecunious life, mostly in Andalusia. Here, on long mule-back journeys, on the benches of crowded posadas, haggling over prices, he wore out the best years of his middle age. There were frequent money difficulties, for he was not paid regularly: there were law suits, for he was rash and unbusinesslike, and above all there was the terrible question of a deficit, in which, owing to a bank failure and to the fecklessness he may have inherited from a Micawberish father, he lost a large sum of Government money that had been entrusted to him. This led to a period of acute poverty and to at least one spell of imprisonment. One may judge his social position from the fact that, though his headquarters during most of this time was Seville, he seems never to have known any of the distinguished group of writers and poets who lived there. Yet he never gave up. Elderly, shabby, obscure, disreputable, pursued by debts, with only a noisy tenement room to work in, he was still, in whatever spare time he could find, carrying on his unescapable vocation of literature. We owe *Don Quixote*, as we owe Joyce's *Ulysses*, to its author's having been a man of quite extraordinary persistence and optimism.

For Cervantes had never entirely stopped writing. The things he found it easiest to do were verse plays, and all through the nineties he was turning out *comedias* for the theatre at Seville. But Lope de Vega's new technique was making his pieces look stilted and old-fashioned. With more leisure now that he had lost his job, he took up again the art of novel writing and began to compose those short stories which he published later under the title of *Exemplary Novels*. They were of different sorts, some being romances in the Italian style, other pictures of criminal life at Seville, others again sketches of extraordinary events or characters, taken from actual life. One of the subjects that most interested him was madness. This was a taste of the time: the liking for calm and ideal scenes and generalized characters was giving place to a craving for the bizarre and extraordinary. The idea came to him—actually he seems to have taken it from an *entremés*, or one-act play—to write a short story about an amusing madman who imagined himself to be a knight-errant, carrying on the feats recorded in the novels of

Chivalry. The date is thought to have been 1597, when Cervantes was fifty: the place, as he half-tells us himself, a prison—either that of Argamasilla de Alba or of Seville—and the title *Don Quixote de la Mancha*. Its first part, for it grew into a long book, came out in 1605.

Never, perhaps, before or since has a writer had such an extraordinary stroke of luck. The vein Cervantes had hit on was not only a wonderfully rich and productive one, leading to unexpected depths and possibilities, but it was one which he himself was peculiarly fitted to explore. So from the first chapter, with its plain and balanced portrait of the hero, we get a feeling of assurance: in the second, with Don Quixote's arrival at the inn and mistaking it for a castle and coming out with one of his magniloquent speeches, we begin to have some idea of the delicious consequences that could be drawn from his madness. But Cervantes had not yet hit on the device that would enable him to realize the full possibilities of his theme. The knight alone was not a sufficiently strong thread on which to string the incidents. It took a few chapters for him to discover this: then, bringing his hero home, he sent him out again with Sancho Panza. After that there are no more hesitations: master and man by their wonderful powers of conversation are sufficient to sustain the interest. It is this duality of heroes that turns what would otherwise be a short entertaining story into a long and very great book.

Don Quixote was conceived in prison at a low-water mark in Cervantes' life and he tells us that in writing it he "gave play to his melancholy and disgruntled feelings." Something more then than a skit on the novels of Chivalry must have been intended. I think therefore, that we ought to take note of the fact that the famous knight had many features in common with his creator. We learn, for example, that Don Quixote was of the same age as Cervantes when he set out on his adventures and that he had the same physical appearance: we read of his wits being dry and sterile and his head turned by too much reading, just as we are told in the preface that his author's were. Moreover, he was the incorrigible optimist and idealist who set out to reform the world by force of arms and instead was beaten by it. Must not this, or something like it, have been Cervantes' view of his own history? It is true that these similarities are accompanied by even greater dissimilarities. But if the writer was in some sense "putting himself" into his hero, that is precisely what we should expect. When novelists seek to create characters who will represent the deepest things in themselves, they start by delineating something very different. It is by wearing masks that one obtains freedom of self-expression. I suggest, therefore, that one of the sources of Don Quixote's power to move us comes from his being a projection of a discarded part of Cervantes himself: that is to say, of the noble intentions and failure of his life. It is for this reason that the irony in this most ironical of books has often the deep and searching quality of self-irony. It accounts too for that curious animosity against his hero which, as Sr. Madariaga has pointed out, often seems to harden Cervantes' pen. When he thought of the harm his generous illusions had done him, he felt bitterly and took it out on the figure who represented them. But he was not the kind of man to remain embittered for long: his temperament was too buoyant, besides which the zest of such triumphant creation naturally made him well disposed to the most successful of his characters. The result is an ambivalence of attitude that runs through the book and adds to its complexity. Among other things it helps to determine what sort of life Don Quixote is to be allowed at each moment—whether the daemonic vitality of the puppet (that sure sign of his projection from great depths) or the wise and mature reflections that come direct from Cervantes' experience and reading. That is to say, in so far as Cervantes intended the figure of Don Quixote to stand for anything, it was quite simply for the man who ruins himself and others by his romantic and generous illusions and by his over-confidence in the goodness of human nature. If this conception is somewhat deepened in the second part, we must at least be careful not to read into the text as some people have done, a political or social allegory on the Spain of Philip II.

But let us look at the book itself and forget the writer. We see then the knight and his squire wandering across Spain in search of adventures, the road they take picked out for them by the whim of Rocinante, the only horse in literature to have a character. As they go they talk—never was there book so full of discussion and argument—yet their conversation does not, as in most novels, appear to further the progress of the plot, but is concentrated round the great fantastical theme of knight-errantry. We watch the fluctuations of Don Quixote's far from robust faith, the wonderful crop of rationalizations by which he defends and preserves it, the effects of all this on Sancho, the constantly shifting relations of the pair to one another, and last, the gradual weakening of the knight's belief in himself, with his death when it fails and returns him to the empty state of sanity. This rake's progress of the believing man, passing from the wealth of total conviction to the bankruptcy of ut-

ter scepticism, with its deep pathos and sadness, has been so well
brought out and analysed in Sr. Madariaga's brilliant study that I
shall not attempt to recapitulate it.[2] But *Don Quixote* is a complex
and even a baffling book, presenting many different facets. Let us
therefore try and approach it from some other angles.

We spoke just now of the felicity of the general theme. One of its
merits is the way in which, in every incident that comes along, it
stimulates the reader's interest. It does this by providing a series of
fixed contrasts that set up between them a tension. For example,
there is the contrast between the actual situation and what it appears to be to Don Quixote: there is that between his noble and
exalted way of feeling and Sancho's peasant shrewdness and self-
interest: and, if one likes, that between the knight's wise and sane
ratiocinations and his violent fantasies whenever the subject of
Chivalry enters his head. Every situation that turns up brings at
least two of these into play and the reader is kept in suspense until
he knows precisely how it will be decided. By this means the weakness inherent in the picaresque form—a chain of events loosely
strung together—is overcome and the greatest concentration brought
to bear on each incident. Note too—a stylistic contrast—that this
madness of the principal character has a language of its own: the
archaic magniloquence of the books of Chivalry provides a sort of
upper floor of pomp and imagery standing above the ordinary idiom
of the book. This was a great discovery, made possible by the
example of Ariosto in *Orlando Furioso*. For one feels not only the
delicious irony of the knight-errantly speeches, but also the beauty
of a stately feudal language rising out of the plain and habitable
level of Cervantes' prose.

The point about which everything in the book revolves is of
course Don Quixote's madness. Among other things it raises—and
not simply in the obvious way—the question of the nature of Truth.
At first we may say to ourselves that there is no real problem here:
the Knight of the Doleful Countenance is mad, and that's that. But
presently it dawns on us that his madness is confined to one thing—
the belief, not itself irrational by the standards of that age, that the
books of Chivalry were true histories. Once this is granted, it was
no more mad for him to attempt to revive the profession of knight-
errantry than it was for a monk to imitate the Fathers of the desert.
Now the innkeeper, who was perfectly sane, also believed in the
truth of the books of Chivalry, though since the things described

---

[2] *Don Quixote: An Introductory Essay in Psychology*, by Salvador de Madariaga
(1934).

in them had never fallen within his experience, he drew the (purely empirical) deduction that they had ceased to take place. What caused the two men to disagree was not therefore any greater degree of rationality on one side than on the other, but simply a difference of propensity or inclination. Don Quixote had a strong desire to play a noble and heroic part in life—to right wrongs and assist the unfortunate and by so doing become famous—whereas the inn-keeper was content to take the world as he found it so long as he could go on cheating it. The knight's madness is thus the direct consequence of his nobility of character whilst the innkeeper's sanity is due to his being commonplace.

We can explain Sancho's mixture of belief and disbelief in pre-cisely the same way. When he is in the believing mood, it is because he is under the double influence of Don Quixote's superior rhetoric and of his own greed and ambition; and when he is sceptical it is because he lacks his master's sense of a high vocation as well as his years of browsing among the books of Chivalry. For once one grants the historical character of those books, the feats of enchanters in changing the appearance of things in order to thwart knights-errant become just as credible as those of the devils and witches in which, in theory at least, everyone believed. It is thus inexact to speak of Don Quixote as lacking in shrewdness or being gullible by nature. His delusion is the result of a long secretly sustained wish to rise above the dullness of his monotonous life, have adventures and distinguish himself. But Cervantes, in presenting to us his episte-mological riddle, has gone further. For not only has he made his knight nobler and, for all his craving for renown, more distinter-ested than any of the persons who are shown to us as sane, but he has made him more intelligent. A good example of this will be found in those delicious passages where Don Quixote pours out a flood of subtle and convincing arguments to support a view that anyone can see is erroneous. His mind works more lucidly when it has a worse case to defend. If we stop to think a moment, we may well wonder where the author is taking us.

As we have said, the making of the novel lies in its having two contrasted heroes or principal characters—Don Quixote and Sancho. The best parts, those passages one reads again and again with never failing delight, are the conversations between them. One represents altruism, the other self-interest: one wisdom and learning, the other the practical intelligence: one is mad and the other is sane. And yet—this is an example of the subtle quality of Cervantes' observa-tion—as the book progresses, they are constantly affecting and even invading one another. The simple contrast between them with which it started breaks down and we get what Sr. Madariaga has called the sanchification of Don Quixote and the quixotification of Sancho. This leads to moments in which they almost appear to have changed places.

Such, it might be said, are the ordinary effects of living together. But the spell, the ideology, that binds them is important too. Whether one thinks of them as two partners of a firm dealing in futures, or as two members of a sect who must gather the rewards of their faith in this world (glory pure and simple for the one, wealth and power for the other) they march forward side by side, talking and arguing all the time, with their eyes fixed on the distance. This at least is the position in the second part, where Sancho's self-importance swells out till at moments he feels himself the equal, or superior even, of his master. It is then that one comes across those touches of mutual jealousy and rivalry—Don Quixote showing peevishness when Sancho is given his island, Sancho discovering for the first time the Quixotic pleasures of fame and glory—that make this book such a continually unfolding revelation of human nature. Once more one sees what treasures of subtlety and irony a theme based on simple contrasts can throw into the lap of a discerning novelist.

But perhaps the relationship between the pair may best after all be compared to that most intimate of partnerships, marriage. The long dialogue between them that takes up the principal part of the book suggests, in a more ceremonious key, the familiar dialogue of married couples. It is made up of the same inconclusive wranglings, the same recriminations and *tu quoques*, the same fixed recollections and examples dragged out again and again from the past to clinch an argument. Thus the fact that Sancho was tossed in a blanket early in their travels and that his master failed to rescue him and, to conceal his impotence, put the whole thing down to the work of enchanters, is brought up by the squire every time the question of enchantments is raised in the course of the book. It is one of the two rocks upon which his unbelief, when he is in the unbelieving mood, is founded. Just as in married life, every disagreement leads back to some classic precedent or "You said so-and-so."

And this has the effect of lacing together in an extraordinary way the various incidents. One of the most admirable things about this novel, which at first sight seems to be composed of a number of separate episodes, strung together like beads on a thread, is that few things in it are really finished with when they have occurred. On the contrary, they are taken up into the minds of the two protagonists and reappear later on as a part of their argument. This not only gives the plot a greater unity, but it makes it more subtle. Every striking event has, as it were, a succession of echoes and it is these echoes that make the book what it is. It would be hard to find a novel in which the psychological repercussions of happenings had a greater importance.

We have suggested that the relations of the knight to his squire have some resemblance to those of a married couple. And this comparison has perhaps more to it than might appear at first sight. In their peripatetic ménage, Don Quixote plays the part of the unmitigated male and Sancho that of the semi-dependent female. Hence the long story of Sancho's fidelities and infidelities, which is one of the most revealing things in the book. How true to life, too, it is that, as the spiritual potency of the male declines, the female should rise and spread herself and dominate! Through almost the whole of the second part it is Sancho who is the leading figure, and in the last chapters we see him, in spite of his touching devotion to his master, getting ready for a prosperous widowhood. The knight dies as all men die, when—sane, empty, deflated—he has fulfilled his role of impregnator. In this capacity one might say that Sancho symbolizes the passive and feminine world, which requires heroes and men of ideas to fertilize it.

But to return to the text—for the temptation to allegorical interpretation must be resisted—let us note how all the interest is deliberately concentrated upon these two. The outer world, in the form of innkeepers, muleteers, duchesses, distressed damsels and so forth, is brought in only to provide incentives, to put them through their paces.[3] In itself it is of no consequence: what alone matters is the performance of the preposterous couple and the discussion on the nature of reality and on the means of apprehending it that their mishaps invariably give rise to. It is not of course a purely philosophic discussion: rather it is a marvellous display of human prej-

[3] Cervantes tells us that he often found the boredom of keeping the light focused on his two heroes intolerable. For this reason he introduced pastoral episodes, where they took a back seat. But his readers objected to this. In the second part, therefore, he allowed the plot gradually to lose all pretence of naturalness and to become a machine for producing situations that would extract every drop of humorous reaction from the pair. If this injures the unity of tone of the book, as the practical joking of the Duke and Duchess certainly does, it gives us in exchange a rich and complex development of the two principal characters such as the more cumbersome plot evolution of the naturalistic novel can rarely furnish.

udices, delusions, doubts, sagacity, stupidity, self-deception, shrewdness, arranged by a master of ironic perception to delight us by its
contradictions and incompatibilities. We watch the give and take
with all the amused superiority and detachment of people who see
through the disputants' motives and know the real answers. And
then, with a shock of surprise, we realize that, even though these
particular answers may be known to us, we are looking on at a
puppet show in which the puppets represent ourselves and that it
is our own faith and doubt and certainty and ignorance that are
being shown to us.

That is why we can speak of the profundity of this book: the
gracia[4] of some particular remark by Don Quixote or Sancho sets
up a pulse of delight that goes echoing through our minds and
drawing out our thoughts towards their frontiers. We scarcely need
to ask how far the author intended this. It is in the nature of poets
to say more than they know and Cervantes was carried by the current of the theme he had discovered far out of his depth. How
could he have supposed that, in revealing the psychological mecha-
nism of one particular faith, it was necessarily faith in general and
even the possibility of knowledge that he was questioning? His
book is one that will be reinterpreted by every age because it is
continually suggesting very much more than it says.

And yet we cannot escape from this question of intention so
easily. Here we have a writer, who in all his other works seems so
limited in imagination, producing effects of a subtlety that make
most other novelists appear crude. The natural properties of the
theme are not in themselves enough to account for it: only an artist
of abnormal fineness of perception could have made use of its
powers of suggestion as he has done. But this seems to demand an
illustration. I will take the adventure of Montesinos' Cave, which
is one of the high-water marks of the book.

Montesinos is a knight who figures in a number of Spanish
ballads that deal with the Carolingian legends. The most famous
of these shows him following the blood-stained trail of his friend
and cousin, the paladin Durandarte, as he flees from the field of
Roncesvalles. After crossing the greater part of France at the gallop,
he comes up with him near Paris. The paladin is lying mortally
wounded *debajo una verde haya,* under a green beech tree, and
with his last breath adjures him to cut out his heart with his dagger
and to carry it to his lady Belerma, whom he had served for seven

---

[4] [Opportune or unexpectedly just wittiness—ED.]

years without success. Montesinos does this, Belerma weeps tears of pure blood and faints—*vencida de un gran desmayo*.

The absurdity of the story and its great popularity had some time before tempted Góngora to write a parody of it. A cave by the ruined castle of Rocafrida in La Mancha was known as Montesinos' Cave. What could be more natural than that Cervantes should lead his hero to the place? And so in chapter xxii of the second part he does. The knight arrives, accompanied by Sancho and another person, and after an invocation of exquisite absurdity to Dulcinea (it suggests a parody of one to the Virgin) is lowered on a rope down the shaft and at the end of half an hour is pulled up again unconscious. His companions revive him, he sits up and asks for food. As soon as he has eaten he describes his experiences.

These really amount—as we can see, but he could not—to his having had an extraordinary dream. On reaching the bottom of the cave, so he tells us, he swooned and then, opening his eyes, found himself a green meadow, at the end of which stood a castle whose walls seemed to be made of transparent crystal. As he looked at it, its gates opened and out of them came a venerable old man, clad in a long mulberry gown with a white beard that fell below his waist and—an absurd touch—a rosary whose every tenth bead was as large as a "middle-sized ostrich egg." Greeting Don Quixote by name, he told him that he and those who dwelt in these enchanted solitudes had long been awaiting his arrival, for it was to his invincible heart and prodigious spirit that the task of delivering them had been reserved. And he informed him that he was Montesinos.

A conversation followed in which Don Quixote questioned him about the events described in the ballad and Montesinos replied, correcting the text in one instance: in removing his cousin's heart from his body, he said, he had used a fine poignard and not a dagger. They then entered the palace and in a hall paved with alabaster came to a magnificent tomb. On the top of it lay the figure of a man made, not of bronze or marble, but of flesh and bone. "This," declared Montesinos, "is my friend Durandarte, flower and mirror of all the valiant knights and lovers of his day and kept here by the enchanter Merlin." And he went on to relate once more the scene of his death, giving, as guides do, certain prosaic details, such as that his heart weighed at least two pounds. On this a surprising thing occurred: Durandarte in a loud voice, as if mechanically repeating a part, began to recite the actual words attributed to him by the ballad. On which his cousin knelt down and with streaming eyes assured him that his commands had been carried out, that his heart, carefully salted to preserve it, had been carried to his lady Belerma and that they all with their squires and attendants were waiting to be released from their enchantment. "And now," he continued, "I have news to tell you, for here you see that doughty Knight, Don Quixote de la Mancha, of whom so many things have been foretold, who has revived with greater glory than ever the forgotten order of knights-errant and by whose strength and valour it may well be that we shall be delivered from our enchantment." To which Durandarte in a hollow voice replied, "And even if this were not so, O Cousin, even if this were not so, patience, I say, and shuffle the cards." And turning over, he relapsed into his former silence.

We are now shown in charade the last scene mentioned in the ballads—the procession of Belerma and her maidens, bearing Durandarte's heart and singing dirges. Their dress is strange and antiquated, for they wear black robes and white turbans, and Don Quixote with his matter-of-fact eye notes that Belerma is not the great beauty he had expected, but that she has a yellow colouring and lines under her eyes. Reading his thoughts, Montesinos explains that this is due, not, as might be supposed, to her monthly periods —for it is many years since she last had them—but to her great grief. Otherwise one would see that even Dulcinea del Toboso scarcely equalled her in beauty.

After the tension caused by this *gaffe* has subsided—for Don Quixote was committed by his vows to maintaining in single combat that his lady excelled all other women in beauty—another dream charade begins. Dulcinea and her two maidens, dressed as common village girls, appear leaping and capering through the meadow like goats. This is a recollection of an incident that had occurred a few days previously, when Don Quixote and his squire had visited Toboso. Sancho, to conceal a previous deception of his, had pointed out three ugly village girls whom they had met riding on donkeys as being Dulcinea and her maidens, and had described their princess-like beauty and apparel. When the knight had protested that he saw only village girls, Sancho had assured him that that must be because he had been put under an enchantment. Rather unwillingly Don Quixote had accepted this explanation. It is for this reason that they appear in his dream in this form. They caper past, and Dulcinea turns her back rudely when he speaks to her. But now a very odd thing happens. No sooner have they gone than one of the maidens returns and approaches him. On behalf of her mistress she asks for a small loan—six *reals,* as security for which she offers a dimity petticoat. Don Quixote gives her all he has—four: the girl, instead of a curtsey, leaps six feet in the air and goes off. On this Montesinos offers some plausible reasons for their enchantment and the knight's account of his dream ends. During the three days and nights he has spent underground, he has seen and learned, he says, an infinite number of marvels, but he postpones their description to another occasion.

Let us now look at this adventure of the Cave a little more closely. At first sight it may seem to be just one more mock-heroic episode in the style of Ariosto. A chapter from a Grail-legend story, which, without losing all its poetic strangeness and beauty, has been brought down to earth and made ridiculous by a number of small touches. But how is it that these touches are given us by, of all people, Don Quixote? One explanation is that we have here the author's satirical humour breaking out through the mouth of his hero and making him parody himself. But this surely is to neglect Cervantes' perfectly clear statement that he was giving us Don Quixote's vision or dream. And in fact a dream atmosphere of wonderful verisimilitude envelops the whole chapter and gives to these absurd touches—which, if they were intrusions of the author's wit, would surely strike a false note—their peculiarly subtle flavour. Since this is, as we already know, a psychological novel, we must expect this dream to throw some new light upon Don Quixote's character. Let us see if it does so.

The magic castle, the enchanted Montesinos and his speech of welcome require no special interpretation: they are part of the knight's romantic fantasy and of his boundless self-esteem, and therefore already familiar to us. But note the realistic touches: the correction over the dagger, the weight of the heart, the speculation upon the yellowness of Belerma's skin, and so forth. These affect us not merely by their sudden reduction of high romance to the crudest reality: their comedy is finer than that, for it consists in their being indications of a fundamental dryness and prosaicness in the mind of this man who has set himself up against the prosaic scheme of things. It is a quality we have noted in him before, but which in the freer atmosphere of the dream takes on a greater latitude.

There is then that disconcerting remark of the recumbent Durandarte. Not only does he express doubt about the ability of Don Quixote to release him from his enchantment, but he puts his doubt into a popular proverb "Patience and shuffle the cards," which startles us by its cynical inappropriateness. We are reminded of some of the remarks of the Red Queen in *Alice in Wonderland*.[5]

The incident of Dulcinea's maid asking for the loan of a few shillings is another example of the same enigmatic inconsequence. There is of course an insinuation under it. Many of the fair ladies of Madrid and Seville must have been in the habit of treating elderly gallants in just this way—only of course the "loans" they asked for would have been considerably larger. But the incident has been caught up and absorbed into the dream, so that the insinuation is felt to be, not a satirical stroke of the author's, but a subversive whisper that has come from some small voice in Don Quixote himself. A whisper reminding the dreamer that, if any Dulcinea is ready to listen to his advances, it will be because she is mercenary.

We get then, through the device of a dream, an oblique yet penetrating glimpse into the deeper layer of Don Quixote's mind. We see that his knight-errantly fantasy, even in its moment of triumph, when freed by sleep from all the trammels of reality, has not achieved the conquest of every portion of his mind. There is a dry matter-of-factness that contrasts oddly with it and which one guesses may originally have led him, by its very dullness, to take this escape. And there is also the voice of common sense and reason, living on like a fifth column within him, disguised and in hiding, yet ready to seize every suitable opportunity for sabotage. One does not need to have read modern books of psychology to recognize the symptoms as they show themselves in the dream language, or the delicate exactness with which Cervantes has recorded their appearance.

There remains the question, how could a Spanish writer of the seventeenth century have such an understanding of the secret processes of the mind? The answer is, no doubt, that the instinct of a writer of genius may lead him a long way if he is prepared to trust himself to it freely. But a certain social climate is required if he is to be given the encouragement to do this. I believe that this climate existed in the peculiar kind of wit or humour for which Seville, and indeed most of Andalusia, is famous, and which is known as *gracia*. It is the humour of an imaginative people given over to the charms of social life in an easy climate, with the spectator's attitude to what goes on round them and little sense of responsibility. De-

[5] Durandarte had reasons that were not known to Cervantes for taking a cynical view of knight-errantry. He owed his own existence to a misunderstanding about Durendal, the name given in the French *Chansons de geste* to Roland's sword, which some Spanish jongleur had taken to be a person.

cription being impossible, I will only say that one of its features
s a disinterested delight in the absurd (English and French humour
.ave generally some moral implications), and another, an oriental
ove of double meanings, of suggestion rather than statement, of
mbiguity and subtlety used for their own sake. And all expressed
n that tone of slyness and ironic reserve known as *discreción*. It
vas on this humour, if I am right, that Cervantes drew what drafts
ie needed for his many-storied novel, just as Shakespeare drew many
lements in his style from the witty jargon of courtiers, so that what
o our minds seem far-reaching innuendoes, full of metaphysical or
)sychological import, were often in their original intention mere
iumorous contrasts and whimsicalities, intended for immediate
lelight yet all the more agreeable to their readers because they
:ontained unexplored possibilities of interpretation. To an author
vho chose his theme well, this Andalusian *gracia* gave an unusual
)pportunity for working his conscious and unconscious faculties in
iarness, and on, as it were, two levels. Not in vain, we may say, had
Cervantes spent so many years beside what an earlier poet had called
as aguas del rio sotil Sevillano, "the waters of the subtle Sevillian
iver."

We have seen that *Don Quixote* grew out of Cervantes' long and
painful experiences of frustration and failure. It thus deals with one
)f the classic themes of Spanish literature—disillusion. Spaniards,
who commonly set their hopes too high and expect a miracle to
fulfil them, often come to feel themselves deceived by life. Cervantes
had also started off in a very optimistic frame of mind, but it had
become too much a part of his nature to be given up. It will be
remembered that we spoke of his having been educated by a school-
master who had Erasmist leanings. Now there is very much in his
novel that calls up the humanistic spirit of Charles V's reign. There
is the Renaissance notion of the perfection of Nature and of the
supremacy of Reason: there is the optimistic attitude to life and
the commonsense morality, without a trace of mysticism. Most significant of all is the absence of any sign of belief in original sin.
This dogma, which expressed in theological terms the sense that
there is a sort of inertia limiting the growth of reason and virtue
in human beings, had lain dormant through the Middle Ages to
burst up with terrifying force among the Lutherans and Calvinists.
From them it had spread to Spain, carried in a modified form by
the Jesuits. But in Cervantes we do not come across any trace of it.
He remained what one might call a natural Liberal, living on in
an age when the last spark of the Liberal spirit was dead. It is for

this reason that he seems to have been regarded by his contemporaries as a man of old-fashioned views, half pedant and half, as we should say, Victorian, writing in a smooth, balanced style that had dated. And that, of course, is precisely one of the reasons why he is alive to us. We only partly understand the Southern Baroque writers, though we find them exciting. They lived in a tight, guilt-ridden world, turned in on itself and alternating between a superficial hedonism and a profound pessimism. Although in some respects it was like our own, it differed by having a certain stifling feeling in its air that was the result of the steady decrease of intellectual liberty. But Erasmus joins hands across a gulf with the eighteenth and nineteenth centuries. It is the background of his reasonableness and moderation that makes Cervantes a universal writer, as Calderón and Quevedo for all their genius could never be. Indeed it was in the countries north of the Pyrenees that his greatness was first recognized at a time when south of them his novel was still regarded as light literature.

One qualification: *Don Quixote,* as we have seen, came into the world like Montaigne's *Essays,* on the last wave of humanistic feeling and values. Yet it has seventeenth-century features. The hero himself belongs to the violent dream-world of Baroque hagiography. He is first cousin to the ecstatic saints of Zurbarán or Ribera, though painted without chiaroscuro and in comic guise. He is martyred under our eyes and by our laughter. The whole tendency of the book too, with its epistemological queries and its psychological subtleties, proclaims a more complex age than that of the Renaissance. We should remember this in speaking of Cervantes' dependence on the past.

Cervantes' powers of comic invention are bound up with his skill in using language to convey fine shades of feeling. One example of this is the tone of his narrative passages. He is the first prose-writer, I think, to understand that, in telling a story, one must gain the attention and confidence of the reader by one's manner. How he does this is more easily felt than described. But open *Don Quixote* almost anywhere and one will see how by the mere intonation, as it were, of his sentences he conveys a deliberation and assurance, a sense of being completely at ease with his audience that one does not find in earlier writers. Sometimes this is carried too far for modern taste, which does not like any trace of showmanship in its literary entertainers. But generally speaking the zest and enjoyment of the man, and his assumption that you are going to enjoy yourself too, give one an appetite to go on reading him. Then he is a master—and what a great one!—of the art of dialogue. It was only to be expected that he should have done this well, because one of the particular pleasures to be derived from his book comes from the continual victories we witness of words over facts. Some new situation arises which we know that Don Quixote must interpret in accordance with his peculiar fantasy, and we wait to see how he will do it. Then, no sooner has his interpretation been given than the inevitable insurmountable objection is made by Sancho or some other person, and at once the question is how he will get round it. That he always does so, and far better than one could have hoped, and in quite unsuspected ways, is due not only to his ingenuity in argument, supported by the wide range of his mind and reading, but to his remarkable rhetorical powers. The knight, who loses every time he takes to the sword, wins a battle whenever he opens his mouth. But the battle won by Cervantes is greater still, because he must not only take care of his hero's dialectic, but also convey to us, the principal observers, something more, something finer about the unconscious motives of the actors. We are made to be deliciously "in on" every episode.

Another thing to be particularly noted in Cervantes' style is the confident way in which he places his characters before us and makes them talk or perform some action, so that we really see them all the time and believe in them. There are no extraordinary flashes, no sudden revealing phrases, such as the Baroque writers favoured, but a steady even light. The speed too with which everything happens is just what it should be—an important thing in a novel, for it is this that keeps the attention stretched. In short we have in *Don Quixote* a classic model of novelist's style as it existed down to the nineteenth century. How remarkable an achievement that was will be seen if one looks at any of the novels, *contes* or romances, in any language whatever, before him, and notes the baldness with which they are written.

The English novel owes a great deal to Cervantes. Fielding, Smollett, Scott and Dickens came out of him. For more than two hundred years he has been more read and admired in this country than any other foreign writer. Yet today his stock is low. The ordinary reader of robust appetite may continue to enjoy him, but the intellectual, after a first youthful perusal, leaves him on the shelf. Now there are, I think, a number of reasons for this. In the first place it must be admitted that, like all very well written books, *Don Quixote* loses much of its savour in translation, and also that even in Spanish some parts of it are tedious. Then we are put off by the slapstick, though why we should refuse to accept from Cervantes what we gladly put up with from Charlie Chaplin, I do not know. However, there are some people who maintain that it is the author's evident enjoyment of the knight's drubbings that repels them. This seems to me to be based on too literal a reading: Don Quixote is a symbol before he is a man and his defeats are the defeats of the principle for which he stands. In a book whose subject is right thinking, the author must necessarily take sides with— to use Freudian language—the Reality Principle against the ragings of the Super-Ego. The significant thing about this novel—its claim to be twice over a tragedy—is that it not only shows us the defeat of the man of noble feelings by the second-rate and vulgar, but that it convinces us that that defeat was right.

But the chief reason for the neglect of *Don Quixote* today is, I think, that we allow the too simplified picture that the Victorians had of it, and which is confirmed by our first youthful reading, to stand between us and the original. This is a pity because it is really a book that has more to say to us than it had to them. Its subject is militant—which is as much as to say revolutionary—faith. It explains the psychology of the believing and half-believing man with a subtlety and penetration not approached by any other writer. If one wanted a modern equivalent, one could rename it the adventures of the party man and his fellow traveller. And where do its sympathies lie? The revolutionary is the hero of the book, yet its author has not only made him mad, but has cast doubts on the purity of his motives. Don Quixote may be inspired by a passion for justice, but he is also vain and egoistic and cut off by his obsession from an understanding of human life. The condemnation of his mission is expressed by his niece in the question, "Would it not be better to stay peacefully at home than to go gadding about the world in search of *pan de trastrigo?*"—which Shelton translates "better bread than is made from wheat." Yet we never doubt that Cervantes was a man of goodwill: he is emotionally on his knight's side, though he pronounces judgment against him. With all his failings, Don Quixote towers above the other characters as the one great and noble man in the book.

Lastly we may take this book on a metaphysical plane. Although in doing this we are going far beyond the author's intentions, the material for such an interpretation is there and there is pleasure to be got from the queries it raises about human certainties. If we cannot pin down this most elusive of writers to any definite attitude, we may at least say that he contrasts the biological need which man has for faith with the difficulty his intellect has in finding grounds for one. Don Quixote dies when he loses his illusion—a commentary on Baudelaire's *Il faut être ivre*—whilst Sancho, who has no intellect, lives on and flourishes. We may sum up Cervantes' contribution to philosophy by saying that, like Montaigne and Descartes, he set in motion a chain reaction of doubt.

Perhaps we have now reached a point when we can pull all these strands together and say what the author of *Don Quixote* was really like and how his book grew out of him. By temperament a positive, sanguine man with a strong will to live and high ambitions, he was secretly riddled, as one might expect from his early life and parentage, with uncertainty and self-doubt. At Lepanto and still more at Algiers he silenced these doubts by the means that are open in wartime to every man of spirit—that is, by reckless displays of gallantry. But back in Spain this comparatively easy way was no longer feasible. The chasm between what he was and what he wanted to be began to grow wider. A failure in love, a failure in literature, a failure even in the very ordinary job he had taken on, sinking deeper every day into shabbiness and disreputability and seeing round him a family even more disreputable than himself (his sisters had made their living out of rich men, just as his only daughter was soon to do), he yet found late in life the luck, the talent and the courage—for all were required—to face up to his predicament and express his tragic sense of it in a novel. And so we have *Don Quixote*, a book written, as a learned oriental critic has said, with the pen of doubt upon the paper of conviction, a profoundly human book, crude and tedious perhaps at times, but shot through with lights of marvellous subtlety and delicacy, and with this special characteristic—that it generates in the mind of everyone who reads it as it should be read new thoughts and reflections. It has the ambiguity, the faculty for being endlessly interpreted, of myths, so that one might almost say that the author wrote it in collaboration with his readers.

There is one last aspect I would like to touch on. The Russian novelists have accustomed us to expect that a great novel should portray in a broad way the life and character of the country where it was written. This is certainly done by *Don Quixote*. With the exception of the *Canterbury Tales,* there is no English book that conveys half as immediately or abundantly the flavour of England. Its scene of action lies for the most part on the roads and in the roadside inns or *ventas*. Along these roads there passed, generally on mules or asses and invariably at foot-pace, everyone who had any reason for travel, and this was an invitation to Cervantes to bring almost every well-known type or profession into his picture. A few episodes occur in more solitary places, among that inextricable tangle of hills and valleys that is known as the Sierra Morena. But, wherever we are, we feel the Spanish landscape with its treeless plains or poplar-fringed streams or valleys dotted with ilex trees— *toda la espaciosa y triste España,* as Luis de León called it—looking, as it were, over our shoulder. Though never described to us, it is always present.

There are then the two chief actors. I need not say that Sancho, with his strings of proverbs and his ready wit and his shrewdness and his obstinacy, is a national product. Starting off as the type of stage *gracioso,*[6] he develops as the book goes on into the most complete and detailed portrait of a peasant or working man ever painted. (His appearances in the second part and those of his wife Teresa are especially delightful.) The knight too with his gravity and courtesy, and a certain plainness and bareness of mind that tells us that he also has been conditioned by the scenery, is made in the Spanish mould. And where else but in Spain could the friendship that unites master and man be found? In England or France it would, then or at any other time, have been unthinkable. It says worlds for the temper of Spanish society that such mutual loyalty and affection should have been able to transcend the barriers of rank and fortune. This was possible because the innate sense of dignity and self-esteem that are peculiar to Spaniards and to some of the Balkan peoples prevent them from thinking that any profession, however humble, can demean them. Even today, in out-of-the-way places, the servant who has eaten of his master's bread is a member of his family.

But, it will be asked, is not Don Quixote himself, with his delusions and his wisdom, his violence and his courtesy, his egoism and his moral fervour, in some sort the type and symbol of the Spanish character? That is what the Spaniards of today, moved by the insatiable passion for understanding and explaining themselves that has come over them since the turn of the century, have declared, and, so long as we are careful not to attribute this view to Cervantes, I do not see why we should not agree with them. For Don Quixote is the incarnation of the spirit of non-compromise. When the fit is on him, he believes in his own absolute rightness and virtue, and then nothing can deflect him from the course he has chosen. We

[6] [Stage fool in the Spanish *comedia*—Ed.]

call his moral passion and inflexibility noble because it appears to override self-interest, though modern psychologists have given a different interpretation of such states of mind. And we notice that whatever he does at such times ends in failure, because it takes no account of reality.

Now most people would agree that something of this sort is to be found among Spaniards. They hold their opinions, not merely obstinately and rigidly, but with a sort of *brio,* as though they held them for the express purpose of challenging other people. That is to say, they are often less interested in the truth of what they are maintaining than in the fact that it is they who are maintaining it. An opinion for them is much more than an estimate of probabilities; it is something you wear on your helmet when you want to give battle, something with which your honour, which is another word for your personality, is associated. You like to display it because you are proud of it, and you cannot compromise on it. Now this state of affairs leads to the Spaniards being a very frank people, but it also puts them in danger of being fanatical. No one who has read Spanish history since the time of the Catholic Kings can doubt that there is a strong tendency to fanaticism in Spanish life. But when they have not been roused and challenged, they display very different characteristics, such as tolerance, kindness, humanity, prudence and oriental passivity. What, in my opinion, makes *Don Quixote* such a good allegory of the Spanish character is its demonstration of how the visionary, aggressive and fanatical element in Spaniards comes out of and recedes into the wise, patient and pacific one. No better example could be given of the faculty that some great writers have of creating scenes and characters that far transcend in depth and range anything that they may have consciously aimed at.

The Example of Cervantes

by Harry Levin

I

To crown him with an adjective of his own choosing, Cervantes
continues to be the exemplary novelist. It is a truism, of course, that
he set the example for all other novelists to follow. The paradox is
that, by exemplifying the effects of fantasy on the mind, he pointed
the one way for fiction to attain the effect of truth. We state his
achievement somewhat more concretely when we say that he created
a new form by criticizing the old forms. *Don Quixote,* in terms of
its intention and impact, constituted an overt act of criticism.
Through its many varieties of two-sided observation, there runs a
single pattern: the pattern of art embarrassed by confrontation with
nature. This is the substance of the critical comment that every
chapter makes in a differing context. We can test it by considering
the implications of two such passages, taken from familiar and typical episodes, widely separated yet closely related. (With some cross-
reference to the original Spanish in the interests of semantics, and
a good deal of paraphrase in the interests of condensation, I shall
be quoting Cervantes from the contemporaneous English translation
of Thomas Shelton. Spelling will be modernized, and parenthetical
numbers will refer to any standard text.)

Our first passage occurs in Chapter XXII of the First Part, which
is entitled "Of the liberty Don Quixote gave to many wretches, who
were a-carrying perforce to a place they desired not." Let us pause
for a moment over this heading. It turns into a characteristically
dry understatement as soon as we realize that "the place they desired not" was the galleys. But the emphasis falls on the two com-

"The Example of Cervantes." From *Contexts of Criticism* by Harry Levin
(Cambridge, Mass.: Harvard University Press, 1957), pp. 79–96. Copyright ©
1957 by the President and Fellows of Harvard College. Reprinted by permission
of the publishers.

mon nouns in the main clause, "liberty" and "wretches." *Libertad!*
The very word, which was to reverberate with such easy sonority
for Walt Whitman, carried a poignant overtone for Cervantes. After
the famous battle of Lepanto in which he lost the use of his hand,
as he never tires of retelling, he had been captured by pirates and
sold as a slave, and had perforce spent five long years in Algerian
captivity. That enslavement, in a place Cervantes desired not, must
have lent special meaning to Don Quixote's gesture of liberation.
The tale later told by the Captive—the Spanish Captain enslaved
at Algiers who recovers his greatest joy, lost liberty—is highly ro-
manticized; but it hints that the actual truth was stranger than the
incidental fiction when it mentions a certain Cervantes (*"tal de
Saavedra"*) and the deeds he did—and all to achieve liberty (*"y todas por alcanzar libertad,"* I, xl).

Hence the wretches are more to be pitied than scorned; and here
the key word, *desdichados,* is not so much a term of contempt as
an ironic expression of fellow feeling. It may not be irrelevant to
recall that *El Desdichado* is also the title Gérard de Nerval gives
to his melancholy sonnet on the romantic hero. A similar ambiguity
characterizes the French *les misérables* or the Russian *neschastniki.*
The undertones of humanitarian sympathy, implied when Don
Quixote liberates the convicts, come to the surface when he finally
reaches Barcelona, and we are brought face to face with galley
slaves. Again we cannot help thinking of the author—not because
his book is, in any sense, autobiographical; but because it is, like
most great books, the unique distillation of mature experience.
Behind the book stands a soldier of misfortune who had encountered many setbacks on his personal journey to Parnassus. Having
tried his one good hand at virtually all the flowery forms of the
artificial literature of that baroque period, he had addressed himself
to the hazards of the road in the uncongenial guise of tax collector.
And again it is of himself that he speaks with rueful humor, when
the Priest and the Barber hold their inquisition over the books in
Don Quixote's library. Among those which are set aside from the
burning is the pastoral romance of *Galatea* by Miguel de Cervantes
Saavedra. The Priest mitigates his criticism with a pun: this author
is *"más versado en desdichas que en versos"*—better versed in mis-
fortunes than in verses (I, vi).

Don Quixote's ideal of humanistic perfection is to be equally
well versed in arms and letters. It might be opined that he fails
because his military training has lagged so far behind his literary
preparation. Something like the contrary might be maintained

about his creator. At all events, after all he had been through, Cervantes would have been the very last man to cherish romantic illusions on the subject of adventure. He was therefore just the man to dramatize a distinction which has since become an axiom, which has indeed become so axiomatic that it might well be called Cervantes' formula. This is nothing more nor less than a recognition of the difference between verses and reverses, between words and deeds, *palabras* and *hechos*—in short, between literary artifice and that real thing which is life itself. But literary artifice is the only means that a writer has at his disposal. How else can he convey his impression of life? Precisely by discrediting those means, by repudiating that air of bookishness in which any book is inevitably wrapped. When Pascal observed that true eloquence makes fun of eloquence, he succinctly formulated the principle that could look to Cervantes as its recent and striking exemplar. It remained for La Rochefoucauld to restate the other side of the paradox: some people would never have loved if they had not heard of love.

The chapter that sees the convicts liberated is rather exceptional in its direct approach to reality. The preceding chapter has been a more devious and characteristic excursion into the domain of romance. Its theme, which has come to be a byword for the transmuting power of imagination, as well as for Don Quixote's peculiar habit of imposing his obsession upon the world, is the barber's basin he takes for the fabulous helmet of Mambrino, stolen from Rinaldo by Sacripante in the *Orlando Furioso*. If the recovery of this knightly symbol is effected without undue incident, it is because the barber has no wish to fight; subsequently, when he returns to claim his property, he allows himself to be persuaded that it is really a helmet which has been enchanted to look like a basin. Such is the enchantment Don Quixote invokes to rationalize his defeats and embarrassments. Delusions of grandeur, conveniently enough, are sustained by phobias of persecution; somehow hostile enchanters always manage to get between him and the fulfillment of his ideals. Cervantes borrowed his plot from an interlude about a peasant bemused by popular ballads; and though that *donnée* is elaborated through an infinite series of variations, it remains almost repetitiously simple. Each episode is a kind of skit in which the protagonist, attempting to put his heroic ideals into action, is discomfited by realities in the shape of slapstick comedy.

Thus deeds, with a vengeance, comment on words; and Cervantes' formula is demonstrated again and again. Afterward there are more words, pleasant discussions, *"graciosos razonamientos"*—which naturally require the presence of an amusing companion, an interlocutor, a *gracioso*. The hero of cape-and-sword drama is squired by such a buffoon; the courtier is often burlesqued by the zany who serves him; Don Quixote's servant—like Figaro or Jeeves—is cleverer, in some vital respects, than his master. Much, possibly too much, has already been written on the dualism of Don Quixote and Sancho Panza as a symbolic representation of soul and body, past and present, poetry and prose, the inner dilemmas of psychology, or the all-embracing antitheses of metaphysics. We need only remind ourselves in passing that, within this eternal comedy team, Sancho Panza's role is to assert a sense of reality. The incident of the windmills provides him with his usual cue and his classical response. When the knight beholds these machines in the distance, and asks the squire whether he too does not behold those monstrous giants, it is Sancho's function to reply with an other question: "What giants?" In his person the challenging voice of empiricism does its best and its worst to refute the aprioristic frame of mind, which has since become so closely identified with the Don that we sometimes term it *Quixotry*.

Now, on the comic stage, Sancho would have the final word. In the pictorial vision of Daumier, the pair coexist within the same frame of reference as the bourgeoisie and the caricatured intellectuals. Yet in a book, where words are the only medium, Don Quixote enjoys a decided advantage; the very weakness of his position in life lends strength, as it were, to his position in literature; in the field of action he may encounter discomfiture, but in the verbal sphere he soon resumes his imaginary career. When Sancho is skeptical about the basin and goes on to doubt the rewards of knighthood, the Don simply lapses into his autistic fantasies of wish-fulfillment; and his conversation during the next few pages spins out another romance in miniature. The most elaborate of the many little romances that run through his head and through the novel figures in his argument with the Canon of Toledo at the end of the First Part, and offers Cervantes occasion to develop his theory of the comic epic in prose. The Canon, on his side, is a more erudite humanist than Sancho Panza; but he casts the weight of his learning in favor of what the critics have labeled "probability"; and he pertinently distinguishes between fictitious and truthful histories (*historia imaginada, historia verdadera*).

Don Quixote's answer is a powerful statement of the appeal of romance. Freud would have diagnosed it as the purest indulgence in the pleasure-principle, the sheerest escape from the reality-principle. It is the daydream of a golden world of gardens and castles where art improves upon nature, where blandishing damsels await the errant adventurer and every misadventure leads toward a happy ending. It is a heady and concentrated restatement of the ever-appealing myth that, in Cervantes' day, incarnated its bland arche-type in Amadís of Gaul. Amadís, like every true cavalier, was by definition a paragon who surpassed all other cavaliers; his invul-nerable prowess was an unparalleled as the peerless beauty of his lady, Oriana, or the perfect faithfulness of his squire, Gandalín. He was predestined to triumph over an all but endless sequence of rivals and obstacles, and to be united with his heroine in an en-chanted chamber which only the bravest and fairest could enter, somewhere out of this world on an uncharted island misleadingly named Terra Firma. Meanwhile the chronicle of his adventures and those of his progeny, prolonged through five generations and twenty-four volumes, furnished the primary source of inspiration for Don Quixote, whose pattern of behavior is—to speak it pro-fanely—a kind of *imitatio Amadís*.

Imitation is the test that Cervantes proposes, knowing full well that when nature imitates art, art reveals its innate artificiality. Literally his hero reënacts episodes from the life-cycle of his own hero, as when he assumes the name of Beltenebros and undergoes penance in the Sierra Morena. But since he aspires to combine the virtues of other heroes—the Nine Worthies, the Twelve Paladins, the aggregate muster-roll of knight errantry—he must likewise emu-late Ariosto's Orlando. And since Orlando went mad for love of the fair Angelica, Don Quixote must rage in order to prove his devo-tion to the fair Dulcinea del Toboso. The place-name he attaches to his kitchen-maid heroine is less aristocratic than anticlimactic, particularly when it is left to dangle as the refrain of one of the poems addressed to her. The process of emulation, dedicated to a whole set of models at once, going through their motions so pedanti-cally and overstating their claims so fanatically, tends to reduce them all to absurdity. Because this tendency is deliberate, the pre-vailing method is that of parody: a marvelous gift, according to Ben Jonson, which makes a work "absurder than it was." But *Amadís de Gaula* could hardly have been absurder than it was; its innumerable sequels might almost have been parodies; while *Don Quixote* might be no more than another sequel, if it had no ob-jective vantage-point from which to chart the deviations of its sub-jective course.

Its protagonist sallies forth at the outset, talking to himself—as

will be his wont—about the historian who will have the honor of
recording the exploits he is about to accomplish (I, ii). With a diz-
zying shift of the time-sense, he looks back from the future upon
events which have yet to take place. From first to last the narration
is colored by his own self-consciousness. A much later sally is introduced by this mock-heroic sentence:

> Scarce had the silver morn given bright Phoebus leave with ardor of
> his burning rays to dry the liquid pearls on his golden locks, when
> Don Quixote, shaking off sloth from his drowsy members, rose up
> and called Sancho his squire, that still lay snorting (II, xx).

Here, with the calculated anticlimax of the last word, all the mytho-
logical ornamentation sinks into bathos. Actuality, suddenly intervening, restores our perspective to a more firmly grounded base of
observation. The high-flown monologue becomes a pedestrian dialogue, which in turn restates the dialectical issue of the book. Sancho
Panza, the principal dialectician, is quite aware of that variance
which makes his fall into a mere hole so utterly different from Don
Quixote's exploration of the Cave of Montesinos: "There saw he
goodly and pleasant visions and here, I believe, I shall see nothing
but snakes and toads (II, lv)." The pleasant visions are abstract and
remote: the snakes and toads are concrete and immediate; the variance is all in the point of view.

The psychological contrast is reflected in the stylistic texture
from the opening page, where the first paragraph is straight factual
exposition, while the second echoes two florid sentences from Don
Quixote's reading. Diction shows the increasing influence of Sancho's viewpoint when—amid bouquets of poetic conceit and parades
of learned authority, the regular mental context of Don Quixote—
Cervantes apologizes for using the homely substantive *puercos,* and
thereby calling a pig a pig. Once this sort of interplay has been
established, Don Quixote himself can take the metaphorical step
from the sublime to the ridiculous. When Sancho reports that
Dulcinea's visage is slightly blemished by a mole, he can respond
with an inappropriate amplification—"Though she had a hundred
moles as well as that one thou sawest in her, they were not moles
but moons and bright stars"—a pretty picture which outdoes even
Shakespeare's hyperbolic gibes against the Petrarchan sonneteers
(II, x). The gravity of his demeanor is matched by the grandiosity
of his rhetoric, a manner of speaking broadly connoted by the rhetorical term *prosopopeya.* His dead-pan humor would not be humorous were some one else not there to see the joke, to watch the

imitation becoming a parody by failing to meet the challenge at hand. As his purple passages are juxtaposed with Sancho's vernacular proverbs, the bookish and sluggish flow of his consciousness is freshened and quickened; flat assertion is rounded out, and soliloquy is colloquialized.

Cervantes, whose *Colloquy of the Dogs* we must not forget, was well schooled in those mixed modes of Erasmus and Lucian which —linking the early modern spirit to the late Greco-Roman—seem to express the self-questionings of a traditional culture during an epoch of rapid and far-reaching change. The literature of the Renaissance, which moves from one extreme to the other so readily, is the register of a violent effort to catch up with the expanding conditions of life. With its realization that certain themes are still untreated goes the feeling that certain techniques are becoming outmoded. The needed renewal and the strategic enlargement begin by adapting, experimenting, cross-fertilizing, and incidentally producing giants and dwarfs whose incongruous qualities merely bear witness to the overplus of creativity. Extraordinary combinations of language, such as macaronics, waver between Latinity and the vulgar tongues. Poetry, evoking the legendary past, varies its tone from nostalgia to facetiousness. Prose impinges, entirely unaware of its hybrid possibilities as an imaginative medium. A transitional sense of disproportion makes itself felt, not only in mannerist painting, but in complementary literary genres: mock-epic, which magnifies vulgarity, applying the grand manner to commonplace matters; and travesty, which minimizes greatness, reclothing noble figures in base attire.

It will easily be seen, from page to page, how Cervantes ranges between these two reductive extremes. One of his own descriptions of his style, at the beginning of the chapter before us, oscillates from high-sounding (*"altisonante"*) to trivial (*"minima"*). This oscillation puzzled Shelton so much that he translated the latter word by one more congruent to the former: "divine" (*divina*). However, Cervantes encompasses many such disparities, bridging the gap between style and subject by the continual play of his irony. Rabelais could revel in the *mélange des genres,* parodying the quest for the Holy Grail in the cult of the Holy Bottle. A lesser writer, Robert Greene, could live between two worlds and keep them apart: first-hand journalistic accounts of the London underworld and mannered pastoral romances set in some escapist Arcadia, with very little intermixture of styles. The immeasurable contribution of Cervantes was to broaden the province of prose fiction by bringing both realms together, not in a synthesis perhaps, but in the most durable antithesis that literature has known; by opening a colloquy between the romance and the picaresque, so to speak, between *Amadís de Gaula* and *Lazarillo de Tormes*. Spain, with its strongly marked chiaroscuro of contrasts, social as well as cultural, presented the pertinent matter of fact along with the far-fetched matter of fiction. The first-person narrative of the little beggar, Lazarillo, whose harsh masters taught him to cheat or be cheated, gave Cervantes the fructifying example for an exemplary novel to which *Don Quixote* refers, *Rinconete and Cortadillo*—a tale endearing to American readers as a Sevillian adumbration of *Tom Sawyer* and *Huckleberry Finn*.

II

Having proceeded discursively, after the fashion of Rocinante, we have come back to our starting point and are ready to set out once again. Our preliminary amble has not been wasted if it has confirmed our awareness of the "disorderly order" that regulates the imaginary gardens of Cervantes, and that may emerge from the passage to which we now return. After the gang of unfortunates bound for the galleys is released through the officiousness of Don Quixote, he is confounded by reality, in the shifty person of their ringleader: a rogue indeed, the authentic picaroon, Ginés de Pasamonte. Ginés, among his other dubious traits, harbors pretensions as a man of letters; to beguile the time in prison, he declares, he has made a book out of the story of his life. This may strengthen the bonds of affinity that connect the present chapter with the life of Cervantes; for we know that the author was imprisoned, through some bureaucratic complication, during the period when he was writing *Don Quixote*; and he may be referring to that circumstance, with his genius for rising above a situation, when his prologue alludes to "some dark and noisome prison." In any case, Don Quixote is curious about this particular product of incarcerated endeavors.

"Is it so good a work?" said Don Quixote.

"It is so good," replied Ginés, "that it quite puts down *Lazarillo de Tormes* and as many others as are written or shall write of that kind: for that which I dare affirm to you is that it treats of true accidents, and those so delightful that no like invention can be compared to them."

"And how is the book entitled?" quoth Don Quixote.

"It is called," said he, *"The Life of Ginés of Pasamonte."*
"And is it yet ended?" said the knight.
"How can it be finished," replied he, "my life being not yet ended?"

To mention a work of fiction in the course of another work of fiction can be a two-edged device. It can show up the book that is mentioned, thereby sharpening the realism of the book that does the mentioning. This is what Ginés does for his own work at the expense of Lazarillo, and what Cervantes is doing for *Don Quixote* at the expense of *Amadís de Gaula,* expressly invoked by his own commendatory verses. Conversely, the invidious comparison can glance in the other direction, as in the case of many a derivative academic novel today: the pale reflection of a dream of the shadow of Henry James. But that is unmitigated imitation, and it produces a conventional literature, circumscribing novelists to the point where even their titles must be quotations from other books. The method of Cervantes utilized literary means to break through literary conventions and, in the very process, invented a form substantial and flexible enough to set forth the vicissitudes of modern society. Parody, explicitly criticizing a mode of literature, developed into satire, implicitly criticizing a way of life. Developing out of the debris of feudalism, the novel has waxed and waned with the middle class. Yet in the twentieth century, according to Thomas Mann's contemporary Faust, the arts tend more than ever to parody themselves. The writer's problem, as André Gide has rephrased Cervantes' formula, is still the rivalry between the real world and the representation we make of it.

It is significant that Gide's most serious novel, which likewise probes the theme of how novels come to be written, is called *The Counterfeiters*; and that Mann's last fragment—begun forty years before and completed only, in the peculiar sense of Ginés, by the author's death—is a reversion to the picaresque cycle, *Confessions of Felix Krull.* For trickery is inherent, as artists recognize, in their business of dealing with illusion. We do well then to scrutinize some of their tricks rather closely; and Cervantes is well justified in conveying this caveat, or insight, through the mouth of an incorrigible charlatan. After all, no one can express what is by nature inexpressible. Life itself is infinitely larger than any artistic medium. However, by revealing the limitations of their medium, writers like Cervantes heighten our consciousness of what existence means. The real story of Ginés de Pasamonte, comparatively more real than the imagined *Life of Lazarillo de Tormes,* is bound to be incomplete because life is endless. It lasts forever, as Tolstoy's peasant says just before he dies in *War and Peace*. In all sincerity, therefore, we cannot say *finis;* we can only write "to be continued." And so with Cervantes, like Ginés writing in prison, and breaking off his First Part with a provisory ending and a cautionary moral: Beware of fiction! It is fictitious; that is to say, it is false. Don't let it mislead you!

The ironic consequence of his warning was the creation of an archetype, a fictional personage destined to be far more influential than Amadís of Gaul. The remarkable success of the First Part was the precondition of the Second, which is consequently more deliberate in its artistry. By that time, the latter volume announces, the fame of its predecessor has spread so widely that any lean horse would be hailed as Rocinante. The earlier conclusion, in which so little was concluded, clearly invited some continuation. Before Cervantes could take up his own tale again, the interloper who signed himself "Avellaneda" brought out his notorious sequel: an imitation of a parody. Because the impersonation had to be imitative, it could not be organic; it could not live and grow as Cervantes' original would do in his Second Part. The mysterious Avellaneda, when Cervantes finally caught up with him, all but took the place of Amadís as a satirical target, and as a measure of the distance between echoed phrases and lived experiences. Adding insult to injury, he had not only plagiarized; he had also criticized his victim for not keeping his own brain-children in character, and—even more significantly—for introducing Ginés. That scoundrel had shown a comparable ingratitude when he rewarded his liberator with a shower of stones, absconding with Don Quixote's sword and —temporarily—Sancho Panza's ass. But the Second Part arranges a further encounter and, for the knight, an opportune revenge.

This involves our second illustration, a rather more extended example which need not be cited at length, since it figures so prominently in the celebrated episode of Master Peter's puppet-show. Poetic drama—another genre which Cervantes had practiced with indifferent results—is here reduced to its most elementary level, just as prose fiction was in the instance we have been discussing. The link between these two passages, as we learn from the next chapter, is Maese Pedro himself, who turns out to be none other than Don Quixote's old enemy, Ginés. Always the escape-artist, he is now an itinerant showman, and more of a dealer in deception than ever. One of his other exhibits happens to be a fortune-telling ape, whose roguish trick is subsequently exposed. Now Cervantes was obviously fond of animals; a dog-lover and a master of the beast-fable, he satirizes war in a parable about braying asses and courtly love in a serenade of cats; the dramatis personae of his book include a traveling menagerie; but the ape, above all, is the parodistic animal. When the lovelorn Dorothea joins the friendly conspiracy to bring the knight to his senses, she poses as the Infanta Micomica of Micomicón ("Princess Monkey-Monkey of Monkeyland"). Actually a damsel in distress, she acts the part of a damsel in distress; and the make-believe story she recounts to Don Quixote is the parody of a parody, her own story.

This monkey-business, if it may be so designated, accelerates to its climax through a sequence of scenes at the inn. There the incidental stories accumulate, and there the actual personages who tell or figure in them are interrelated through the fiat of romantic coincidence. Viktor Shklovsky has aptly described this meeting-place as "a literary inn," though another emphasis would interpret it as a social microcosm. On the one hand, the relationship between letters and arms is the appropriate topic of Don Quixote's discourse; on the other, the crude farce of the wineskins and the stern intervention of the Holy Brotherhood, searching for the importunate busybody who freed the convicts, underline the romance with a touch of reality. The central interpolation is a tale which comes out of the same bag of manuscripts as some of Cervantes' *Exemplary Novels* —or so the literary host very plausibly informs his guests. It is the tale of the so-called Curious Impertinent, an almost Proustian study in point of view, wherein Anselmo's universal suspicion functions as a sort of mirror-opposite for Don Quixote's ubiquitous credulity. Characterization of the protagonist gains in depth as he passes through the levels of the characters who surround him, in their assumed roles, with their recounted adventures—sometimes tales within tales. As in Chaucer's *Canterbury Tales,* the story-tellers take on an extra dimension against the formal backdrop of their stories.

Part I situates these episodes, within the tradition of the frame-story, at an extra remove from the reader. In Part II, as the narrator proudly explains, they are unified by the divagations of a single plot. Where the First Part centered upon an inn, which the hero insisted on taking for a castle, the Second Part leads to a long sojourn at a genuine castle, where the conversation is less inspired and the horseplay heavier than at any other juncture of the book. Castles in Spain, for non-Spaniards, have proverbially symbolized the veritable fabric of romance. "Castle-building," in the library at Waverley Honour, was the state of mind that engendered the latter-day romances of Sir Walter Scott. The terrain of Don Quixote, the arid region of La Mancha, overlaps Castile, which is quite literally the land of castles. But Cervantes' castle seems to mark an anticlimactic turning point, a release from mental imprisonment, the beginning of an undeception for the knight; while it bewitches the squire, offering him a brief chance to go his own way and to impose the rough justice of the common man on the neighboring dependency of Barataria. Overshadowed by that glimpse of a democratic community, or the disillusioning city of Barcelona just ahead, chivalric entertainment may well pall. Not that the Duke and Duchess have spared any courtesy; they have humored their fantastic guest with such labored vivacity that they are accused of being madder than he; there has been more manipulation and masquerading, more play-acting and practical joking, at the castle than at the inn.

The effectiveness of the play-within-the-play lies in making the main drama more convincing: when the King interrupts the Players in *Hamlet,* we feel that at last we have come to grips with reality. One way of attaining this effect is to make the theatrical figures unconvincing; and when these are puppets rather than actors, wooden dolls imitating human beings, everything undergoes a reduction of scale; their performance becomes a mode of ridicule, as Bergson has suggested in his essay on laughter. Hence, among the many stratagems that Cervantes employs against the romance, none is more sharply conceived nor more skillfully executed than the puppet-play. His description of it commences in epic style, with the spectators—Tyrians and Trojans—falling silent, and the youthful reciter appealing to the authority of old French chronicles and Spanish ballads (II, xxvi). The setting is a city whose ancient name, Sansueña, suffuses a dreamy atmosphere. The plot concerns the Princess Melisendra, imprisoned by the Moors even as Cervantes himself has been, and her knightly rescuer, Gaiferos, who must accomplish his task by fighting the Moors as Cervantes has done—but with a difference, that crucial difference between fantasy and actuality which it is his constant purpose to emphasize.

For once Don Quixote has no need to superimpose his fancies; he need only take the presentation literally. As a matter of fact, he starts by criticizing certain details of Moorish local color. Gradually he suspends his disbelief—which has never been too strong—and enters into the spirit of the occasion so actively that, before the others can stop him, he has begun "to rain strokes upon the puppetish Moorism." The puppeteer, Ginés, alias Pedro, cries:" Hold, Señor Don Quixote, hold! and know that these you hurl down, destroy,

and kill, are not real Moors but shapes made of pasteboard." And
reality is restored no less abruptly than it is when Alice cries out to
the creatures of Wonderland: "You're nothing but a pack of cards!"
Pedro-Ginés, the arch-manipulator, the ever versatile illusionist, la-
ments his loss for an operatic moment or two, and then shrewdly
reckons it up: so much for Charlemagne split down the middle, so
much for Melisendra without a nose, and so on down to the last
marivedí, paid in full by Don Quixote in coin of the realm. Such
mercenary language contrasts with another aspect of the show: the
puppets were knocked down, we are told, "in less than two credos."
This is rather a figure of speech than an article of belief; and the
wax candles probably have no ritual significance; yet it is worth re-
membering that the word *retablo,* applied to the puppet-show,
signifies primarily an altarpiece. I do not want to place undue stress
on symbols which prove so brittle; but we cannot altogether ignore
the iconoclasm of Cervantes, since the Inquisition did not.

In the next chapter, when the narrator swears to his own veracity
as a Catholic Christian, the author himself feels obliged to point out
that this protestation comes from an unbelieving Moor (II, xxvii).
Elsewhere he repeatedly warns us that Moors are not to be trusted:
they are "cheaters, impostors, and chemists" (II, iii). Cervantes'
fictional narrator is one of these elusive infidels: an "Arabical and
Manchegan historiographer" named the Cide Hamete Benengeli,
who does not appear in the opening pages of the book. Don Quixote
completes his first sally, saunters forth again, challenges the Biscayan, and is left sword in air by the break between the seventh
and eighth chapters. In a digression, Cervantes tells us that his
documentation has run out, and that we might well have been left
in suspense forever; again, as in the later colloquy between Don
Quixote and Ginés, life is conceived as an unfinished book. Happily,
in a bazaar at Toledo, Cervantes has chanced upon an Arabic manuscript which will supply the rest of the story; and from now on the
Cide Hamete will be responsible for it, even as Captain Clutterbuck
or Jedediah Cleishbotham would be responsible for Scott's narra-
tions, and other pseudonymous narrators for Stendhal's and Man-
zoni's. Since the author presents himself as editor, assuming the intervention of a Spanish translator from the Arabic, the text stands
at three removes from ourselves, enriched with afterthoughts like a
palimpsest. This procedure has the advantages of enabling the author to digress more freely, to blame his source for indiscreet remarks, and to cultivate an air of authenticity.

But authenticity is deeply called into question on one problematic occasion, when the whole trend of the book is reversed, turning back from pragmatic demonstration to metaphysical speculation, or—in the more incisive phrase of Américo Castro—from a critique of fiction to a critique of reality. Can men's lives be so sharply differentiated from their dreams, when all is said and done? Can we live without illusion? we are asked. Don Quixote may be right, the rest of us wrong. Many of the philosophers, most of the poets, would take his side. Spanish imagination is not unique in having been fascinated by Calderón's refrain: *La vida es sueño,* life is a dream. Even Shakespeare conceded the possibility: "We are such stuff/As dreams are made on . . ." Who are we, in that event, to look down upon puppets imprisoned within the dream-city of Sansueña? May it not be that the images of ourselves created by writers, as Pirandello would urge, are more real than we are? For example, *Don Quixote.* The chapter that explores such ultimate doubts is admittedly apocryphal; it may be an intermixture of truth and falsehood, as pantomimed by Maese Pedro's ape. We are tempted to believe that Don Quixote's descent into the Cave of Montesinos is a return to the deep well of the past, the unconscious memory of the race, and that the mythical heroes sleeping there personify the ideals he struggled to practice, the ideology of the Golden Age. Yet the simple and brutal alternative persists that he may have been caught in a lie and have become a party to the general imposture.

In the absence of other witnesses, certainty continues to elude us. The best advice Don Quixote can report is the gambler's maxim spoken, curiously enough, by the flower and mirror of chivalry, Durandarte: *Paciencia y barajar,* patience and shuffle, go on with the game (II, xxiii). After the underground interview with the dead heroes, the next stage is the fable about the asses, and then the puppetry of Pedro-Ginés; and each successive chapter is a station on the pilgrimage of disenchantment. Disarmed, dismounted, and finally discomfited, the former knight is on his way homeward, when the sight of shepherds rouses his flagging impulses to their last wish-dream. Sancho, of course, has an important part in it:

> I'll buy sheep and all things fit for our pastoral vocation; and calling myself by the name of shepherd Quixotiz and thou the shepherd Pansino, we will walk up and down the hills, through woods and meadows, singing and versifying and drinking the liquid crystal of the fountains, sometimes out of the clear springs and then out of the swift-running rivers . . . (II, lxvii).

But Don Quixote has come to the end of his life and, accordingly, of his book. It remained for other books to parody the pastoral romances, as his had parodied the romances of chivalry: notably a French disciple of Cervantes, Charles Sorel, who wrote a novel entitled *Anti-Romance,* and subtitled *The Wayward Shepherd (L'Anti-roman, ou le berger extravagant).* That would be another story; but perhaps the term *anti-romance* might be usefully borrowed to generalize a major premise of the modern novel, from Fielding, who began as Cervantes' professed imitator by lampooning Richardson, to Jane Austen, who sharpened her acute discriminations on Gothic romances and novels of sensibility:

> Charming as were all of Mrs. Radcliffe's works, and charming even as were the works of all her imitators, it was not in them perhaps that human nature, at least in the midland counties of England, was to be looked for.

The time, the place, and the style of *Northanger Abbey* have little in common with Cervantes; but his protean formula has held, as it has been readjusted to varying situations through the lengthy record of Don Quixote's posthumous adventures. One of the many female Quixotes has been Madame Bovary; one of the many Russian Quixotes has been Prince Myshkin. Heinrich Heine summed up the romantic movement as a school of Quixotry when he exclaimed: "Jean-Jacques Rousseau was my Amadís of Gaul!" In a parallel vein, it might be argued that Voltaire's Amadís of Gaul was Leibniz, that Tolstoy's was Napoleon, or Mark Twain's Baedeker. The number of specific instances would seem to indicate some broader principle, such as André Malraux has recently formulated in his illustrated treatise on the creative imagination. His dictum—that every artist begins with *pastiche*—is highly illuminating, so far as it goes; it has to be qualified only by recognizing that *pastiche* implies both activities which we have associated and distinguished, imitation and parody. The novelist must begin by playing the sedulous ape, assimilating the craft of his predecessors; but he does not master his own form until he has somehow exposed and surpassed them, passing from the imitation of art through parody to the imitation of nature.

Voyage with Don Quixote

by *Thomas Mann*

May nineteenth, 1934

It seemed a good idea to begin it by drinking a vermouth in
the bar; accordingly we did so, while quietly awaiting the moment
when the ship should start. I had taken out of my travelling-bag this
notebook and one of the four little orange linen volumes of *Don
Quixote*, the chosen companions of my trip. More unpacking was
uncalled for at that moment. We had nine or ten days before us
until we should land on the other side of the world. Another Saturday would come round, another Monday and Tuesday, before this
well-conducted adventure of ours should reach its goal. The easy-
going Dutch boat whose gangplank we had just mounted does not
do it faster—why should she? The speed corresponding to her com-
fortable medium size is certainly saner and more natural than the
shattering, record-breaking pace of those colossi which in six or even
four days madly overlap the vast spaces that lie before us. *Piano,
piano!* Richard Wagner thought that *andante* was the true German
tempo. Well, there is something very arbitrary about all these
half-way answers to the question "What is German?" And in the
end it remains unsettled, leaving a negative impression because they
appear to condemn as un-German all sorts of things that are not so
at all—as, for instance, the *allegretto,* the *scherzo,* and the *spiritu-
oso!* This remark of Wagner's would have been happier if he had
left out all reference to the national—a sentimentalizing idea any-
how—and confined himself to the objective value that I ascribe

to the quality of slowness. All good things take time; so do all great things. In other words, space will have its time. It is a familiar feeling with me that there is a sort of *hubris,* and a great superficiality, in those who would take away from space or stint it of the time naturally bound up with it. Goethe, who was certainly a friend of man, yet did not like to use artificial aids to his powers of perception, such as the microscope and telescope, would probably have agreed with this scruple. Of course, the question arises where the line is to be drawn and whether ten days are not just as bad as six or four. To be strictly orthodox, one would have to give the ocean as many weeks instead, and travel by the wind, which is a force of nature, just as steam is. As a matter of fact, we are using oil fuel. But these speculations approach the fantastic.

And yet my flights of fancy are explainable enough: their source is my own inward excitement. I have, quite simply, stage fright. And what wonder? My maiden voyage across the Atlantic, my first encounter with the mighty ocean, my first knowledge of it—and there, on the other side of the curvature of the earth, above which the great waters heave, New Amsterdam the metropolis awaits us! There are only four or five such in the world, only four or five of this unique and monstrous breed of cities, extravagant in size and kind, standing out even among what we call capital cities, just as in the natural kingdom, among the features of the landscape, the mountain, the desert, and the ocean belong in a category by themselves. I grew up on the Baltic, a provincial body of water. And the traditions of my blood are those of the small and old-established city, civilized and gentled, whose inhabitants are endowed with sensitive imaginations and capable of feeling for the elemental both a sense of awe and a sort of ironic distaste. Ivan Goncharov was once on the high seas during a violent storm. The captain had him fetched from his cabin to behold it: Goncharov was a writer, he said, the storm was magnificent, he ought not to miss it. The author of *Oblomov* came on deck, looked about him, and said: "Yes, it's a nuisance, isn't it?" And went below again.

*   *   *

Shipboard reading—it falls into a category generally despised. The usual view is that reading for a journey must be of the lightest and shallowest, mere foolery to pass the time. I cannot understand it. In the first place, this so-called light reading is the dullest stuff in the world; but even aside from that I cannot see why, especially upon a serious occasion like this voyage, one should decline below the level of one's intellectual habits and go in for the silly and jejune. Perhaps the conditions of life on shipboard, at once removed from the everyday and full of excitement, produce a mental and nervous condition in which silliness disgusts us less than usual . . . *Don Quixote* is universal; just the right reading for a trip to the end of the world. It was no small adventure to write it; the passive adventure of reading it will worthily correspond. Strangely enough, I have never gone through the masterpiece systematically, from beginning to end. I will do so on board and in ten days come to the rim of this ocean of a book, at the same time as we come to the other rim of the Atlantic.

The windlass was making a din as I wrote down this resolve. We went on deck, to look back and forward.

* * *

May twentieth

* * *

Yesterday afternoon, and last night in the blue salon, to the accompaniment of the music, I read *Don Quixote*. I will now continue to read, sitting in my deck-chair, a transmogrification of Hans Castorp's excellent reclining-chair. What a unique monument is this book! More conditioned in taste by its time than the deliberate satire against that taste would indicate; the whole spirit of the work utterly sycophantic in its protestations of loyalty; yet how its creative genius, critical, free, and human, soars above its age! Tieck's translation, the spirited medium of the classic romantic period, enchants me more than I can say. It is a beautiful instrument wherewith to render the spacious humour of this style—which is almost impressive enough to make me wonder whether humour after all is not the great essential element of the epic. Or even to make me consider them one and the same, though the statement could probably not be objectively sustained. A style that mingles the humorous and the romantic is surely well calculated to make the whole "great and remarkable historie" pass as a translation and commentary of an Arabic manuscript composed by a Moor, Cid Hamete Benengeli. Upon this manuscript the translator is supposed to base his tale. Indeed, the story often employs the indirect forms; as, for instance, he will say: "The story goes on to tell" or " 'Allah be praised!' cried out Benengeli three times at the beginning of this chapter, after which he continued," and so forth. Immensely funny are the summary chapter-heads: "Of the wise and pleasant discourse which passed between Sancho Panza and his wife Teresa Panza, as well as other matters worthy of record"; or, with burlesque humour: "Of things which Benengeli says, he will learn who reads them, if he reads with attention." Humorous, finally, in the highest sense, is the portrayal of the two principals, so human and lively is the author's perception of character in all its many-sidedness and depth. He himself is proudly aware of this excellence, when he dwells on the despised and worthless sequel to his first part. This sequel was the work of an impudent bungler, who was tempted by the world-wide fame of Cervantes's novel to seek success with a continuation of it. The plagiary drove Cervantes to compose a second part himself, books seven to twelve in the completed work—though, as Goethe remarks, the theme was really exhausted in the first part. The author of the first sequel saw in Don Quixote naught but a gaby whom only the lash could cure of his delusions, in Sancho Panza merely a glutton. In more than one place, in the second part of the true sequel Cervantes protests with jealous scorn against such a simplification. Likewise he embarks upon controversy, which is a model of dignity and moderation, though only in form. It needs the aid of rhetoric to incite a reader to take up the cudgels, while at the same time to preserve a dignity worthy of the man from La Mancha himself. "You would like it well, were I to attack him [the author of the false second part] with adjectives like 'silly,' 'impudent,' 'limited.' But it does not occur to me. His sin be on his own head; he has to answer to himself for what he has done, and that is the end of the matter." Very Christlike and very scrupulous. What really galls Cervantes is simply that "this gentleman" calls him an old cripple—as though it were in the power of genius to hold back time that it should not go over his head; or as though he had got his mutilated hand in a tavern brawl and not in the glorious day of battle (referring to the naval battle of Lepanto). "And besides," he says with spirit, "we assume that a man composes not with his grey hairs but with his understanding, the which commonly improves with the years." That is delightful. But all the mildness and enlightenment of his grey hairs do not prevent him from setting forth the coarsest and most offensive tales of the reader as "the gentleman's" work, and as evidence that it is "one of the most devilish of the Devil's wiles to put it into a man's head that he too can write a book and get it printed and gain money and fame by it." Certainly they betray anger, furious hatred, and a spirit of revenge, these tales; they betray the half-unconscious pain of the artist when he sees confusion in men's minds between that which has success although it is good and that which has success because it is bad.

For it befell Cervantes that a plagiarism that gave itself out as a sequel to his book "went all over the world" and was as eagerly read as the original. It imitated the grosser and more popular qualities of the genuine work, seizing upon the folly of the hero and its inevitable nemesis, as well as upon the gluttony of Sancho Panza. But that was all. It could not attain to the deep human feeling, the melancholy, or the great art—nor, frightful to say, were these much missed. The public, it seems, saw no difference between the two versions. That is depressing for an author. When Cervantes talks about the disgust, the bad taste in his mouth, felt by the reader of the pseudo-*Quixote*, he is speaking for himself and not for his public. He had to write the second part to drive away the bad taste, not from his readers' mouths, but from his own; and it came there not alone from the badness of the performance but also on account of the success of his own first part. The reader must remember that the second part, "written down by the same artist and from the same matter" as the first, was composed in order to rehabilitate the success of the earlier one, to rescue its endangered honour. The second part has no longer the happy freshness and carelessness of the first, which shows how, *par hasard et par génie,* a blithe and vigorous satire grew into the book of a whole people and of all humanity. It would be less weighted down with humanism, cultural elements, and a certain literary frigidity if the ambition to achieve distinction had not played a part in its composition. But in especial the author labours in the second volume to bring out more clearly and consciously that depth and diversity in his delineation of the main characters of which I have already spoken. In this above all he would bear witness to "the same artist and the same matter" as in the first volume. Don Quixote is of course a simpleton; that is clear from his mania of knight-errantry. But his obsolete whimsy is also the source of such true nobility, such purity of life, such an aristocratic bearing, such winning and respect-compelling traits, physical and mental, that our laughter over his grotesque and doleful countenance is always mingled with amazed respect. No one can know him and not feel drawn to the high-minded and pathetic man, mad in one single point but in all others a blameless knight. It is pure spirit, disguised as fantasy, that sustains and ennobles him, that

carries his moral dignity unscathed out of each and every humilia
tion. I find it exquisite that Sancho Panza the potbellied, with his
proverbs, his mother wit, his shrewd peasant judgment of human
nature, who has no use for the "idea" that results in beatings, but
rather for the skin of liquor—Sancho Panza has feeling for this
spirit. He loves his good albeit ridiculous master despite all the
hardship that loyalty to him incurs; does not leave him nor stir
from his side, but serves him with honest and admiring fealty—even
though sometimes he may lie to him at need. All that makes even
Sancho Panza worthy of our affection; it rounds out his figure with
humanity and lifts it out of the sphere of the merely comic into
that of genuine humour.

Certainly Sancho Panza is national in that he represents the attitude of the Spanish people towards the noble madness of chivalry.
This is for good or ill his function. Since yesterday I have been
pondering the fact. Here is a nation presented with a travesty of
tragedy, a *reductio ad absurdum* of its national qualities, which it
turns into its most prized classic masterpiece. Gravely, calmly,
proudly, it looks as into a mirror at its own *grandezza,* its idealism,
its lofty impracticality, its unmarketable high-mindedness—is this
not strange? The historical greatness of Spain lies in bygone centuries. In ours it has to struggle with problems of adaptation. But as
for me, what interests me is precisely the difference between what
we pompously call history and our own inward, human history.
Freedom, light-hearted self-criticism, probably do not ensure a
people a prominent role in history. But they give it charm; and,
after all, in the end even charm and its opposite play their roles in
history. Whatever pessimistic historians may say, human beings have
a conscience, even if only an æsthetic one, a feeling for good taste.
They bow, of course, before success, before the *fait accompli* of
brute force, even of successful crime. But at bottom they do not lose
sight of the humanly beautiful, the violently wrong and brutalizing,
which has happened in their midst; and in the end without their
sympathy might and brute force can reap no lasting success. History
is ordinary reality, to which one is born, to which one must be
adequate. Upon it Don Quixote's inept loftiness of soul suffers
shipwreck. That is winning, and ridiculous. But what would a Don
Quixote at the other extreme be like? Anti-idealistic, sinister, a
pessimistic believer in force—and yet a Don Quixote? A brutalized
Don Quixote? Even Cervantes, with all his melancholic humour,
had not gone so far as to conceive that.

May twenty-first

* * *

I have diverted myself the whole day with the epic wit of Cervantes, in making the adventures of the second part, or at least some of them, grow out of Don Quixote's literary fame, out of the popularity that he and Sancho enjoy, thanks to the earlier part, "their novel," the great history wherein they were first portrayed. They would never have got so far as the ducal court if the distinguished persons there had not know the extraordinary pair so well from reading about them and been enchanted to see them in the flesh and amuse themselves by giving them entertainment. That is new, and unique. I know nowhere else in literature where the hero of a novel lives on his own fame, as it were upon the reputation of his reputation. The simple reappearance of well-known characters in novel sequences, as in Balzac, is after all something quite different. Their existence is confirmed, their personalities achieve greater depth by virtue of our old acquaintance with them and the fact that they were there before and have come back. But they do not change their level; the order of illusion to which they belong remains the same. In Cervantes it is more than this: a sort of romantic illusion, a trick with an ironic undertone. Don Quixote and his squire, in this second part, quit the sphere of reality where they belonged, the novel where they first had their being, to move in person, as more lively realities, through a world which paid them joyous homage. And that world, in its turn, represents a higher stage of reality, although even it is a depicted world, the illusional evocation of a fictive past. Sancho Panza, in the presence of the Duchess, permits himself to jest: "That squire of his, who is, or ought to be, in the same history, called Sancho Panza, that am I, unless I was changed in the cradle, I mean in the press." Yes, Cervantes even evokes a figure out of the detested false sequel, and makes it convict itself out of its own mouth and show that the Don Quixote created by the same author cannot possibly be the right and true one. These are devices after the heart of E. T. A. Hoffmann himself. Indeed, they may be a clue to the source of much in the writers of the romantic school. It cannot be said that they were the greatest artists. But they have thought the most fruitfully about the weird depths, the trick mirrors and false bottoms of artistic illusion;

and it is precisely because they were artists in and beyond art that they came so dangerously near to the ironic dissolution of form. It is well to be constantly aware that this is the intimate pitfall of every technique that seeks to combine the humorous with the realistic. From the comic touch of certain epic means of producing reality to the word-plays and artifices of downright buffoonery, faithful to form and yet amorphous, it is only a step. I do indeed give my reader an unexpected opportunity of seeing with his own eyes Joseph, son of Jacob, sitting by the well in the moonlight, and of comparing his bodily presence, fascinating if also humanly incomplete as it is, with the ideal renown that centuries have woven about his figure. But I hope that the humour of this method of seizing the occasion to evoke reality may still deserve the honourable name of art.

May twenty-second

* * *

As for *Don Quixote,* it is indeed a strange product: naïve, unique, arbitrary and sovereign in its contradictions. I cannot but shake my head over the single tales scattered through it, so extravagantly sentimental they are, so precisely in the style and taste of the very productions that the poet had set himself to mock. He crams his hosts of readers full to their hearts' content with the very diet from which he would wean them—a pleasant cure! In those idylls he resigns his earlier role, as though to say that if the age wanted that sort of thing he could give it them, yes, even be a master at it. But I am not so clear about the position with regard to those humanistic speeches which he sometimes puts in his hero's mouth; whether he does not thereby distort the character, overstep its limits, and inartistically speak for himself. They are excellent, these speeches; for instance, upon education, and upon the poesy of nature and of art, which the knight in the green mantle gets to hear. They are full of pure reason, justice, human benevolence, and nobility of form, so that he in the green mantle is justly astonished, "and indeed so much that he wavered in his earlier opinion that the man must be foolish." Quite rightly so, and the reader should waver too. Don Quixote is a bit cracked but not in the least stupid, though the fact was not so clear, even to the author himself, in the beginning. His respect for the creature of his own comic invention grows during the narrative. This process is perhaps the most fascinating thing in the whole novel; it is a novel in itself, waxing proportionately with his regard for his work, which at first he conceived modestly, as a pretty crude and downright satire, without a notion of the extent to which his hero was destined to grow in stature, symbolically and humanly. The change in the point of view permits and even causes a considerable identification of the author with his hero, an inclination to assimilate his intellectual attainments to the author's own, to make him the mouthpiece of Cervantes's convictions and to heighten by cultural and intellectual gifts the picturesque charm which, despite his doleful exterior, his own mad idea develops in Don Quixote. It is his master's elegance of thought and diction that is often the source of Sancho's boundless admiration—and he is not the only one to be fascinated by it.

May twenty-third

*　　*　　*

At odd times I read in my orange-coloured volumes and am appalled at Cervantes's intemperate cruelty. For despite that considerable assimilation of the hero to his creator, of which I wrote yesterday, despite the author's high respect for the work of his brain, his inventiveness runs riot in ridiculous and humiliating pitfalls, into which the high-minded hero then tumbles and most comically disgraces himself—as in the adventure with the cheeses, which the "low-minded" Sancho Panza put into Don Quixote's helmet and which began to melt at the moment of high pathos and send streams of curd over the knight's eyes and beard, so that he thinks his brains are softening or he is sweating some horrible sort of sweat— whereat he forfends the thought that it might be a sweat of fear. There is something sardonic and desperately funny in such inventions—as, for another instance, that about the wooden cage in which Don Quixote was "cooped up" and dragged about. Humiliation could not further go. He gets endless beatings, almost as many as Lucius in the story of the Ass.[1] And yet his creator loves and honours him. Does not all this cruelty look like self-flagellation, self-revilement, castigation? Yes, it seems to me as though here the author abandons to scorn his oft-flouted belief in the idea, in the human being and his ennoblement; that this grim coming to terms with reality is actually the definition of humour.

[1] The reference here is to *The Metamorphoses,* otherwise known as *The Golden Ass,* by Apuleius, the novelist of late Roman Antiquity—ED.

Cervantes puts into Don Quixote's mouth an admirable critique of the nature of translation. It seems to him, he says, that a translation from one language into another is like a Flemish carpet looked at on the wrong side: "for though the figures come out, they are full of threads which mar them and show them not in full beauty and completeness as on the right side. But I will not say that on that account translation is not a praiseworthy work." The metaphor is striking. Only two Spanish translators are exempted, Figueroa and Xauregui. With them one can scarcely distinguish between translation and original. They must have been extraordinary, those two. But in the name of Cervantes I should like to except another name: that of Ludwig Tieck, who in the German *Don Quixote* has made another right side to the carpet.

May twenty-fourth

Yesterday *The Golden Ass* came into my head and ran off my pen—not quite by chance, since I came upon certain affinities between the late-classic novel and *Don Quixote;* though in my ignorance I do not know if others have not found them before. The scenes and episodes I mean become striking by their inherent oddness and lack of motivation, indicating a diffused origin. It is significant that they are in the second, intellectually more ambitious part of the book.

There is, in the first place, in the ninth book, the story of "The Wedding of Camacho, with Other Delightful Incidents." Delightful? Why, this wedding is a frightful affair; but the word as it stands in the chapter-head anticipates the *blague,* the delusion, the secret mockery and farce, the tragic practical joke, which await the reader and most of the characters as well. In the end everything gives place to bewildered laughter. The rustic betrothal feast of the beautiful Quiteria with the rich Camacho is described with florid extravagance. Camacho is the happy rival of the scorned but stouthearted Basilio, who is only scorned by command, for he has loved his neighbour's daughter Quiteria since childhood and she loves him in turn, so that they really belong together before God and man. The union of the fair one with the rich Camacho happens only by the iron command of the bride's father. The festivities have got as far as the betrothal when amid great outcry the unhappy Basilio appears, "clad in a black jacket, all welted with crimson in flames," and in a trembling voice makes a speech. He says that he, the moral obstacle to the full and undisturbed happiness of the pair, will put himself out of the way. He cries:

> "Long live the rich Camacho with the ungrateful Quiteria! Many and happy ages may they live; and let poor Basilio die, whose poverty clipped the wings of his good fortune and laid him in his grave!" So saying, he laid hold of his truncheon, which was stuck in the ground; and drawing out a short tuck that was concealed in it and to which it served as a scabbard; and setting what may be called the hilt upon the ground, with a nimble spring and determined purpose he threw himself upon it and in an instant half the bloody point appears at his back, the poor wretch lying along the ground weltering in his blood and pierced through with his own weapon.

One cannot imagine a more horrid interruption to a gay and splendid feast. Everyone rushes up, Don Quixote himself dismounts from his Rocinante to assist the unhappy wretch, the priest takes charge of him and suffers no one to draw the dagger from the wound before Basilio has confessed, for the drawing out and the death of the victim would be one and the same thing. The devoted one comes a little to himself and in a faint voice expresses the wish that Quiteria might give him her hand as his bride in the last moments of his life, thus extenuating his sinful death. What can he mean? Shall the rich Camacho resign in favour of Death? The priest warns the dying man to think rather upon his own soul and to confess; but Basilio, rolling his eyes and obviously at his last gasp, swears that he will never confess until Quiteria gives him her hand. This, then, a Christian soul being in the balance, comes to pass, with the consent to boot of the pious Camacho. But scarcely has the benediction been pronounced when up springs Basilio most nimbly, draws out the dagger from his body, which had served it for a sheath, and to the bystanders, who are crying out: "A miracle, a miracle!" pertly responds: "No miracle, only a stratagem." In short, it turns out that the dagger had not gone through Basilio's ribs, but through a lead pipe filled with blood, all this having been a trick arranged between the lovers. Thanks to the good nature of Camacho and the wise and kindly words of Don Quixote the whole results in Basilio keeping his Quiteria and the resumption of the feasting in honour of the bridal pair.

Is this really fair? The suicide scene is painted with complete seriousness and tragic emphasis. The emotions of horror roused not only in the other actors but in the reader as well are quite unequivocal. Yet in the end the whole thing dissolves in laughter and betrays itself as a farce and travesty. It is not a little annoying. The question is: are such practical mystifications really suitable for art —for art as we understand it? I am instructed by Erwin Rohde and by the excellent book which the mythologist and historian of religion Karl Kerenyi wrote in Budapest on the Greco-Roman novel, that the fabulists of late antiquity had an extraordinary love of such scenes. The Alexandrian novel-writer Achilleus Tatius relates in his *History of Leucippe and Cleitophon* how the heroine is slain horribly by Egyptian swamp robbers. The deed is described in all its barbaric detail. It takes place before the eyes of her beloved, who stands separated from her by a wide ditch, and who then is about to slay himself in despair upon her grave. But now companions appear, whom likewise he had thought dead, draw his beloved safe and sound out of the grave, and relate to him that they too had been captured by the natives; that the sacrifice had devolved upon them and that with the help of a property dagger, with the blade on a spring, and a piece of gut filled with blood they had pretended to carry out the deed. Do I deceive myself, or do this blood-filled gut and the trick dagger in *Don Quixote* come from the same school?

The second case is reminiscent of Apuleius himself. I mean the highly remarkable adventure of the ass's bray, which is told in the eighth and tenth chapters of Cervantes's ninth book. Two country justices, the ass of one of whom has run away, go together to the mountains where they think the ass is hiding, and since they cannot find it, try to lure it by imitating its bray, an art in which they are marvellously proficient. One stands here, the other there, and they bray against each other; and always when one makes himself heard, the other runs to the spot convinced that the ass is there, because only he could bray so like life. They overwhelm each other with compliments on their remarkable gifts. But the reason why the ass does not come is that he lies in the bushes devoured by wolves. The magistrates find him at length and, hoarse and exhausted, wend their way homewards. The story of the braying contest spreads abroad, so that the people of the village become the mock of all the neighbouring ones. They are put beside themselves by braying from all sides; bitter quarrels, yes, even passages at arms ensue between village and village, and Don Quixote and Sancho Panza march in upon the sally to one of these. For in the usual way the ass-villagers have made of the jest an honour and a watchword: they issue forth with a white satin banner upon which a braying ass is painted, under which emblem they march towards the anti-asses with lances, crossbows, partisans, and halberds to deliver them a battle. But Don

Quixote puts himself in the way. He makes a lofty speech, wherein he admonishes them in the name of reason to desist from their purpose and not let it come to bloodshed for such trifles. They seem willing to listen to him. But now Sancho mixes in to clinch the matter and says that not only would it be folly to be angered at the sound of a bray, but that also he himself in his youth could bray with such infectious verisimilitude that all the asses in the village answered him. And in token that it is an art, which, like swimming, once learned is never forgotten, he holds his nose and brays till all the near-by valleys echo—to his own huge undoing. For the villagers, not being able to bear hearing it, thrash him soundly, and even Don Quixote, quite contrary to his practice, must flee from the threat of their crossbows and partisans. He makes himself scarce; and Sancho, whom, scarcely come to himself, they have "set on his ass" and suffered to follow his master, joins him in flight. Moreover the squadrons, after they have waited the night in vain for the enemy, who have not come out, "returned to their homes joyful and merry" and, adds the scholarly poet, "had they known the practice of the ancient Greeks, they would have erected a trophy in that place."

Extraordinary tale! There are in it associations and affiliations about which I can hardly believe myself mistaken. The ass plays a singular role in the Greco-Roman representational world. He is the animal of Typhon-Set, wicked brother of Osiris; he is the Red One. The mythical hatred of him reached so far into the Middle Ages that the rabbinical Biblical commentaries call him Esau, the name of Jacob's brother, the wild ass. The idea of beating is closely and sacramentally bound up with this phallic conception. The phrase "to beat the ass" has a cult-coloration. Whole herds of asses were ritually beaten as they were driven round the city walls. Also there was the pious custom of pushing the Typhon beast off a rock—just the manner of death which Lucius barely escaped after being turned into an ass in the novel of Apuleius: the robbers threaten him with "*katachremnzesthai*." Moreover he is beaten for braying, just like Sancho Panza, and continues to be beaten all the time that he is an ass—there are fourteen instances. I may add that according to Plutarch the inhabitants of certain villages so hated the voice of the ass that they put trumpeting under a taboo because it sounded like braying. May not the villagers in *Don Quixote* be a reminiscence of these hypersensitive citizens of antiquity?

It is strange to uncover such a primitive mythical inheritance innocently disguised in the Spanish Renaissance author. Did he get it from direct knowledge of classic Roman literature? Or did the

theme come to him by way of Italy, via Boccaccio? Let scholars
decide.

*   *   *

May twenty-fifth

*   *   *

The adventure with the lion is certainly the climax of Don
Quixote's "exploits" and in all seriousness the climax of the novel.
It is a glorious tale, told with a comic pathos, a sympathetic humour,
which betray the poet's genuine enthusiasm for his hero's folly. I
read it twice over and was utterly absorbed in its peculiarly moving,
magnificently ridiculous contents. The meeting with the pennanted
car in which are the African animals, "which the general of Oran
was sending to court as a present to His Majesty," is charming as a
cultural record. It is evidence of his extraordinary art that after all
we have already read of Don Quixote's blind, ill-directed intrepidity,
the author can keep us in breathless suspense throughout this adventure. To the horror of his companions and deaf to any reasonable objections, the knight insists that the keeper should let one of
the ferocious and hungry animals out of the cage to do battle with
him. It is remarkable how Cervantes can sustain a single motive
and keep it fresh and effective throughout. Don Quixote's foolhardi-
ness is so astonishing just because he is by no means so mad as not
to be aware of it. "Encountering the lions," he says later,

> was my unavoidable task, though I knew it to be most extravagant
> rashness, for I was very well aware that fortitude is a virtue placed be-
> tween the two vicious extremes of cowardice and foolhardiness. But
> it is better the valiant should rise to the high pitch of temerity than
> sink to the low point of cowardice. For as it is easier for the prodigal
> to become liberal than for the covetous, just so it is much easier for
> the rash to hit upon being truly valiant than for the coward to rise to
> true valour.

What moral intelligence! The observation of the man in the green
mantle is most pertinent: "What he said was coherent, elegant, and
well said; what he did was extravagant, rash, and foolish." One
almost gets the impression that the author put it forward as a natural and unavoidable antimony of the higher life.

The classic scene, depicted a hundred times in pictures, where the
lean hidalgo dismounts from his mare, fearful lest her courage may

not equal his own, and with his trumpery shield and sword, ready for the absurdest duel ever imagined, stands before the open cage full of heroic impatience to get to grips with his enemy—this extraordinary scene lives actually before me in the words of Cervantes. So does the issue of it, which ever so mildly stultifies the knight's heroics. For the king of beasts will not let himself in for such tricks and gambols. He gives one glance, then simply turns his rear foremost and lies unfeelingly down on the floor of his cage. Once more heroics have prosaically missed fire. The whole burden of the theme, all the scorn and mockery of its intent, come down upon Don Quixote's head in the contemptuous, indifferent behavior of the royal beast. The knight is beside himself. He demands of the quaking keeper that he should beat the lion to rouse him to combat. But the man refuses, and at length makes the knight comprehend that he has already displayed the greatness of his courage. No warrior, however doughty, is bound to do more than to challenge his opponent and await him in the open field. If the latter flinches, the blame falls upon him and upon no one else. Don Quixote is finally satisfied. In token of his victory he puts upon his spear the same handkerchief with which he has wiped off his cheesy sweat—whereupon Sancho, who had run away, seeing it from the distance, says: "May I be hanged if my master has not vanquished the wild beasts, for there he summons us." It is a marvel.

In no other place comes out so strongly as here the author's utter readiness to exalt and to abase his hero. But abasement and exaltation are a twin conception the essence of which is distinctly Christian. Their psychological union, their marriage in a comic medium, shows how very much Don Quixote is a product of Christian culture, Christian doctrine, and Christian humanity. It shows as well what Christianity everlastingly means for the world of the mind and of poesy and for the human essence itself and its bold expansion and liberation. I have in mind my Jacob, who whimpered in the dust before the boy Eliphaz, dishonoured to the uttermost, and then, in a dream, out of the very depth of his abased soul produced his great exaltation. Say what you will: Christianity, the flower of Judaism, remains one of the two pillars upon which Western culture rests, the other being Mediterranean antiquity. The denial of one of these fundamental premises of our civilization and education—how much more of both of them—by any group of our European community, would mean its break with that community and an inconceivable, impossible diminishment of its human stature, who knows to what extent? The hectic attack of Nietzsche, the admirer

of Pascal, upon Christianity was an unnatural eccentricity; it has
always puzzled me, like much else in the character of that tragic
hero. Goethe, more happily balanced and physically less hampered,
did not allow his supposed paganism to prevent him from paying
homage to Christianity and speaking out for it as the civilizing
force that it is. Agitated times like ours always tend to confound
the merely epochal with the eternal—as for instance liberalism with
freedom—and to throw out the baby with the bath. Thus each
free and thoughtful person, each mind which does not flicker in the
wind of time, is forced back upon the foundations; driven to become
once more conscious of them and to base more solidly upon them.
The critique of the twentieth century upon Christian ethic (not to
speak of dogma and mythology); the changes that come about naturally with the flow of life; no matter how deep these go, or how
transformingly they work, they are and will remain superficial effects. They can never touch the binding authority of the cultural
Christianity of the Western world, which once achieved cannot be
alienated.

May twenty-sixth

*   *   *

Very arresting and significant is the episode of the Morisco Ricote,
the former shopkeeper from Sancho's village, who has been banished
from Spain by the Edicts and slips back in pilgrim's garb, urged by
homesickness but also in hopes of digging up a buried treasure. The
chapter is a shrewd mixture of professions of loyalty and of the
author's strict adherence to the church, his blameless submission to
the great Philip III—and the most lively human sympathy for the
awful fate of the Moorish people, who, attacked by the Edicts of the
King, are sacrificed to the supposed interests of the state and driven
into misery without regard for individual agony. Through the one
position the author purchases immunity for the other; but I suspect, and it has always been felt, that the first was the political
means to the second and that the sincerity of the author begins only
there. He puts into the mouth of the unhappy Morisco himself an
acceptance of His Majesty's commands, an acknowledgment that
they spring from indisputable right. Many, he says, had not wanted
to believe that the order was seriously meant and considered it a
mere threat. But he saw at once that it was an actual law and as
such would be put into execution at the appointed time. And what

confirmed him in the belief was that he knew of the mischievous extravagant designs "which were such that in my opinion it was a divine inspiration that moved His Majesty to put so brave a resolution into practice." The shameful plots that justify the royal inspiration are not mentioned by name, they remain shrouded in darkness. But not all were guilty. "Some of us," says Ricote, "were steady and true Christian, but these were so few . . . and it is not prudent to nourish a serpent in one's bosom or to keep one's enemies within one's own door." The objectivity and moderation which the author puts in the mouth of the sufferer are most admirable. But gradually and insensibly they are diverted into quite another channel. The Moor says that the punishment was just, a soft and mild one in the opinion of some, but in reality the most terrible that could be inflicted.

> Wherever we are we weep for Spain, for in short here were we born and this is our native country. We nowhere find the reception which our misfortune requires. Even in Barbary, and in all other parts of Africa where we expected to be received, cherished, and made much of, there it is we are most neglected and misused.

Thus the Spanish Moor continues to mourn, so bitterly that it goes to the heart. "We knew not," he says,

> our happiness till we lost it; and so great is the desire almost all of us have to return to Spain that we forsake wife and children and come back again at risk of our lives, so mighty is the love we bear it. And it is now I know, and find by experience, the truth of that common saying: "Sweet is the love of one's country."

Such words as these, the expression of ineradicable natural affinity, obviously give the lie to the phrases about the snake in the bosom, the enemy in the house, the inspired justice of the Edicts, and so forth. The artist's dilemma, expressed in Ricote's speech in the second part of *Don Quixote*, speaks a more convincing language than his careful, obsequious tongue. He sympathizes with the persecuted and banned. They are as good Spaniards as himself or anybody; Spain is their true mother-land; she will not be purer, only poorer, after they have gone, while, once torn from her soil, they are everywhere foreign. Everywhere the words "at home" will be on their lips: "at home in Spain it was thus and thus"—that is, better than where they are. Cervantes, a poor and dependent writer, had all too much need to prove his loyalty; but after he has denied his heart and its honest convictions for only a few moments, he cleanses it again, better than Spain, with all her edicts, can cleanse herself.

He condemns the cruelty of the decree that he has just approved—
not directly, but by stressing the love of the exiles for their home-
land. He even takes it on himself to speak of the freedom of conscience; for Ricote tells how he went from Italy to Germany and
there found a sort of peace. For Germany was a good, tolerant
country, "its people not standing much upon niceties and everybody living as he pleased, for in most parts of it there is liberty of
conscience." Here it was my turn to feel patriotic pride, let the
words be old which awake it in me. It is always pleasant to hear
praise of home out of a stranger's mouth.

May twenty-seventh

*   *   *

I must return to what I wrote yesterday and make clear to myself
how Cervantes's allegiance as Christian and loyal subject enhances
the spiritual value of his freedom, the worth of his criticism. What
concerns me is the relativity of all freedom; the fact that it needs to
be conditioned and checked, not only outwardly but inwardly as
well, in order that it may attain to spiritual worth and be expressive
of a higher form of life. It is hard for us to imagine the state of feudal
dependence in which artists of former times lived, before that
emancipation of the artist ego which has come in with the bourgeois age. One may say that only in very rare cases has this latter
been beneficial to the artist as a type. Once the guild of artists
modestly based itself on its sense of craftsmanship. It was the fundamental constitution even of the greatest, even of that accidental
genius who from time to time got so far as to bow before sovereigns
and flower into supernal worth. The whole conception was probably
more conducive to the sanity of the artist than are the present ones.
In our day we *begin* with emancipation, with the ego, liberty, self-
government. Modest simplicity is no longer the nourishing soil of
greatness. Once, a given painter or sculptor, thinking to dedicate
himself to the calling of beautifying and adorning the world, went
as apprentice to a good master; washed brushes, ground colours,
rose from the ranks. He became a useful help, to whom the old
man doubtless left some work to do, just as the head surgeon at the
end of an operation says to his assistant: "You finish!" Finally he
himself became, if all went well, a master in his calling—and that
was the height of his desire. He was called *"artista"* and the word
covered both conceptions, that of artist and craftsman. Even today

in Italy every master of a trade is so called. The genius, the great ego, the lonely adventurer, was an exception produced out of the modest, solid, objectively skilled cult of the craft; he achieved royal rank, yet even so he remained a dutiful son of the church and received from her his orders and his material. Today, as I said, we begin with the genius, the ego, the solitary—which is probably morbid. Hugo von Hofmannsthal, who, thanks to his Italo-Austrian origins, had much intuitive sympathy with the eighteenth century, once talked to me amusingly and wittily about the pathetic changes that had taken place in the musician's contacts with life. He said that in former days if you visited a musician he talked something like this: "Do sit down, have a cup of coffee, shall I play to you?" Today, he said, they all sit there like ailing eagles. Precisely. Artists have become ailing eagles because art has become solemn. It elevates and dejects the average artist, with unhappy results; it has made art solitary, melancholy, isolated, misunderstood, turned it, in short, into an ailing eagle.

It is certainly true that the poet represents an art world different from the graphic, the plastic, or the musical. Poetic and literary creation have a special place among the arts since in them the mechanical plays a smaller, in any case a different, role, more immaterial, more mental. On the whole its relation to the mind is more immediate. The poet is not artist alone; or rather he is artist in another, more intellectual way, since his medium is the word, his tool of the mind. But even with him it were desirable that liberty and emancipation stood at the end and not at the beginning, so that as a human being the artist would emerge from modesty, limitation, restraint, independence. For, once more, freedom has worth, it confers rank, only when it is won from unfreedom, when it is the process of becoming free. How much more powerful and intellectually significant is Cervantes's human sympathy for the fate of Ricote the Moor and his indirect criticism of the state's harsh attitude, *after* he has expressed the submission which with him is a matter not of hypocrisy but of actual intellectual conditioning! All the human freedom and dignity, the emancipation of the artist spirit; the quixotic audacity that mingles cruel humiliation and moving nobility of soul—all this, the genius, independence, and daring, rests upon reverence before the Holy Inquisition, formal devotion to the monarch, acceptance of the protection of great men and their "well-known generosity," for example Count Lemos and Don Bernardo de Sandoval y Roxas. It soars up from these loyal limitations as involuntarily and unexpectedly as the work itself

grows out of an entertaining, jesting satire—as which it was conceived—and into a monument of universal literature and symbol
of humanity. I take it for a rule that the greatest works were those of
the most modest purpose. Ambition may not stand at the beginning;
it must not come before the work but must grow with the work,
which will itself be greater than the blithely astonished artist
dreamed; it must be bound up with the work and not with the ego
of the artist. There is nothing falser than abstract and premature
ambition, the self-centered pride independent of the work, the pallid
ambition of the ego. So possessed, the artist sits there "like an ailing
eagle."

May twenty-eighth

*   *   *

I am inclined to find the end of Don Quixote a little weak. Death
here assumes the character of a fixation against all unwarranted
literary exploiting, and thereby itself takes on a literary artificiality
that is not very convincing. It is not the same whether a beloved
creation dies to the author or whether he *makes* it die, brings about
and advertises its death, in order that no one else can make it live
again. A literary death born of jealousy. But indeed this very
jealousy betrays once more the poet's inner and proudly defensive
identification with the eternally distinguished creation of his brain.
His feeling is deep; no less sincere in that it expresses itself in
jesting literary precautions against extraneous attempts at galvaniz-
ing the corpse. The priest demands of the notary a certificate "that
Alonzo Quixano the Good, commonly called Don Quixote de la
Mancha, has departed this life and died a natural death; and he
insisted upon this testimonial lest any other author save only Cid
Hamet Benengeli falsely should raise him from the dead and write
endless stories of his exploits." Cid Hamet himself, however, evapo-
rates at this juncture and betrays himself as the whimsical pretext
he always was. He it is indeed who hangs up his pen by a brass
wire upon a spit-rack and charges it to cry out to the presumptuous
or wicked historians who would take it down to profane it:

> Beware, ye poet thieves, beware!
> Nor steal a single line;
> For Fate has made this work its care,
> And guaranteed it mine.

Who speaks? Who says "mine"? The pen? No, it is another speaker who utters the last line. "For me alone was Don Quixote born and I for him; he understood how to act and I to write, we were destined for each other, maugre and in despite of that scribbling imposter of Tordesillas who has dared or shall dare with gross and ill-cut ostrich feather to describe the exploits of my valorous knight; a burden too weighty for his shoulders and an enterprise beyond his dull and frigid genius." Well the poet knows what noble and humanly heavy burden he has borne in this history which has lightened the heart of all the world. He did not know it at the beginning, but he knew it. And how strange! At the very end he does not know it either. He forgets it again.

He says:

> For my only desire was to bring into public abhorrence the fabulous and absurd histories of knight-errantry which, compared with my true and genuine *Don Quixote,* begin already to totter and will doubtless fall, never to rise again. Farewell.

That is a return to the modest satirical parody which was the original intention of a work that grew so much beyond it. The death-bed chapter itself expresses this reversion. For Don Quixote is changed before he dies. The dying man wins—oh, joy!—his sane reason back. He has a long sleep, six hours long, and when he wakes he is by God's mercy mentally healed. His mind is free of the fog that had invaded it by the much reading of those dreadful books of knight-errantry; he sees their senselessness and depravity and will be no longer Don Quixote de la Mancha, knight of the doleful countenance, knight of the lions, but Alonzo Quixano, a reasonable man, a man like other men. That should rejoice us. But it rejoices us strikingly little, it leaves us cold, and to some extent we regret it. We are sorry about Don Quixote—as indeed we were sorry for him when affliction at his defeat stretched him out on his bed of death. For that is actually the cause of his demise; the doctor declares "that melancholy and vexation brought about his death." It is the deep dejection of seeing shipwrecked his mission as knight-errant and light-bringer that killed him. And we, hearing still in our ear that weak and sickly voice speaking the words: "Dulcinea is the most beautiful damsel in the world and I the unhappiest knight, but it is not fitting that my weakness should deny this truth; lay on, knight, with thy lance!"—we share in his defeat, though we know that his mission could not turn out otherwise, being the whimsy and maggot that it was. Even so in the course of the story the whimsy becomes so endeared to us that we are prepared and even eager to let it stand for the spirit, to feel for it as though it were spirit itself—and that we finely owe to the poet.

The case is most difficult. A conflict is present. If the work had only remained true to its original purpose of bringing to scorn the books of knight-errantry, through the ridiculous undertakings and overthrowings of a witless knight, then everything would be simple enough. But since all unexpectedly it expanded so much beyond its fundamental idea, the possibility of a satisfactory ending was destroyed. To let Don Quixote fall and die in one of his senseless enterprises was unthinkable, it would have gone beyond a joke and jarred on Cervantes's audience. To make him live after his return to sanity would not do either; that would be to make the husk survive beyond the soul; would be a degradation of the character below its lofty height—quite aside from the fact that for reasons connected with literary patronage he had to die anyway. I can see that it would have been neither Christian nor edifying to let him die in his delusion, saved indeed from the lance of the knight of the silver moon, but in despair over his downfall. It was needful that his despair be dissipated in his dying hour by the knowledge that it was all madness. But after all is there not death in the revelation that Dulcinea was not an adorable princess but a peasant girl off a dung-hill, and all his actions, griefs, and aspirations were moonshine? Should he not then curse God and die? Certainly it was imperative to save Don Quixote's soul to sanity before he died. But in order that this salvation might be after our hearts, the author should have made his unreason less lovable.

Thus we see that genius may become an embarrassment, and that it can spoil an author's conception. However, not too much is made of Don Quixote's death. It is the sympathetically imagined passing, dignified and Christlike, of a good man, after he has confessed, received ghostly consolation, and set his earthly affairs in order with the notary.

> As all human things, especially the lives of men, are transitory, incessantly declining from their beginning until they arrive at their final period; and as that of Don Quixote had no particular privilege from Heaven, to exempt it from the common fate, his end and dissolution came when he least thought of it.

The reader must take that not too seriously, as did the friends whom Don Quixote left behind, his housekeeper, his niece, and Sancho, his former squire. These indeed mourned him with all their heart;

the reader sees again what a good master he has been; yes, there is the grotesque description of "the sluices of their swollen eyes when the news that he must die forced a torrent of tears from their eyes and a thousand groans from their hearts." It is easy to give a comic turn to the description of sincere sorrow. "Human nature is human nature," "life must go on," and so forth. . . . We are told that during the three days of Don Quixote's agony, though "the whole house was in confusion, yet the niece ate, the housekeeper drank, and Sancho Panza made much of himself; for this business of legacies effaces, or moderates, the grief that is naturally due to the deceased." A mocking tribute to realism, an unsentimental attitude which may once have caused offence. The stoutest and boldest conqueror in the realm of human nature was always well armed with a sense of humour.

*   *   *

May twenty-ninth

The weather is still fine, fresh and slightly misty. Since we took leave at dawn of our beds, where we have rocked so many nights through, the ship, which lay to during the night, so that for the first time we were without the throb of her engines, has slowly got under way. We have breakfasted, given the last touches to our luggage, handed out the final tips. Ready for arrival, we await it on deck. Through the mist rises a familiar figure, the Goddess of Liberty with her crown, a naïve classicistic symbol grown right strange to us today.

I feel dreamy from the early rising and strange experience of this hour. And I dreamed in the night too, in the unfamiliar silence of the engines; now I try to recall the dream which assembled itself from my reading. I dreamed of Don Quixote, it was he himself, and I talked with him. How distinct is reality, when one encounters it, from one's fancy! He looked different from the pictures; he had a thick, bushy moustache, a high retreating forehead, and under the likewise bushy brows almost blind eyes. He called himself not the Knight of the Lions but Zarathustra. He was, now that I had him face to face, very tactful and courteous, so that I recalled with strong emotion the words that I had read about him yesterday:

for in truth, as has been said before, both while he was plain Alonzo Quixano and while he was Don Quixote de la Mancha, he was ever of an amiable disposition and affable behaviour, and was therefore beloved, not only by those of his own family, but by all that knew him.

Pain, love, pity, and boundless reverence filled me altogether as this prescription became real. Dreamily they hover about me in this hour of arrival.

But such thoughts are too European for my surroundings—they face in the wrong direction. Ahead out of the morning mist slowly emerge the skyscrapers of Manhattan, a fantastic landscape group, a towered city of giants.

The Ironic Hero:
Some Reflections on Don Quixote

by W. H. Auden

The following remarks have to assume that the reaction of other readers to *Don Quixote* is the same as mine, namely, that it is a portrait of the Christian Saint. Granted this, it may be interesting to consider:

1. What are the artistic difficulties involved in attempting such a portrait?
2. How does Cervantes solve them?

The Hero

To be the hero or heroine of a book a person must be:

1. Interesting, i.e., either his character or the situation in which he finds himself must be exceptional, even unique.
2. Completely public, i.e., his character, his motives, his actions must become completely manifest to the reader even if they remain hidden from the hero himself, deducible even if not directly stated. This means that anything which happens or might happen to the hero which is not described is of no account.

Heroes are conventionally divided into three classes, the epic hero, the tragic hero, and the comic hero. Don Quixote fits none of them.

The Epic Hero

The epic hero is born with the gift of exceptional *areté*. By birth and breeding he is exceptionally strong, brave, handsome, etc. This

"The Ironic Hero: Some Reflections on Don Quixote" by W. H. Auden. From *Horizon*, Vol. 20 (1949), 86–94. Copyright 1949 by *Horizon*. Reprinted by permission of Curtis Brown, Ltd.

areté is manifested in exceptional deeds, i.e., he performs feats of which the average is incapable. His motive is to win admiration from his equals whether they be friends or foes. The moral standard by which he lives is not a universal requirement, the law, but an individual one, honour. He is not tragic, i.e., he does not suffer more than others; but his death has exceptional pathos—the great warrior comes to the same end as the lowest churl. He exists in the present moment when he comes into collision with another heroic individual.

The Tragic Hero

All tragic heroes must (*a*) have some demonstrated *areté* in the epic sense, (*b*) move from glory to misery; their tragic character is manifested by their suffering more than the average. (*c*) This suffering is caused by a collision with the universal law of justice, which is the same for all. With this in common, there are, however, important differences between the classical and the Christian conceptions of the tragic hero, e.g.:

1. The former is placed in a situation where he is bound to become guilty of manifest sins. The sin for which he is responsible is the subjective sin of hybris. He is made to commit the others as a punishment. The situation of the latter is created partly by others, partly by himself. He is as responsible for the manifest sins he commits as he is for the invisible sin of pride which produces them. Further, there is a difference between hybris and pride. Hybris means believing that you *are* a god, i.e., that you cannot suffer; pride means a defiant attempt to *become* a god, when you secretly know that you are a mortal creature. The classical tragic hero is blind; the Christian tragic hero deceives himself.
2. The former, therefore, must be a fortunate and happy man. The latter (e.g. Richard III) need not be; he must only have an exceptionally strong defiant will.
3. The effect of suffering on the former is to make him humble; through suffering he expiates the past. The effect of suffering on the latter is to harden his heart; for, if he repents, then he ceases to be tragic: e.g. Angelo in *Measure for Measure* and Lear are not tragic heroes. Othello is. The Christian tragic hero is damned.

The Comic Hero

In the comedy of situation (e.g. identical twins) the hero is not properly so called, for he is the average man placed in a less dignified situation than the average. The truly comic hero has less *areté* than the average, e.g., the jealous old husband or the unsuccessful rogue. His attempt to violate the law is thwarted not by the law but by other rogues who are equally outside the law. Like the tragic hero he suffers; but (*a*) the spectator does not suffer sympathetically because he does not identify himself with the comic hero through admiration, (*b*) the suffering is temporary, (*c*) the suffering is educational, i.e., it cures him of his comic madness so that he conforms with the law, either through repentance or out of prudence.

The Christian Saint

The Christian Saint has no special *areté* of power or knowledge (such as he may have is irrelevant), only an obedient will. He is virtuous out of faith in and love of God and his neighbour, not out of a pride which wants him to think well of himself.

To manifest this aesthetically is very difficult because:

(*a*) He must be shown as failing in a worldly sense, i.e., as coming into collision with the law of this world, otherwise there is no proof that he acts out of faith and not mere worldly prudence.

(*b*) Failure and suffering, however, are in themselves no proof of faith, because the collision with the law may also be the result of pride. The visible ends of Christ, the repentant thief and the unrepentant thief are the same, though the third is a tragic figure, the second one a comic figure in the profoundest sense, and Christ is not a hero at all, for he is not the Man-God (Hercules) but the God-Man.

(*c*) The virtues produced by pride cannot be distinguished objectively from the virtues produced by faith. When Becket in *Murder in the Cathedral* is assailed by the fourth tempter, who suggests that he be martyred for self-glorification, it is impossible for Eliot to prove to us that Becket resists the temptation; he can only state that it exists.

(*d*) It is possible, up to a point, to manifest hybris; Agamemnon walks on the purple carpet, Darius attempts to bridge the Hellespont, etc. Pride cannot be directly manifested, for it cannot be directly known even by its victims. I can look in the mirror of my conscience and learn that I am greedy, envious, lustful, etc., and from that infer that I am proud. I cannot, however, learn that I am proud because the pride, if it is there, is in my eye which is looking into the mirror. As Nietzsche says, "He who despises himself nevertheless esteems himself as a despiser."

For the tragic hero suffering is real and destructive; for the comic hero it is unreal or temporary or curative; for both it is a sign that they are not in the truth: both suffer with misunderstanding. The saint, on the other hand, is ironically related to suffering; it is real, nevertheless he understands that it is a blessing, a sign that he is in the truth. "I say pain but ought to say solace."

The Knight Errant

The Knight Errant, whom Don Quixote wishes to become and actually parodies, was an attempt to christianize the pagan epic hero, i.e., the Knight Errant,

(*a*) possesses epic *areté* of good birth, good looks, strength, etc.

(*b*) This *areté* is put in the service of the law, to rescue the unfortunate, protect the innocent, and combat the wicked.

(*c*) His motives are three: (i) the desire for glory.
                                          (ii) the love of justice.
                                          (iii) the love of an individual woman who judges and rewards.

(*d*) He suffers exceptionally, first in his adventures and collisions with the lawless, secondly in his temptations to lawlessness in the form of unchastity and, thirdly, in his exceptionally difficult erotic romance.

(*e*) In the end he succeeds in this world. Vice is punished, and virtue is rewarded by the lady of his heart.

When we first meet Don Quixote he is (*a*) poor, (*b*) not a knight, (*c*) fifty, (*d*) has nothing to do except hunt and read romances about Knight-Errantry. Manifestly, he is the opposite of the heroes he admires, i.e., he is lacking in the epic *areté* of birth, looks, strength, etc. His situation, in fact, is aesthetically uninteresting except in one thing: his passion is great enough to make him sell land to buy books. This makes him aesthetically comic. Religiously he is tragic; for he is a hearer not a doer of the word, the weak man guilty in his imagination of Promethean pride. Now suddenly he goes mad, i.e., he sets out to become what he admires. Aesthetically this looks like pride; in fact, religiously, it is a conversion, an act of faith, a taking up of his cross.

The Quixotic Madness and the Tragic Madness

The tragic hero is tempted by an *areté* he possesses to conquer this world, whose nature he knows. His decisions are the result of a calculation of the probabilities of success, and each success increases his madness (e.g., Iago). Don Quixote is (*a*) lacking in *areté*, (*b*) has a fantastic conception of this world, (*c*) always meets with failure yet is never discouraged, (*d*) suffers himself intentionally and makes others suffer only unintentionally.

The Quixotic Madness and the Comic Madness

The comic rogue declares: The World = that which exists to give me money, beauty, etc. I refuse to suffer by being thwarted. He is cured by being forced to suffer through collision with the real world.

Don Quixote declares: The World = that which needs my existence to save it at whatever cost to myself. He comes into collision with the real world but insists upon continuing to suffer. He becomes the Knight of the Doleful Countenance but never despairs.

Don Quixote and Hamlet

Hamlet lacks faith in God and in himself. Consequently he must define his existence in terms of others, e.g., I am the man whose mother married his uncle, who murdered his father. He would like to become what the Greek tragic hero is, a creature of situation. Hence his inability to act, for he can only "act," i.e., play at possibilities.

Don Quixote is the antithesis of an actor, being completely incapable of seeing himself in a role. Defining his situation in terms of his own character, he is completely unreflective.

Madness and Faith

To have faith in something or someone means:

(*a*) that the latter is not manifest. If it becomes manifest, then faith is no longer required.

(*b*) The relation of faith between subject and object is unique in every case. Hundreds may believe, but each has to believe by himself.

Don Quixote exemplifies both. (*a*) He never sees things that aren't there (delusion) but sees them differently, e.g., windmills as giants, sheep as armies, puppets as Moors, etc. (*b*) He is the only individual who sees them thus.

Faith and Idolatry

The idolater makes things out to be stronger than they really are so that they shall be responsible for him, e.g., he might worship a windmill for its giant-like strength. Don Quixote never expects things to look after him; on the contrary he is always making himself responsible for things and people who have no need of him and regard him as an impertinent old meddler.

Faith and Despair

People are tempted to lose faith (*a*) when it fails to bring worldly success, (*b*) when the evidence of their senses and feelings seem against it. Don Quixote (*a*) is constantly defeated yet persists, (*b*) between his fits of madness sees that the windmills are not giants but windmills, etc., yet, instead of despairing, says, "Those cursed magicians delude me, first drawing me into dangerous adventures by the appearances of things as they really are and then presently changing the face of things as they please." His supreme test comes when Sancho Panza describes a country wench, whom Don Quixote sees correctly as such, as the beautiful Princess Dulcinea and in spite of his feelings concludes that he is enchanted and that Sancho Panza is right.

Don Quixote and the Knight Errant

Don Quixote's friends attack the Romances he loves on the grounds that they are historically untrue, and lacking in style.

Don Quixote, on the other hand, without knowing it, by his very failure to imitate his heroes exactly, at once reveals that the Knight Errant of the Romances is half-pagan, and becomes himself the true Christian Knight.

Epic Dualism

The world of the Romances is a dualistic world where the completely good and innocent fight the completely evil and guilty. The Knight Errant comes into collision only with those who are outside the law, giants, heretics, heathens, etc. Don Quixote when in one of his spells, under the illusion that he is showing the righteous anger of the Knight Errant, comes into collision with the law, i.e., he attacks innocent clerics and destroys other people's property.

When he is not deluded as to the nature of those he is trying to help, e.g., the convicts or the boy being thrashed, he only succeeds in making things worse and earns enmity, not gratitude.

Frauendienst

Don Quixote affirms all the articles of the Amor religion, namely, that (*a*) the girl must be noble and beautiful, (*b*) there must be some barrier, (*c*) the final goal of the Knight's trials is to be rewarded by having his love reciprocated.

In fact, the girl he calls Dulcinea del Toboso is "a good likely country lass for whom he had formerly had a sort of inclination, though 'tis believed she never heard of it." She is of lower social status, and he is past the age when sexual love means anything to him. Nevertheless, his behaviour has all the courage that might be inspired by a great passion.

Again, Don Quixote expects to be tempted to unchastity so that, in the inn when the hunchback maid is trying to reach the carter's bed, he fancies that she is the daughter of the Governor of the Castle, who has fallen in love with him and is trying to seduce him. Bruised and battered as he is, even Don Quixote has to admit that for the moment he has no capacity.

The language is the language of Eros, the romantic idolization of the fair woman, but its real meaning is the Christian Agape, which loves all equally irrespective of their merit.

Snobbery

The true Knight Errant has nothing to do with the Lower Orders and must never put himself in an undignified position, e.g.,

Launcelot is disgraced by riding in a cart. Don Quixote attempts to do likewise but with singular unsuccess. He is constantly having to do with the Lower Orders under the illusion that they are the nobility. His aristocratic refusal to pay, which he adopts out of literary precedence, not personal feeling, never works out—he ends by overpaying. Again the language is the language of the feudal knight, but the behaviour is that of the Suffering Servant. This may be compared with the reverse situation in *Moby Dick,* when Captain Ahab leaves his cabin boy in his captain's cabin and mounts the look-out like an ordinary seaman: here the behaviour is apparently humble, but in fact the extremity of pride.

This-Worldliness

The Knight Errant is this-worldly in that he succeeds in arms and in love. Don Quixote professes a similar hope but in fact is not only persistently defeated but also cannot in the end even maintain in combat that Dulcinea is without a rival. Thus, he not only has to suffer the Knight's trials but also must suffer the consciousness of defeat. He is never able to think well of himself. He uses the language of the epic hero, but reveals himself to us as the Knight of Faith, whose kingdom is not of this world.

Sancho Panza and Don Quixote

Without his comic lymphatic squire, the Knight of the Doleful Countenance would be incomplete. Sancho Panza's official motive for following Don Quixote is the promise of a governorship. But this is a purely imaginary idea to the former, and in the end he reveals his motives, which are (*a*) for the excitement, (*b*) for love of his master. Sancho Panza sees the world that requires changing as it is, but has no wish himself to change it. Yet it turns out that he is the one who has to play the part of the Knight Errant and rescue his distressed master from misfortune. Don Quixote wishes to change the world but has no idea what the world is like. He fails to change anything except Sancho Panza's character. So the two are eternally related. Don Quixote needs Sancho Panza as the one creature about whom he has no illusions but loves as he is; Sancho Panza needs Don Quixote as the one constant loyalty in his life which is independent of feeling. Take away Don Quixote, and Sancho Panza is so nearly pure flesh, immediacy of feeling, so nearly without will that he becomes a hedonist pagan who rejects everything but matter. Take away Sancho Panza, on the other hand, and Don Quixote is so nearly pure spirit that he becomes a Manichee who rejects matter and feeling and is nothing but an egotistic will.

Don Quixote's Death

However many further adventures one may care to invent for Don Quixote—and, as in all cases of a true myth, they are potentially infinite—the conclusion can only be the one which Cervantes gives, namely, that he recovers his senses and dies. Despite the protestations of his friends, who want him to go on providing them with amusement, he must say: "Ne'er look for birds of this year in the nests of the last: I was mad, but I am now in my senses: I was once Don Quixote de la Mancha, but am now the plain Alonso Quixano, and I hope the sincerity of my words and my repentance may restore me the same esteem you have had for me before."

For, in the last analysis, the saint cannot be presented aesthetically. The ironic vision gives us a Don Quixote, who is innocent of every sin but one; and that one sin he can put off only by ceasing to exist as a character in a book, for all such characters are condemned to it, namely, the sin of being at all times and under all circumstances interesting.

Analogy is not identity.

Art is not enough.

On the Significance
of *Don Quijote**

by Leo Spitzer

. . . The task before us this evening is to explain the historical
and international significance of the Spanish novel, "El Ingenioso
Hidalgo Don Quijote de la Mancha." Let us start with the most
modest aspect which this great book offers us.

The average European meets the ingenious *hidalgo* Don Quijote
for the first time as a child. This is not so of the average American;
in America the *Don Quijote,* along with other things Spanish, became a victim of the philosophy of the Enlightenment; but in Europe the *Don Quijote* is first of all a children's book—a significant
fact which must not be forgotten in our learned disquisitions. Several great books of world literature, not purposely written for children, have reached this consecration as books able to form the
sensitivity of man in the making: *Don Quijote, Robinson Crusoe,
Gulliver's Travels, Moby Dick, Gil Blas,* and *Tartarin* (that French
pocket-edition of the *Quijote*). The reason must be that these
works contain certain elements which adults and children have in
common, in other words, which appeal to human wisdom at the
child stage: these elements are perhaps:

"On the Significance of *Don Quijote*" by Leo Spitzer. From *Modern Language
Notes,* Vol. 77 (Baltimore: The Johns Hopkins Press, 1962), 113–29. Copyright
© 1962 by The Johns Hopkins Press. Reprinted by permission of the publisher.

* This study on the *Quijote* was composed some twenty years ago by Leo
Spitzer as a lecture to be delivered to the members and students of the Spanish
Department of Smith College; in the years that followed the lecture was re-
peated at a number of other colleges and universities in this country.
Though it was never published in its entirety during Professor Spitzer's life-
time, five pages toward the end were quoted, somewhat modified, in *Linguistics
and Literary History,* pp. 68–73, as a conclusion to the chapter "Perspectivism
in *Don Quijote.*"

1. the demonstration of a just world-order in which the future existence of the child will find its place;
2. in contrast to this, the element of the world of faery which tends
   to build up a second world on top of the real one in which the
   child moves;
3. the display of the power of man to master adverse situations,
   whether by skill or critical powers—which makes the child look
   forward hopefully to his own struggle with the life which is to
   come;
4. the element of humor which tends to cushion, or to relativize, the
   hardships of life and to give the child the satisfaction of at least
   a certain mental superiority.

While the fairy tale satisfies the sense of impersonal justice, which
will finally bring about the triumph of Cinderella through the intervention of benign supernatural forces, the adventures of Robinson Crusoe, Gulliver, and Don Quijote abound particularly in the
last two elements (power of man and the humorous display of superiority) which exalt the personal gifts of man. It is the Spanish
novel which is the most sophisticated, since the child does not fully
identify himself with the hero but, while sympathizing with Don
Quijote's character and his will power, takes his stand on the side
of that reality which Don Quijote so contemptuously neglects; and
the child is offered the privilege of feeling superior, intellectually
if not morally, to Don Quijote. It is, indeed, with a certain regret
that he sees, without entirely adopting Sancho Panza's earthiness,
the protagonist mistake windmills for giants, a barber's basin for
a helmet, and a rustic lass for a princess. The child wishes to dominate reality as it is; on the other hand, he will not easily accept its
drabness and limitations, and he sympathizes with Quijote's endeavors to substitute in its place a fanciful reality of the stuff that
dreams are made on; in the challenge which Quijote offers continually to the laws of physics and elementary psychology, there is
enough of the atmosphere of the fairy tale to achieve a transfigura-
tion of the real world. Here Don Quijote stands, with his pitiful
armor, but with every nerve tense, facing with cold bravery the lion
in the open cage—just before the majestic beast will express its
contempt of Quixotism by showing the valorous knight its hind
parts. The child will be by the side of Quijote at the moment the
latter gives his challenge to reality—only to take a stand against
him immediately afterwards, when the hero's will power is thwarted
by triumphant reality. All of Quijote's adventures would show the
pattern of the heroic fight of man against the established world-

order, with the subsequent inevitable, heroi-comical, shattering
defeat—as when the pathetic Quijote must endure the ordeal of
the cheese as it melts and drips down over his eyes and beard, all
because his rustic squire Sancho, heedless of knightly propriety, has
stowed away the cheese in his master's helmet; and to crown his
punishment, Don Quijote is made to feel that his brain, already
dried out by much reading, is also melting . . . Such violent scenes
reveal the workings of an inexorable world-order which adds contempt to punishment; but the momentary indulgence in cruelty will
quickly give way to compassion, as by a catharsis. If the child follows well the lesson he has learned in this book, he will, in later
life, adapt his own will power to criticism, and be able to understand reality, without despising too much the imaginative type of
man who is a failure in dealing with life, and without sympathizing too readily with the so-called "successful realist" who knows only
the laws of mechanics and of behaviorism. He will, perhaps, remember the words of Don Quijote after the adventure of the lion: that
valor is a virtue halfway between cowardice and temerity, and that
it is easier for temerity, than for cowardice, to convert itself into
valor. He will realize that the Knight of the Green Cloak is right
when he says that the *words* of Don Quijote are all good and wise,
and all his *deeds* senseless and silly. Obviously, life asks for a harmony between words and deeds.

Now, lifting our eyes above the horizon of the child, what is still
to be seen in this book that is essential to mankind? In order to
inform ourselves, let us consult the author. This is a good method
for the literary critic since, as Joseph Bédier, the French scholar in
medieval epic poetry, has said, the most awkward narrator understands still more of his tale than even the most intelligent critic:
a rule often wrongly disregarded by critics overreliant on their own
wits. In the preface to the First Part, Cervantes begins by describing
his own attitude toward his book, upon completing it: he felt that
his sterile and uncultivated mind could engender only a meagre,
fantastical thing, dry as a hazelnut, full of weird imagination: an
offspring engendered in a prison, as it were, and toward which,
though seemingly the parent, he feels rather like a step-father, in
no wise bound to conceal its faults from the reader—for the reader
will be in possession of his own soul and in command of his free
will, and is not to be asked to refrain from voicing his own opinion.
Cervantes goes on to say that it was his original intention to offer
the reader his child, naked as it was born, without the usual adorn-
ment of a preface, of learned marginal notes, of laudatory sonnets

and epigrams; while he was trying to make up his mind to act against the established tradition, he tells us that he was joined by a friend, who dispelled all lingering doubts by telling him that his book needed no further recommendation or decoration, and by pointing out to him its real purpose: *derribar la máquina mal fundada de los libros de caballerías,* to produce the downfall and destruction of that mischievous mass of absurdities in the romances of chivalry which, though despised by some, were admired by many —"and if successful, believe me, you will have performed a service of no mean importance." Cervantes, convinced by his friend, immediately converts this discussion into his preface.

Thus it would seem that Cervantes wrote his novel solely for *literary* purposes, in order to destroy a literary genre; it would be a caricature of a man whose brain has been infected with the virus caught from reading such romances as Lancelot, Tristan, Palmerín, Belianís etc.,—of which an *auto da fé* is arranged in Chapter VI.

Now it has been the general trend among critics (including that poet-critic Unamuno) to brush aside, as of no central significance for our novel, the critical program proclaimed by the author of the *Quijote: derribar la máquina* of the romances of escapism. After all, they argue, the centuries-old fashion of these romances had reached its height a century before *Don Quijote,* and was already in its decline by 1560; how then should Cervantes have been impelled to attack its influence in 1605? Or, even if this was his initial purpose, it was soon lost sight of, as the novel gradually developed beyond its original didactic scope, growing in breadth, and vision and humanity.

But I beg to disagree: too much has Cervantes, in the preface written at the completion of the First Part, and on the last page of the whole book, insisted on his *literary* program. And if the critics have been so eager to disregard his expressly stated purpose, in favor of one supposedly more closely allied to human nature and life, it has been, perhaps, because they have failed to grasp the magnitude of this purpose, and the human problem implied therein. For what Cervantes did was to *posit the problem of the book,* and of its influence on life—a problem that has developed in the course of the last centuries, a problem as challenging today as it was to Cervantes. He was the first to grasp the proportions of this problem; seventy years earlier Rabelais had written a novel of human cognizance, celebrating within the framework of a popular story, the giant forces of man who seeks for knowledge—and for knowledge in books. Rabelais is still a Utopian humanist of the

sixteenth century; his Spanish successor, though much more classicistic in his aesthetics than Rabelais, has thoroughly experienced
the disillusionment of the Baroque Age (the *desengaño,* as the
Spaniards call it)—and disillusionment, too, at the Humanistic insistence on books.

From the moment when, through the invention of printing, reading became a privilege granted to the masses, a privilege which was
not in general existence in the Middle Ages; from the moment
when cultural values came to be disseminated, not through the ear,
the musical, religious, and communal sense (*fides ex auditu,* says
St. Paul), but through the eye, the rational, analytic, and individ-
ualistic sense, there was born the peril of wrong application of literature in life by individuals reading alone, severed from society
—the more so since mankind is no longer, as was the case in the
Middle Ages, in quest of the eternal verities beyond discussion, but
is resolved to progress, in its own strength, by application of reason
and analysis, and the dead weight of tradition looms heavily over
our individual outlook on life—which implies the ever-necessary
sifting of values of an outworn tradition. After Cervantes, many
writers, Molière, Rousseau, Goethe, Chateaubriand, Nietzsche, and
the Flaubert of *Madame Bovary* and of *Bouvard et Pécuchet,* will
exercise the right of the "literary politician" to sift traditional literature and to pronounce a verdict on that part of literature which
they believe has, in the process of time, become detrimental to the
community. The problem posited by Cervantes can never die in a
civilization which is predicated on progress, and on "book-learn-
ing," and which consequently is constantly threatened by the continued reading of obsolete books—or, also, by the failure to read
certain books: the two bourgeois Bouvard and Pécuchet have read
too much undigested "progressive" science and, actually, one night,
in the Père Lachaise cemetery, they come to dig a grave for poetry.
Since our children are born into a bookish and progressive civilization, the problem of the "danger of the book" is a permanent one.
(Also today there is sometimes more to be feared from the books
of science in which Bouvard and Pécuchet delighted, than from
poetry.)

It was the deed of a genius to visualize, as Cervantes did, the
danger inherent in what is one of the basic tools of our civilization:
reading. In fact, he must have sensed this danger in his own case;
he tells us, for example, that he used to pick up on the street any
printed scrap of paper—obviously not with the worship which Saint
Francis had for anything written because it could contain one of

the holy truths, but because of his desire to steep himself in a fictitious world (like his own Quijote). This victim of the book virus is of course only one specimen in the gallery of fools which the Baroque Age was wont to pillory; by that time it had become the usual tendency to portray not only Renaissance-like figures of an ideal balance, but equally classic representatives of the bizarre; Montaigne had already shown an interest in the transient, the odd, the whimsical in man, this being *ondoyant et divers;* in Rome an academy of the *Umoristi* had been established, which entertained its members with portrayals of the humor originating in the various extravagant humors; Ben Jonson had created his comedy *Everyman in His Humour.* One humor in particular, the melancholic, was considered to be not altogether bad, but generative as well of scholarship and wisdom as of madness and whimsicality: the Spanish physician Dr. Huarte had shown, shortly before the *Don Quijote* appeared, that melancholy and its "capricious" derivatives, are helpful to the talent, to the *ingenio,* of the scholar. The knight of La Mancha is an *ingenioso* and a capricious man, a bizarre melancholic—the version of a frustrated humanistic scholar, who is cured only on his deathbed (after a purging fever) of his acquired "dryness" of temper, i.e., of his book-conditioned melancholy. The combination of melancholy, eccentricity, and bookishness which leads to abortive action is Cervantes' own idea, just as it was Shakespeare's to have his Hamlet's melancholy, eccentricity, and meditative scholarship result in inaction; and both the inaction of the melancholy Hamlet and the hasty action of the melancholy Don Quijote show the life-destroying effects of an in-itself noble scholarly temperament when overdeveloped without mental discipline.

Thus the *Don Quijote* is a novel written against a certain type of novel deemed detrimental to the community because it may warp the minds of its noblest members: a critique of a literary genre condemned by the author, written in the form of a parodistic novel which, in a sort of parasitic manner, had to adopt all the situations and devices of the type of novel ridiculed. Thus Cervantes, this extravagant inventor of plots as garnered in his pastoral novel *La Galatea* and in his numerous plays, deliberately imprisoned himself in the *Quijote,* in a seeming subservience to a stale pattern of adventures, situations, themes—even words. The novel-of-chivalry-to-end-all-novels-of-chivalry must adopt a particular technique: it must allow the story to unfold as if for the enjoyment of the credulous reader, at the same time suggesting slyly the reaction of the critic-author, which will often consist only of an ironical under-

scoring, whereby he achieves an original creation composed of in-
gredients borrowed from the works criticized: a re-creation of the
old subject matter. There will be on the stage a wild, exuberant,
fantastic pageant of ineptitudes ostensibly endorsed by an ironical
prompter. There will be the cage of the lion, and the doughty
knight to do battle with the beast—who, however, better informed
by Cervantes, will refuse, for all the proddings of the jailors, to
take up the challenge of the self-styled gladiator, opposing the majestic contempt of Nature to Quixotic extravaganza; the lion will
refuse to be a lion of romance and will force Quijote back into
reality.

And the genre created by Cervantes to lead humanity back to
reality, the type of the counter-novel, the anti-novel, this could not
die with its creator: perhaps the novel, as a genre, is always likely
to produce toxins which must be counteracted by antitoxins. The
genre of the novel in itself is a hybrid, somewhat anarchic genre
which was unknown to classical aesthetics and to the literary canons
of the ancients: a hybrid genre which came to life in the late period of Greek literature, again in the later Middle Ages and, once
more, in modern times, where it seems to have come to stay: that
is, at periods weary of pure poetry. For that hybrid genre of the
novel is born of poetry and of something else, of an extrapoetic
factor, of a tendency to encroach upon life, along with an inborn
striving toward pure art, a nostalgic yearning back to epic beauty.
The older form of narrative art is everywhere epic poetry, epic
poetry that maintains itself in the spheres of pure art, of a stylization of life, without any direct imitation or caricature of life—as
its versified form testifies: epic poetry presents us with the great
legendary or mythical past in its beauty as past (in the tense, so
to speak, of the French *passé défini*, not the *passé indéfini* which
draws inferences for the present).

But the novel can offer a vicarious life to sap our actual life,
and produce an illusion in which the things narrated appear as
present, and the lines between romance and reality are blurred.
The prosaic form contributes to this illusion, making romance appear as authentic, unaltered reality. The Arthurian novel of *Galeotto* was the reason that Dante's Paolo and Francesca "read no
more that day" but kissed in sin (*quel giorno più non vi leggemmo
avante*). Because, while they were reading, their lives had become
penetrated by the novelistic substance, they had dreamed themselves
into the parts of the loving protagonists: they were Quijotes *avant-
la-lettre,* indulging in the *pestilencia amorosa* (as our virtuous

knight would call it), obviously because they did not know where
to distinguish between dreams and reality. And the novel was a
Galeotto, a pander (as Dante says, *Galeotto fu il libro*), which, in
making the past appear as present, induced Paolo and Francesca
into sin. (If an average American [less sinful than Paolo and Francesca, but no less romantic] should take along a copy of *Gone With
the Wind* or *Anthony Adverse* to while away a train trip to California, he would do this with the intention of replacing his "traveling" present by a narrated past, of inhabiting this book instead
of the railroad coach: the purpose would not be that of enjoying a
piece of art *qua* art.) It is told that Balzac, to a friend who called
upon him while he was working at his novel *Eugénie Grandet,* exclaimed, with the eye of one looking upon an hallucination, "elle
est morte!"; the hallucination of reality in the novel may be so
complete that it takes hold of the author himself. We may imagine
that Homer or the author of the *Song of Roland* was soberer!

To the illusionistic element of the Spanish romance of chivalry,
to the element of day-dreaming in the French *roman romantique,*
Cervantes and Flaubert oppose their disillusioning technique. In
their counter-novels there is present, to the same degree as in their
models, an extra-poetic element, this time, that of criticism. If the
idealistic models tend to lure us into artificial and vicarious para-
dises, the derivative sceptical anti-novel would make us realize the
dangerous pitfalls of credulity. Both genres place us on the plane
of action: our interest is not "disinterested," as Kant asks enjoyment of art to be, and as it is when we are faced with purely narrative, epic art. We must accept the birth of the novel as a fact
of modernity, and the existence of its two sister-variants (the earlier
born out of the craving for an escape into a vicarious life—the
chivalric, pastoral, adventure novel; the latter intended to dispell
the illusionment afforded by the former) as a necessary polarity in
post-epic narrative art.

Cervantes, in that one Spanish book which, as Montesquieu has
said, caused all the previous Spanish books to be forgotten, has
created the second variety of the novel: the critical novel. This
Cervantine variety has been expanded in the nineteenth century
to criticism not only of the pernicious effect of literature on life,
as in *Madame Bovary,* but criticism of certain ways of life itself, of
whole civilizations. This we find in Balzac, Maupassant, Thackeray,
Tolstoy, Proust, Thomas Mann, Faulkner; and more and more the
two elements, the illusioning and the disillusioning, tend to be
fused: the novelist's imitation of present reality is so excellent that

we could easily be lured into the snares of illusion, were it not for his warning finger which we see lifted above the pages. The nostalgia for epic beauty manifests itself in illusionary devices even when the end is disillusion—as when Flaubert adopts the extreme measure of creating poetic beauty out of the ugly and the foolish. Today we prefer in the novel a clear-cut, rigorous, critical exactitude, but nevertheless, out of the criticism of a civilization, there may emerge, as it often happens in novels of Steinbeck, Hemingway, and Faulkner, the beauty of a positive counterpart: pure eternal epic beauty.

What we have just said would seem to encourage the belief that Cervantes, in his counter-novel, or critical novel, wished only to destroy: is there, in the *Quijote,* nothing of that striving back toward poetic beauty, implied in our definition of the hybrid genre of the novel? The very opposite is true. First of all, in the narrative of Cervantes, in his art of periodizing, in the interspersed poetry and, particularly, in the speeches of the protagonist, there is poetic beauty; since, as we have said, Don Quijote is always right in what he says, less so in what he does, he is given an opportunity to say beautifully what is denied to him to do with equal grace: to couch in a noble (and not always self-parodistic) style the noblest emotions of his author's times, and to treat of the themes which predominated with the Renaissance thinkers. What Américo Castro has taught us about *el pensamiento de Cervantes* is mainly drawn from Don Quijote's orations: as he delivers his speech on the Golden Age, against the background of the placid beauty of night and stars, in the company of primitive shepherds, frugally dining on acorns and wine, Don Quijote will gaze at the acorns meditatively, like Hamlet at poor Yorick's skull, and see in them the symbols of a lost age of simplicity and natural goodness: instead of Hamlet's baroque split vision of the world (here death, here life!), we witness in this scene a noble Christian melancholy, a classical restraint, a harmonious fusion of protagonist and environment, of thought and feelings. It has been the artistic achievement of Cervantes to transform the raw material of Renaissance philosophical themes into poetry, turning ideas into poetry, making the "intellect" sing (*faire chanter les idées,* as Valéry says), just as Rabelais had done in an earthy, and Dante in a transcendent manner. And finally there is, at least in the first part of the *Don Quijote,* the elusive poetic beauty of the interpolated short stories, those tales which, far from imitating the genre of the main plot, precipitate us into an atmosphere of romantic nowhereness, where the laws of realism have ceased to exist, and where imagination alone holds sway—as, for example the story of the roving Amazon of the mountains, Marcela, or that of the Moorish girl Zoraida who, by her conversion to Christianity, has become María. This by-play, afforded by the presence in the *Quijote* of independent stories similar to those published by Cervantes under the title of *Novelas ejemplares* (the story of Zoraida-María is somewhat akin to that of Preciosa *la gitanilla*), has always puzzled the commentators: if Cervantes started out with the intention to *derribar la máquina* of the romance of chivalry, why does he let in, by a side-door, the *máquina* of stories written in precisely the spirit of the romances of chivalry? If it was his desire to warn us of fanciful interpretations of reality by his protagonist, why is it that the stories, quite to the contrary, generally justify facts which at first seem to be fanciful, but later are proved to be entirely true? The explanation of this contradictory procedure can only be that Cervantes anticipated the feeling of disharmony or incompleteness which would be produced in the reader by an anti-novel in pure form, and that Cervantes' harmonious nature asked for an equilibration of the critical sense by the beauty of the fabulous. The whole of the Cervantine novel falls then into two parts: the one teaches criticism before imaginative beauty, the other re-establishes imaginative beauty in the face of all possible scepticism. But since the illusionistic stories are interpolated into the critical novel (not the reverse) and since they are found only in the first part of the novel, we must assume that Cervantes, while desiring to counterbalance the corrosive effects of the anti-novel by the admixture of traditional illusion, did not hesitate to subordinate the older approach to the new: with him criticism is victorious in the century of Descartes—even in Spain.

It is one of the miracles of history (which is generally regarded by professional historians as rather deterministic, as enclosing individual phenomena and figures within tight compartments) that the greatest deeds sometimes occur at a place where and at a time when the historian would least expect them. It is a historical miracle that in the Spain of the Counter-Reformation, when the trend was toward the re-establishment of authoritarian discipline, an artist should have arisen who, thirty-two years before Descartes' *Discours de la méthode* (that autobiography of an independent philosophical thought), was to give us a narrative which is simply one exaltation of the independent mind of man—and of a particularly powerful type of man: of the artist. It is not Italy with its Ariosto and Tasso, not France with its Ronsard and d'Urfé, not Portugal with its

Camões, but Spain which gave us a narrative which is a monument
to the narrator *qua* narrator, *qua* artist. For, although the protagonists of our novel seem to be Quijote, with his continual misrepre-
sentation of reality, and Sancho with his sceptical half-endorsement
of Quixotism, they are overshadowed by CERVANTES, the artist of
the word, who combines a critical and an illusionistic art according
to his free will. From the moment we open the book to the moment
we put it down, we are given to understand that an almighty over-
lord is directing us, who leads us where he pleases. (Surely, this
authoritarian trend in itself would be in line with the spirit of the
Counter-Reformation; but, in our case, the man in whom such
power is lodged is the artist.) The prologue which I have mentioned
shows us Cervantes in the perplexity of an author putting the final
touches to his work, and we understand that the friend who seemingly came to his aid with a solution was only one voice within the
freely fabricating poet. The first sentence of the narrative proper:
"En un lugar de la Mancha de cuyo nombre no quiero acordarme"
is further evidence that Cervantes is insisting on his right to free
invention. While I accept recent suggestions by Casalduero and
María Rosa Lida de Malkiel that we have here to do with a device
usual in simple folktales and opposed to the elaborate technique
of the romances in which the place of origin of their heroes was
clearly stated—I feel that there is also present in this beginning of
the novel an emphasis on the right of the narrator to state or omit
the details he pleases, a device which has been imitated in the
eighteenth century by Sterne and Goethe ("Eduard—so nennen wir
einen reichen Baron im besten Mannesalter") and in the nineteenth century by Melville ("Call me Ishmael"), a device by which
the narrator reminds the reader of his dependence upon him. Furthermore, Cervantes feigns not to know definitely the name of his
protagonists: was the knight called Quijada, Quijano, or Quijote?
Was Sancho called Panza or Zancas? Was his wife called Teresa
Panza, Mari-Gutiérrez or Juana Gutiérrez? Cervantes pretends that
he does not know or that his sources give divergent names. These
variations are nothing but vindications of his artistic liberty to
choose the details of his story among infinite possibilities. And on
the last page of the book, when, after Quijote's Christian death,
Cervantes has that Arabian historian Cide Hamete Benengeli
(whose chronicle he supposedly had used as a source) lay away his
pen, which will rest forever on top of the cupboard, in order to
forestall any spurious continuation of the novel in the genre of
Avellaneda's piratical undertaking, we know that the reference to

the Arabian pseudo-historian is only a pretext for Cervantes to reclaim for himself the relationship of real father (no longer the step-father!) to his book. Then the chronicler's pen delivers itself of a long speech, culminating in the words: "For me alone Don Quijote was born and I for him; his task was to act, mine to write. For we alone are made for each other." ("Para mí sola nació don Quijote, y yo para él; él supo obrar, y yo escribir; solos los dos somos para en uno.") An imperious "alone" (*solos*) which only Cervantes could have said and in which there not only appears what we would call today an author's claim for intellectual property rights in the invention of a character, but in which all the Renaissance pride of the poet asserts itself: the poet who was the traditional immortalizer of the great deeds of historical heroes and princes. This was, as is well known, the economical background of the Renaissance artist; he was given sustenance by the prince in return for the immortal glory which he bestowed upon his benefactor. But Don Quijote is no prince from whom Cervantes could expect to receive a pension, not a doer of great deeds in the outer world (his greatness lay only in his warm heart), and not even a being who could be attested in any historical source—however much Cervantes might pretend to such sources. Don Quijote acquired his immortality exclusively at the hands of Cervantes, as the former well knows and admits. Obviously, Quijote wrought only what Cervantes wrote, and he was born for Cervantes as much as Cervantes was born for him. In the speech of the pen of the pseudo-chronicler we have a discreet but at the same time outspoken self-glorification of the artist. Furthermore, the artist Cervantes grows by the glory which his characters have attained; and in the novel we see the process by which the figures of Don Quijote and Sancho become living persons, stepping out of the novel, so to speak, to take their place in real life—finally to become immortal historical figures. Thomas Mann, in his essay on the *Quijote,* has said: "This is quite unique. I know of no other hero of a novel in world literature who would equally, so to speak, live off the glory of his own glorification ("ein Held der von seinem Ruhm, von seiner Besungenheit lebte"). In the second part of the novel, when the Duke and Duchess ask to see the by now historical figures of Quijote and Panza, the latter says to the Duchess; "I am Don Quijote's squire who is to be found also in the story and who is called Sancho Panza —unless they have changed me in the cradle—I mean to say, at the printers'." In such passages, Cervantes willingly destroys the artistic illusion: he, the puppeteer, lets us see the strings of his puppet-show:

"see, reader, this is not life, but a stage, a book: art. Recognize the life-giving power of the artist as a thing distinct from life!" By multiplying his masks (the friend of the prologue, the Arabian historian, sometimes the characters who serve as his mouthpiece) Cervantes seems only the more to strengthen his grip on that whole artistic cosmos which his novel represents. And the strength of the grip is enhanced by the very nature of the protagonists: Quijote is what we would call today a split personality, sometimes rational, sometimes foolish; Sancho, too, at times no less Quixotic than his master, is at other times incalculably rational. In this manner the author makes it possible for himself to decide when his characters will act reasonably, when foolishly (no one is more unpredictable than a fool who pretends to wisdom). At the start of his journey with Sancho, Don Quijote promises his squire an island kingdom to be ruled over by him, just as was done in the case of numerous squires in chivalric literature. But, acting on his critical judgment (of which he is not entirely devoid), Don Quijote promises to give it to him immediately after their conquest, instead of waiting until the squire has reached old age, as is the custom in the books of chivalry. The Quixotic side of Sancho accepts this prospective kingdom without questioning its possibility, but his more earthly nature visualizes—and criticizes—the actual scene of the coronation: how would his rustic spouse Juana Gutiérrez look with a crown on her head? Two examples of foolishness, two critical attitudes: neither of them is the attitude of the writer, who remains above the two split personalities and the four attitudes. Cervantes sometimes does not even decide whether the wrong inferences his Don Quijote draws from what he sees are totally preposterous: he gives to understand that the barber's basin appears to Don Quijote as a helmet and it may appear to others as something else: perspectivism is what he teaches and there may even exist a *baciyelmo,* a basin that is at the same time a helmet—the word-coinage itself reflecting the hybrid shapes of reality. But my point is that this perspectivism enhances the figure of the novelist.

With this tolerance toward his characters which is also a somewhat Machiavellian principle of "divide and conquer," the author succeeds in making himself indispensable to the reader: while, in his Prologue, Cervantes calls for a critical attitude on our part, he makes us depend all the more on his guidance through the psychological intricacies of the narrative: here, at least, he leaves us no free will. We may even infer that Cervantes rules imperiously over his own self: it was he who felt his self to be split into a critical and an illusionistic part (*desengaño* and *engaño*); but in this baroque Ego he made order—a precarious order, it is true, which was reached only once by Cervantes in all his works, and which was reached in Spain only by Cervantes (for Calderón, Lope, Quevedo, Gracián decided, in medieval manner, that the world is only illusion and dreams, *que los sueños sueños son*). And indeed only once in world literature has this precarious order come into being. Later thinkers and artists did not stop at proclaiming the inanity of the world: they went so far as to doubt the existence of any universal order and, when imitating Cervantes' perspectivism (Gide, Proust, Conrad, Joyce, Virginia Woolf, Pirandello) they failed to sense the unity behind perspectivism—so that, in their hands, sometimes the personality of the author himself is allowed to disintegrate. Cervantes stands at the other pole from that modern dissolution of the personality of the narrator: his attempt—made in the last moment before the unified Christian vision of the world was to fall asunder —was to restore this vision on the artistic plane, to hold before our eyes a cosmos split in two separate halves, disenchantment and illusion, which, nevertheless, as by a miracle, do not fall apart. Modern anarchy checked by a classical will to equipoise: the baroque attitude! We recognize now that it is not so much that Cervantes' nature is split in two (critic and narrator) because this is required by the nature of Don Quijote, but rather that Don Quijote is a split character because his creator was a critic-poet who felt with almost equal strength the need of illusionary beauty and that of pellucid clarity.

To modern readers the "pathological character" of Don Quijote might seem to be a typical case of social frustration: a person whose madness is conditioned by the social insignificance into which the caste of the knights had fallen, with the beginning of modern, somehow already mechanized, warfare—just as in Flaubert's *Un cœur simple,* we are meant to see as socially conditioned the frustrations of Félicité, the domestic servant, which lead to the aberration of her imagination. I would, however, warn against interpreting Cervantes in terms of the nineteenth-century sociological resentments of a Flaubert, since Cervantes himself has done nothing to encourage such a sociological approach. Don Quijote is able to recover his sanity, if only on his death-bed, and his erstwhile madness is but one reflection of that generally human lack of reason—above which the author has chosen to take his stand.

High above the world-wide cosmos of his making, in which hundreds of characters, situations, vistas, themes, plots and subplots are

merged, Cervantes' artistic self is enthroned, an all-embracing creative self, a visibly omnipresent artistic Creator who graciously takes
the reader into his confidence, showing him the work of art in the
making, and the laws to which it is necessarily subjected. This artist
is in a way God-like, but not deified; far be it from us to conceive
of Cervantes as attempting to dethrone God, replacing him by an
artistic demi-god. On the contrary, Cervantes always bows before
the supernal wisdom of God, as embodied in the teachings of the
Catholic Church and the established order of the state and of society. But, on the other hand, the novelist has extended, by the
mere art of his narrative, the demi-urge-like independence of the
artist. His humor, which admits of many strata, perspectives, masks,
of relativization and dialectics, bears testimony to his high position
above the world. His humor is the freedom of the heights, a freedom
beneath the dome of that religion which affirms the freedom of the
will.

There is, in that world of his creation, accessible to adults and
children alike, the bracing air with which we may fill our lungs
and by which our individual senses and judgment are sharpened,
and the crystalline lucidity of an artistic Maker in its manifold
reflections and refractions. Perhaps the child in us that wants to
fight its way, through the maze of the world, toward intellectual
clarity, without impoverishment of the heart, under orderly benign
stars, is not unappreciative of an artistry whose sophistication makes
the world richer, more interesting, and more habitable. The greatest
works of art have, indeed, the power, after making us see the most
unexpected perspectives, of restoring, to the renewed world, that
primeval simplicity and richness which it must have had on the
first day of creation, that inner beatitude of self-enjoying beauty
that is as well God-like as child-like.

As you may have seen, my historical interpretation of the *Quijote* is at the opposite pole from that of Unamuno who believes
that the story of the life of Don Quijote and of Sancho Panza was
dictated to Cervantes' pen by the suprapersonal and perennial
Spanish national character, by the innate Spanish will to immortality through suffering: the *sentimiento trágico de la vida* of the
Spanish race embodied in the figures of the quasi-saint *Nuestro
Señor Don Quijote de la Mancha* and his evangelical squire. In my
opinion, it is Cervantes, the artistic dictator, who dictated the story
to his pen, and Cervantes, no semi-Christian like Unamuno, knew
of no quasi or "quotation-mark" saints, being able to distinguish

clearly the earthly plane from the transcendental; and, on the former plane, he obeyed his own sovereign reason. We must not deny to Unamuno his right to build his own poetic vision on top of Cervantes' novel (since Cervantes himself, as we have seen, built his critical vision on top of previous literatures), but we may question the historical validity of the Unamunesque interpretation of the Quijote novel—and perhaps also question the wisdom of making out of a novelistic character, outspokenly condemned or questioned by Cervantes, a national hero of Spain; was it in the interests of the moral regeneration of the Spanish nation to present an amusing fool in a novel as a true national hero? It seems to me then that Cervantes does not belong to the family of the desperate God-seekers Pascal or Kierkegaard, but to that of Erasmus, Descartes, and Goethe, of the serene humanists and quiet worshippers of the divine, who saw it in all its variety of earthly forms.

The Enchanted Dulcinea

by Erich Auerbach

—Yo no veo, Sancho, dijo Don Quijote, sino a tres labradoras sobre tres borricos.

—Ahora me libre Dios del diablo, respondió Sancho; ¿y es posible que tres hacaneas, o como se llaman, blancas como el ampo de la nieve, le parezcan a vuesa merced borricos? Vive el Señor, que me pele estas barbas si tal fuese verdad.

—Pues yo te digo, Sancho amigo, dijo Don Quijote, que es tan verdad que son borricos o borricas, como yo soy Don Quijote, y tú Sancho Panza: a lo menos a mí tales me parecen.

—Calle, señor, dijo Sancho, no diga la tal palabra, sino despabile esos ojos, y venga a hacer reverencia a la señora de sus pensamientos, que ya llega cerca: y diciendo esto se adelantó a recebir a las tres aldeanas, y apeándose del rucio tuvo del cabestro al jumento de una de las tres labradoras, y hincando ambas rodillas en el suelo, dijo:

—Reina y princesa y duquesa de la hermosura, vuestra altivez y grandeza sea servida de recebir en su gracia y buen talante al cautivo caballero vuestro, que allí está hecho piedra mármol, todo turbado y sin pulsos de verse ante vuesa magnífica presencia. Yo soy Sancho su escudero, y él es el asendereado caballero Don Quijote de la Mancha, llamado por otro nombre el Caballero de la Triste Figura.

A esta sazón ya se había puesto Don Quijote de hinojos junto a Sancho, y miraba con ojos desencajados y vista turbada a la que Sancho llamabra reina y señora; y como no descubría en ella sino una moza aldeana y no de muy buen rostro, porque era carirredonda y chata, estaba suspenso y admirado, sin osar desplegar los labios. Las labradoras estaban asimismo atónitas viendo a aquellos dos hombres tan diferentes hincados de rodillas, que no dejaban pasar adelante a su compañera; pero rompiendo el silencio la detenida, toda desgraciada y mohina, dijo:

—Apártense nora en tal del camino, y déjenmos pasar, que vamos de priesa.

A lo que respondió Sancho:

—Oh princesa y señora universal del Toboso, ¿cómo vuestro magnífico corazón no se enternece viendo arrodillado ante vuestra sublimada presencia a la coluna y sustento de la andante caballería?

Oyendo lo cual otra de las dos dijo:

—Mas yo que te estrego burra de mi suegro: mirad con qué se vienen los señoritos ahora a hacer burlas de las aldeanas, como si aquí no supiésemos echar pullas como ellos: vayan su camino, y déjenmos hacer el nueso, y serles ha sano.

—Levántate, Sancho, dijo a este punto Don Quijote, que ya veo que la fortuna, de mi mal no harta, tiene tomados los caminos todos por donde pueda venir algún contento a esta ánima mezquina que tengo en las carnes. Y tú, oh extremo valor que puede desearse, término de la humana gentileza, único remedio de este afligido corazón que te adora, ya que el maligno encantador me persigue, y ha puesto nubes y cataratas en mis ojos, y para sólo ellos y no para otros ha mudado y transformado tu sin igual hermosura y rostro en el de una labradora pobre, si ya también el mío no le ha cambiado en el de algún vestiglo para hacerle aborrecible a tus ojos, no dejes de mirarme blanda y amorosamente, echando de ver en esta sumisión y arrodillamiento que a tu contrahecha hermosura hago, la humildad con que mi alma te adora.

—Toma que me agüelo, respondió la aldeana, amiguita soy yo de oír resquebrajos. Apártense y déjenmos ir, y agradecérselo hemos.

Apartóse Sancho y déjola ir, contentísimo de haber salido bien de su enredo. Apenas se vió libre la aldeana que había hecho la figura de Dulcinea cuando picando a su hacanea con un aguijón que en un palo traía, dió a correr por el prado adelante; y como la borrica sentía la punta del aguijón, que le fatigaba más de lo ordinario, comenzó a dar corcovos, de manera que dió con la señora Dulcinea en tierra: lo cual visto por Don Quijote, acudió a levantarla, y Sancho a componer y cinchar el albarda, que también vino a la barriga de la pollina. Acomodada pues el albarda, y queriendo Don Quijote levantar a su encantada señora en los brazos sobre la jumenta, la señora levantándose del suelo le quitó de aquel trabajo, porque haciéndose algún tanto atrás tomó una corridica, y puestas ambas manos sobre las ancas de la pollina dió con su cuerpo más ligero que un halcón sobre la albarda, y quedó a horcajadas como si fuera hombre, y entonces dijo Sancho:

—¡Vive Roque, que es la señora nuestra ama más ligera que un alcotán, y que puede enseñar a subir de la jineta al más diestro cordobés o mejicano; el arzón trasero de la silla pasó de un salto, y sin espuelas hace correr la hacanea como una cebra, y no le van en zaga sus doncellas, que todas corren como el viento!

Y así era la verdad, porque en viéndose a caballo Dulcinea todas
picaron tras ella y dispararon a correr, sin volver la cabeza atrás por
espacio de más de media legua. Siguiólas Don Quijote con la vista,
y cuando vió que no parecían, volviéndose a Sancho le dijo:

—Sancho, ¿qué te parece, cuán mal quisto soy de encantador-
es? . . .

("I see nothing," declared Don Quixote, "except three farm girls
on three jackasses."

"Then God deliver me from the devil!" exclaimed Sancho. "Is
it possible that those three hackneys, or whatever you call them,
white as the driven snow, look like jackasses to your Grace? By the
living God, I would tear out this beard of mine if that were true!"

"But I tell you, friend Sancho, it is as true that those are jackasses, or she-asses, as it is that I am Don Quixote and you Sancho
Panza. At least, that is the way they look to me."

"Be quiet, sir," Sancho admonished him, "you must not say such a
thing as that. Open those eyes of yours and come do reverence to the
lady of your affections, for she draws near."

Saying this, he rode on to meet the village maids and, slipping down
off his donkey, seized one of their beasts by the halter and fell on his
knees in front of its rider.

"O queen and princess and duchess of beauty," he said, "may your
Highness and Majesty be pleased to receive and show favor to your
captive knight, who stands there as if turned to marble, overwhelmed
and breathless at finding himself in your magnificent presence. I am
Sancho Panza, his squire, and he is the world-weary knight Don
Quixote, otherwise known as the Knight of the Mournful Countenance."

By this time Don Quixote was down on his knees beside Sancho.
His eyes were fairly starting from their sockets and there was a
deeply troubled look in them as he stared up at the one whom Sancho
had called queen and lady; all that he could see in her was a village
wench, and not a very pretty one at that, for she was round-faced and
snub-nosed. He was astounded and perplexed and did not dare open
his mouth. The girls were also very much astonished to behold these
two men, so different in appearance, kneeling in front of one of them
so that she could not pass. It was this one who most ungraciously
broke the silence.

"Get out of my way," she said peevishly, "and let me pass. And bad
luck go with you. For we are in a hurry."

"O princess and universal lady of El Toboso!" cried Sancho. "How
can your magnanimous heart fail to melt as you behold kneeling before your sublimated presence the one who is the very pillar and support of knight-errantry?"

Hearing this, one of the others spoke up. "Whoa, there, she-ass of my father!" she said. "Wait until I curry you down. Just look at the small-fry gentry, will you, who've come to make sport of us country girls! Just as if we couldn't give them tit for tat. Be on your way and get out of ours, if you know what's good for you."

"Arise, Sancho," said Don Quixote, "for I perceive that fortune has not had her fill of evil done to me but has taken possession of all the roads by which some happiness may come to what little soul is left within me. And thou, who art all that could be desired, the sum of human gentleness and sole remedy for this afflicted heart that doth adore thee! The malign enchanter who doth persecute me hath placed clouds and cataracts upon my eyes, and for them and them alone hath transformed thy peerless beauty into the face of a lowly peasant maid; and I can only hope that he has not likewise changed my face into that of some monster by way of rendering it abhorrent in thy sight. But for all of that, hesitate not to gaze upon me tenderly and lovingly, beholding in this act of submission as I kneel before thee a tribute to thy metamorphosed beauty from this humbly worshiping heart of mine."

"Just listen to him run on, will you? My grandmother!" cried the lass. "Enough of such gibberish. We'll thank you to let us go our way."

Sancho fell back and let her pass, being very thankful to get out of it so easily.

No sooner did she find herself free than the girl who was supposed to have Dulcinea's face began spurring her "hackney" with a spike on the end of a long stick that she carried with her, whereupon the beast set off at top speed across the meadow. Feeling the prick, which appeared to annoy it more than was ordinarily the case, the ass started cutting such capers that the lady Dulcinea was thrown to the ground. When he saw this, Don Quixote hastened to lift her up while Sancho busied himself with tightening the girths and adjusting the packsaddle, which had slipped down under the animal's belly. This having been accomplished, Don Quixote was about to take his enchanted lady in his arms to place her upon the she-ass when the girl saved him the trouble by jumping up from the ground, stepping back a few paces, and taking a run for it. Placing both hands upon the crupper of the ass, she landed more lightly than a falcon upon the packsaddle and remained sitting there astride it like a man.

"In the name of Roque!" exclaimed Sancho, "our lady is like a lanner, only lighter, and can teach the cleverest Cordovan or Mexican how to mount. She cleared the back of the saddle in one jump, and without any spurs she makes her hackney run like a zebra, and her damsels are not far behind, for they all of them go like the wind."

This was the truth. Seeing Dulcinea in the saddle, the other two prodded their beasts and followed her on the run, without so much as turning their heads to look back for a distance of half a league.

Don Quixote stood gazing after them, and when they were no longer
visible he turned to Sancho and spoke.

"Sancho," he said, "you can see now, can you not, how the enchanters hate me?" [1]

This is a passage from chapter 10 of part 2 of Cervantes' *Don
Quijote*. The knight has sent Sancho Panza to the hamlet of El
Toboso to call on Dulcinea and announce his intention of paying
her a visit. Sancho, entangled in his earlier lies, and not knowing
how to find the imaginary lady, decides to deceive his master. He
waits outside the hamlet for a time, long enough to make Don
Quijote believe that he has done his errand. Then, seeing three
peasant women on donkeys riding toward him, he hurries back and
tells his master that Dulcinea and two of her ladies are coming to
greet him. The knight is overwhelmed with surprise and joy, and
Sancho leads him toward the peasant women, describing their
beauty and splendid gear in glowing colors. But for once Don
Quijote sees nothing except the actual reality, that is, three peasant
women on donkeys—and this leads to the scene we have quoted.

Among the many episodes which represent a clash between Don
Quijote's illusion and an ordinary reality which contradicts it,
this one holds a special place. First because it is concerned with Dulcinea herself, the ideal and incomparable mistress of his heart.
This is the climax of his illusion and disillusionment: and although
this time too he manages to find a solution, a way to save his illusion, the solution (Dulcinea is under an enchantment) is so intolerable that henceforth all his thoughts are concentrated upon
one goal: to save her and break the enchantment. In the last chapters of the book, his recognition or foreboding that he will never
achieve this is the direct preparation for his illness, his deliverance
from his illusion, and his death. In the second place the scene is
distinguished by the fact that here for the first time the roles appear
exchanged. Until now it had been Don Quijote who, encountering
everyday phenomena, spontaneously saw and transformed them in
terms of the romances of chivalry, while Sancho was generally in
doubt and often tried to contradict and prevent his master's absurdities. Now it is the other way round. Sancho improvises a scene
after the fashion of the romances of chivalry, while Don Quijote's
ability to transform events to harmonize with his illusion breaks

[1] From *The Ingenious Gentleman, Don Quixote de la Mancha*, Vols. 1 and 2,
by Miguel de Cervantes Saavedra, trans. Samuel Putnam (New York: The Viking
Press, Inc., 1949). Copyright 1949 by The Viking Press, Inc. Reprinted by permission of the publisher.

down before the crude vulgarity of the sight of the peasant women. All this seems most significant. As we have here (intentionally) presented it, it sounds sad, bitter, and almost tragic.

But if we merely read Cervantes' text, we have a farce, and a farce which is overwhelmingly comic. Many illustrators have rendered the scene: Don Quijote on his knees beside Sancho, staring in wide-eyed bewilderment at the repellent spectacle before him. But only the stylistic contrast in the speeches, and the grotesque movement at the end (Dulcinea's fall and remounting), afford the fullest enjoyment of what is going on. The stylistic contrast in the speeches develops only slowly, because at first the peasant women are much too astonished. Dulcinea's first utterance (her request to be allowed to pass) is still moderate. It is only in their later speeches that the peasant women display the pearls of their eloquence. The first representative of the chivalric style is Sancho, and it is amusing and surprising to see how well he plays his part. He jumps off his donkey, throws himself at the women's feet, and speaks as though he had never heard anything in all his life but the jargon of romances of chivalry. Forms of address, syntax, metaphors, epithets, the description of his master's posture, and his supplication to be heard—it all comes out most successfully, although Sancho cannot read and owes his education wholly to the example set him by Don Quijote. His performance is successful, at least insofar as he gets his master to follow suit: Don Quijote kneels down beside him.

It might be supposed that all this would bring on a terrible crisis. Dulcinea is really *la señora de sus pensamientos,* the paragon of beauty, the goal and meaning of his life. Arousing his expectations in this way, and then disappointing them so greatly, is no harmless experiment. It could produce a shock which in turn could bring on much deeper insanity. But there is also the possibility that the shock might bring about a cure, instantaneous liberation from his idée fixe. Neither of these things happens. Don Quijote surmounts the shock. In his idée fixe itself he finds a solution which prevents him both from falling into despair and from recovering his sanity: Dulcinea is enchanted. This solution appears each time the exterior situation establishes itself as in insuperable contrast to the illusion. It makes it possible for Don Quijote to persist in the attitude of the noble and invincible hero persecuted by a powerful magician who envies his glory. In this particular case—the case of Dulcinea—the idea of so repellent and base an enchantment is certainly hard to endure. Still, it is possible to meet the situation by means available within the realm of the illusion itself, that is, by means of the knightly virtues of unalterable loyalty, devoted self-sacrifice, and unhesitating courage. And then there is the established fact that virtue will win in the end. The happy ending is a foregone conclusion. Thus both tragedy and cure are circumvented. And so, after a brief pause of disconcerted silence, Don Quijote begins to speak. He turns to Sancho first. His words show that he has recovered his bearings, that he has interpreted the situation in terms of his illusion. This interpretation has become so firmly crystallized in him that even the earthy colloquialism in the directly preceding speech of one of the peasant women—however sharply they may contrast with the elevated style of knightly refinement—can no longer make him doubtful of his attitude. Sancho's stratagem has succeeded. Don Quijote's second sentence is addressed to Dulcinea.

It is a very beautiful sentence. A moment ago we pointed out how cleverly and amusingly Sancho handles the style of the romances of chivalry which he has picked up from his master. Now we see what sort of a master he had. The sentence begins, like a prayer, with an imploring apostrophe (*invocatio*). This has three gradations (*extremo del valor . . . , término . . . , único remedio . . .*), and they are very carefully considered and arranged, for it first emphasizes an absolute perfection, then a perfection in human terms, and finally the special personal devotion of the speaker. The threefold structure is held together by the initial words *y tú*, and ends, in its third, sweepingly constructed division, with the rhythmically conventional but magnificently integrated *corazón que te adora*. Here, in content, choice of words, and rhythm, the theme which appears at the end is already alluded to. Thus a transition is established from the *invocatio* to its obligatory complement, the *supplicatio*, for which the optative principal clause is reserved (*no dejes de mirarme . . .*), although it is still some time before we are allowed to reach it. First we have the multiple gradation—dramatically contrasting with both *invocatio* and *supplicatio*—of the concessive complex, *ya que . . . , y . . . y . . . , si ya también. . . .* Its sense is "and even though," and its rhythmic climax is reached in the middle of the first (*ya que*) part, in the strongly emphasized words *y para sólo ellos*. Only after this entire wonderful and dramatic melody of the concessive clause has run its course, is the long-restrained principal clause of the *supplicatio* allowed to appear, but it too holds back and piles up paraphrases and pleonasms until finally the main motif, which constitutes the goal and purpose of the entire period, is sounded: the words which are to symbolize Don Quijote's present attitude and his entire life, *la humildad con que mi alma te adora*. This is the style so greatly admired by Sancho in part 1, chapter 25, where Don Quijote reads his letter to Dulcinea aloud to him: *¡y como que le dice vuestra merced ahí todo cuanto quiere, y qué bien que encaja en la firma El Caballero de la Triste Figura!* But the present speech is incomparably more beautiful; with all its art it shows less pedantic preciosity than the latter. Cervantes is very fond of such rhythmically and pictorially rich, such beautifully articulated and musical bravura pieces of chivalric rhetoric (which are nevertheless rooted in the tradition of antiquity). And he is a master in the field. Here again he is not merely a destructive critic but a continuer and consummator of the great epico-rhetorical tradition for which prose too is an art. As soon as great emotions and passions or sublime events are involved, this elevated style with all its devices appears. To be sure, its being so long a convention has shifted it slightly from the sphere of high tragedy toward that of the smoothly pleasant, which is capable of at least a trace of self-irony. Yet it is still dominant in the serious sphere. One has only to read Dorotea's speech to her unfaithful lover (part 1, chapter 36), with its numerous figures, similes, and rhythmic clauses, in order to sense that this style is still alive even in the serious and the tragic.

Here, however, in Dulcinea's presence, it simply serves the effect of contrast. The peasant girl's crude, contemptuous reply gives it its real significance; we are in the realm of the low style, and Don Quijote's elevated rhetoric only serves to make the comedy of the stylistic anticlimax fully effective. But even this is not enough to satisfy Cervantes. To the stylistic anticlimax he adds an extreme anticlimax in the action by having Dulcinea fall off her donkey and jump on again with grotesque dexterity, while Don Quijote still tries to maintain the chivalric style. His being so firmly fixed in his illusion that neither Dulcinea's reply nor the scene with the donkey can shake him is the acme of farce. Even Sancho's exuberant gaiety (*Vive Roque*), which after all is nothing short of impertinent, cannot make him lose his bearings. He looks after the peasant women as they ride away, and when they have disappeared he turns to Sancho with words expressive much less of sadness or despair than of a sort of triumphant satisfaction over the fact that he has become the target of the evil magician's darkest arts. This makes it possible for him to feel that he is elect, unique, and in a way which tallies perfectly with the conventions of the knight-errant: *yo nací para ejemplo de desdichados, y para ser blanco y terrero donde tomen la mira y asesten las flechas de la mala fortuna.* And the observation he now makes, to the effect that the evil enchantment affects even Dulcinea's aura—for her breath had not been pleasant—can disturb his illusion as little as Sancho's grotesque description of details of her beauty. Encouraged by the complete success of his trick, Sancho has now really warmed up and begins to play with his master's madness purely for his own amusement.

In our study we are looking for representations of everyday life in which that life is treated seriously, in terms of its human and social problems or even of its tragic complications. The scene from *Don Quijote* with which we are dealing is certainly realistic. All the participants are presented in their true reality, their living everyday existence. Not only the peasant women but Sancho too, not only Sancho but also Don Quijote, appear as persons representative of contemporary Spanish life. For the fact that Sancho is playing a rogue's game and that Don Quijote is enmeshed in his illusion does not raise either of them out of his everyday existence. Sancho is a peasant from La Mancha, and Don Quixote is no Amadís or Roland, but a little country squire who has lost his mind. At best we might say that the hidalgo's madness translates him into another, imaginary sphere of life; but even so the everyday character of our scene and others similar to it remains unharmed, because the persons and events of everyday life are constantly colliding with his madness and come out in stronger relief through the contrast.

It is much more difficult to determine the position of the scene, and of the novel as a whole, on the scale of levels between tragic and comic. As presented, the story of the encounter with the three peasant women is nothing if not comic. The idea of having Don Quijote encounter a concrete Dulcinea must certainly have come to Cervantes even when he was writing the first part of the novel. The idea of building up such a scene on the basis of a deceitful trick played by Sancho, so that the roles appear interchanged, is a stroke of genius, and it is so magnificently carried out that the farce presents itself to the reader as something perfectly natural and even bound to take place, despite the complex absurdity of all its presuppositions and relations. But it remains pure farce. We have tried to show above that, in the case of the only one of the participants with whom the possibility of a shift into the tragic and problematic exists, that is, in the case of Don Quijote, such a shift is definitely avoided. The fact that he almost instantaneously and as it were automatically takes refuge in the interpretation that

Dulcinea is under an enchantment excludes everything tragic. He is taken in, and this time even by Sancho; he kneels down and orates in a lofty emotional style before a group of ugly peasant women; and then he takes pride in his sublime misfortune.

But Don Quijote's feelings are genuine and profound. Dulcinea is really the mistress of his thoughts; he is truly filled with the spirit of a mission which he regards as man's highest duty. He is really true, brave, and ready to sacrifice everything. So unconditional a feeling and so unconditional a determination impose admiration even though they are based on a foolish illusion, and this admiration has been accorded to Don Quijote by almost all readers. There are probably few lovers of literature who do not associate the concept of ideal greatness with Don Quijote. It may be absurd, fantastic, grotesque; but it is still ideal, unconditional, heroic. It is especially since the Romantic period that this conception has become almost universal, and it withstands all attempts on the part of philological criticism to show that Cervantes' intention was not to produce such an impression.

The difficulty lies in the fact that in Don Quijote's idée fixe we have a combination of the noble, immaculate, and redeeming with absolute nonsense. A tragic struggle for the ideal and desirable cannot at first blush be imagined in any way but as intervening meaningfully in the actual state of things, stirring it up, pressing it hard; with the result that the meaningful ideal encounters an equally meaningful resistance which proceeds either from inertia, petty malice, and envy, or possibly from a more conservative view. The will working for an ideal must accord with existing reality at least to such an extent that it meets it, so that the two interlock and a real conflict arises. Don Quijote's idealism is not of this kind. It is not based on an understanding of actual conditions in this world. Don Quijote does have such an understanding but it deserts him as soon as the idealism of his idée fixe takes hold of him. Everything he does in that state is completely senseless and so incompatible with the existing world that it produces only comic confusion there. It not only has no chance of success, it actually has no point of contact with reality; it expends itself in a vacuum.

The same idea can be developed in another way, so that further consequences become clear. The theme of the noble and brave fool who sets forth to realize his ideal and improve the world, might be treated in such a way that the problems and conflicts in the world are presented and worked out in the process. Indeed, the purity and ingenuousness of the fool could be such that, even in the absence

of any concrete purpose to produce effects, wherever he appears he
unwittingly goes to the heart of things, so that the conflicts which
are pending and hidden are rendered acute. One might think here
of Dostoevski's *Idiot*. Thus the fool could be involved in responsibility and guilt and assume the role of a tragic figure. Nothing of
the sort takes place in Cervantes' novel.

Don Quijote's encounter with Dulcinea is not a good illustration
of his relationship to concrete reality, inasmuch as here he does
not, as elsewhere, impose his ideal will in conflict with that reality;
here he beholds and worships the incarnation of his ideal. Yet this
encounter too is symbolic of the mad knight's relationship to the
phenomena of this world. The reader should recall what traditional
concepts were contained in the Dulcinea motif and how they are
echoed in Sancho's and Don Quijote's grotesquely sublime words.
*La señora de sus pensamientos, extremo del valor que puede de-
searse, término de la humana gentileza,* and so forth—alive in all
this are Plato's idea of beauty, courtly love, the *donna gentile* of the
dolce stil nuovo, Beatrice, *la gloriosa donna della mia mente.* And
all this ammunition is expended on three ugly and vulgar peasant
women. It is poured into a void. Don Quijote can neither be graciously received nor graciously rejected. There is nothing but amusingly senseless confusion. To find anything serious, or a concealed
deeper meaning in this scene, one must violently overinterpret it.

The three women are flabbergasted; they get away as fast as they
can. This is an effect frequently produced by Don Quijote's appearance. Often disputes result and the participants come to blows.
People are apt to lose their temper when Don Quijote interferes in
their business with his nonsense. Very often too they humor him in
his idée fixe in order to get some fun from it. The innkeeper and
the whores at the time of his first departure react in this way. The
same thing happens again later with the company at the second inn,
with the priest and the barber, Dorotea and Don Fernando, and
even with Maritornes. Some of these, it is true, mean to use their
game as a way of getting the knight safely back home, but they carry
it much further than their practical purpose would require. In
part 2 the *bachiller* Sansón Carrasco bases his therapeutic plan on
playing along with Don Quijote's idée fixe; later, at the duke's
palace and in Barcelona, his madness is methodically exploited as
a pastime, so that hardly any of his adventures are genuine; they
are simply staged, that is, they have been especially prepared to suit
the hidalgo's madness, for the amusement of those who get them up.
Among all these reactions, both in part 1 and part 2, one thing is

ompletely lacking: tragic complications and serious consequences.
Even the element of contemporary satire and criticism is very
veak. If we leave out of consideration the purely literary criticism, there is almost none at all. It is limited to brief remarks or
occasional caricatures of types (for example the priest at the duke's
court). It never goes to the roots of things and is moderate in at-
itude. Above all, Don Quijote's adventures never reveal any of the
basic problems of the society of the time. His activity reveals nothing
at all. It affords an opportunity to present Spanish life in its color
and fullness. In the resulting clashes between Don Quijote and reality no situation ever results which puts in question that reality's
right to be what it is. It is always right and he wrong; and after a
bit of amusing confusion it flows calmly on, untouched. There is
one scene where this might seem doubtful. It is the freeing of the
galley slaves in part 1, chapter 22. Here Don Quijote intervenes in
the established legal order, and some critics will be found to uphold
the opinion that he does so in the name of a higher morality. This
view is natural, for what Don Quijote says: *allá se lo haya cada uno
con su pecado; Dios hay en el cielo que no se descuida de castigar al
malo ni de premiar al bueno, y no es bien que los hombres honrados
sean verdugos de los otros hombres, no yéndoles nada en ello*[2]—such
a statement is certainly on a higher level than any positive law.
But a "higher morality" of the kind here envisaged must be consistent and methodical if it is to be taken seriously. We know, however, that Don Quijote has no idea of making a basic attack on
the established legal order. He is neither an anarchist nor a prophet
of the Kingdom of God. On the contrary, it is apparent again and
again that whenever his idée fixe happens not to be involved he
is willing to conform, that is only through his idée fixe that he
claims a special position for the knight-errant. The beautiful words,
allá se lo haya, etc., are deeply rooted, to be sure, in the kindly
wisdom of his real nature (this is a point to which we shall return),
but in their context they are still merely an improvisation. It is his
idée fixe which determines him to free the prisoners. It alone forces
him to conceive of everything he encounters as the subject of a
knightly adventure. It supplies him with the motifs "help the distressed" or "free the victims of force," and he acts accordingly. I
think it wholly erroneous to look for a matter of principle here, for
anything like a conflict between natural Christian and positive

[2] "To each his own sin. God is in heaven and does not neglect to punish the
bad and reward the good, and it is not proper that honorable men be the
executioners of other men, it not being up to them."—Ed.

law. For such a conflict, moreover, an opponent would have to appear, someone like the Grand Inquisitor in Dostoevski, who would be authorized and willing to represent the case of positive law against Don Quijote. His Majesty's commissary who is in charge of the convoy of prisoners is neither suited for the role nor prepared to play it. Personally he may very well be ready to accept the argument, "judge not that ye be not judged." But he has passed no judgment; he is no representative of positive law. He has his instructions and is quite justified in appealing to them.

Everything comes out all right, and time and again the damage done or suffered by Don Quijote is treated with stoic humor as a matter of comic confusion. Even the *bachiller* Alonso López, as he lies on the ground, badly mauled and with one leg pinned under his mule, consoles himself with mocking puns. This scene occurs in chapter 19 of book 1. It also shows that Don Quijote's idée fixe saves him from feeling responsible for the harm he does, so that in his conscience too every form of tragic conflict and somber seriousness is obviated. He has acted in accordance with the rules of knight-errantry, and so he is justified. To be sure, he hastens to assist the *bachiller,* for he is a kind and helpful soul; but it does not occur to him to feel guilty. Nor does he feel any guiltier when at the beginning of chapter 30 the priest puts him to the test by telling him what evil effects his freeing of the prisoners had produced. He angrily exclaims that it is the duty of a knight-errant to help those in distress but not to judge whether their plight is deserved or not. And that settles the question as far as he is concerned. In part 2, where the gaiety is even more relaxed and elegant, such complications no longer occur at all.

There is, then, very little of problem and tragedy in Cervantes' book—and yet it belongs among the literary masterpieces of an epoch during which the modern problematic and tragic conception of things arose in the European mind. Don Quijote's madness reveals nothing of the sort. The whole book is a comedy in which well-founded reality holds madness up to ridicule.

And yet Don Quijote is not only ridiculous. He is not like the bragging soldier or the comic old man or the pedantic and ignorant doctor. In our scene Don Quijote is taken in by Sancho. But does Sancho despise him and deceive him all the way through? Not at all. He deceives him only because he sees no other way out. He loves and reveres him, although he is half conscious (and sometimes fully conscious) of his madness. He learns from him and refuses to part with him. In Don Quijote's company he becomes cleverer and

better than he was before. With all his madness, Don Quijote preserves a natural dignity and superiority which his many miserable
failures cannot harm. He is not vulgar, as the above-mentioned
comic types normally are. Actually he is not a "type" at all in this
sense, for on the whole he is no automaton producing comic effects.
He even develops, and grows kinder and wiser while his madness
persists. But would it be true to say that his is a wise madness in the
ironical sense of the romanticists? Does wisdom come to him through
his madness? Does his madness give him an understanding he could
not have attained in soundness of mind, and do we hear wisdom
speak through madness in his case as we do with Shakespeare's fools
or with Charlie Chaplin? No, that is not it either. As soon as his
madness, that is, the idée fixe of knight-errantry, takes hold of him,
he acts unwisely, he acts like an automaton in the manner of the
comic types mentioned above. He is wise and kind independently
of his madness. A madness like this, it is true, can arise only in a
pure and noble soul, and it is also true that wisdom, kindness, and
decency shine through his madness and make it appear lovable.
Yet his wisdom and his madness are clearly separated—in direct
contrast to what we find in Shakespeare, the fools of Romanticism,
and Charlie Chaplin. The priest says it as early as chapter 30 of
part 1, and later it comes out again and again: he is mad only
when his idée fixe comes into play; otherwise he is a perfectly
normal and very intelligent individual. His madness is not such
that it represents his whole nature and is completely identical with
it. At a specific moment an idée fixe laid hold on him; but even so
it leaves parts of his being unaffected, so that in many instances he
acts and speaks like a person of sound mind; and one day, shortly
before his death, it leaves him again. He was some fifty years of
age when, under the influence of his excessive reading of romances
of chivalry, he conceived his absurd plan. This is strange. An over-
wrought state of mind resulting from solitary reading might rather
be expected in a youthful person (Julien Sorel, Madame Bovary),
and one is tempted to look for a specific psychological explanation.
How is it possible that a man in his fifties who leads a normal life
and whose intelligence is well-developed in many ways and not at
all unbalanced, should embark upon so absurd a venture? In the
opening sentences of his novel Cervantes supplies some details of
his hero's social position. From them we may at best infer that it
was burdensome to him, for it offered no possibility of an active
life commensurate with his abilities. He was as it were paralyzed by
the limitations imposed upon him on the one hand by his class and

on the other by his poverty. Thus one might suppose that his mad
decision represents a flight from a situation which has become un-
bearable, a violent attempt to emancipate himself from it. The sociological and psychological interpretation has been advocated by
various writers on the subject. I myself advanced it in an earlier
passage of this book, and I leave it there because in the context of
that passage it is justified. But as an interpretation of Cervantes'
artistic purpose it is unsatisfactory, for it is not likely that he intended his brief observations on Don Quijote's social position and
habits of life to imply anything like a psychological motivation of
the knight's idée fixe. He would have had to state it more clearly
and elaborate it in greater detail. A modern psychologist might
find still other explanations of Don Quijote's strange madness. But
this sort of approach to the problem has no place in Cervantes'
thinking. Confronted with the question of the causes of Don Quijote's madness, he has only one answer: Don Quijote read too many
romances of chivalry and they deranged his mind. That this should
happen to a man in his fifties can be explained—from within the
work—only in aesthetic terms, that is, through the comic vision
which came to Cervantes when he conceived the novel: a tall,
elderly man, dressed in old-fashioned and shabby armor, a picture
which is beautifully expressive not only of madness but also of
asceticism and the fanatic pursuit of an ideal. We simply have to
accept the fact that this cultured and intelligent country gentleman
goes suddenly mad—not, like Ajax or Hamlet, because of a terrible
shock—but simply because he has read too many romances of
chivalry. Here again there is nothing tragic. In the analyses of his
madness we have to do without the concept of the tragic, just as
we have to do without the specifically Shakespearean and romantic
combination of wisdom and madness in which one cannot be conceived without the other.

Don Quijote's wisdom is not the wisdom of a fool. It is the intelligence, the nobility, the civility, and the dignity of a gifted and
well-balanced man—a man neither demonic nor paradoxical, not
beset by doubt and indecision nor by any feeling of not being at
home in this world, but even-tempered, able to weigh and ponder,
receptive, and lovable and modest even in his irony. Furthermore
he is a conservative, or at least essentially in accord with the order
of things as it is. This comes out wherever and whenever he deals
with people—especially with Sancho Panza—in the longer or
shorter intervals during which his idée fixe is quiescent. From the
very beginning—although more in part 2 than in part 1—the

kindly, intelligent, and amiable figure, Alonso Quijano el bueno, whose most distinguishing characteristic is his naturally superior dignity, coexists with the mad adventurer. We need only read with what kindly and merry irony he treats Sancho in part 2, chapter 7, when the latter, on the advice of his wife Teresa, begins to present his request for a fixed salary. His madness intervenes only when he justifies his refusal by referring to the customs of knights-errant. Passages of this kind abound. There is evidence everywhere that we have to do with an intelligent Don Quijote and a mad one, side by side, and that his intelligence is in no way dialectically inspired by his madness but is a normal and, as it were, average intelligence.

That in itself yields an unusual combination. There are levels of tone represented here which one is not accustomed to finding in purely comic contexts. A fool is a fool. We are used to seeing him represented on a single plane, that of the comic and foolish, with which, at least in earlier literature, baseness and stupidity, and at times underhanded malice, were connected as well. But what are we to say of a fool who is at the same time wise, with that wisdom which seems the least compatible with folly, that is, the wisdom of intelligent moderation? This very fact, this combination of intelligent moderation with absurd excesses results in a multiplicity which cannot be made to accord altogether with the purely comic. But that is by no means all. It is on the very wings of his madness that his wisdom soars upward, that it roams the world and becomes richer there. For if Don Quijote had not gone mad, he would not have left his house. And then Sancho too would have stayed home, and he could never have drawn from his innate being the things which —as we find in delighted amazement—were potentially contained in it. The multifarious play of action and reaction between the two and their joint play in the world would not have taken place.

This play, as we think we have been able to show, is never tragic; and never are human problems, whether personal or social, represented in such a way that we tremble and are moved to compassion. We always remain in the realm of gaiety. But the levels of gaiety are multiplied as never before. Let us return once more to the text from which we set out. Don Quijote speaks to the peasant women in a style which is genuinely the elevated style of courtly love and which in itself is by no means grotesque. His sentences are not at all ridiculous (though they may seem so to many readers in our day), they are in the tradition of the period and represent a masterpiece of elevated expression in the form in which it was then alive. If it was Cervantes'

purpose to attack the romances of chivalry (and there can be no
doubt that it was), he nevertheless did not attack the elevated style
of chivalric expression. On the contrary, he reproaches the romances
of chivalry with not mastering the style, with being stylistically
wooden and dry. And so it comes about that in the middle of a
parody against the knightly ideology of love we find one of the most
beautiful prose passages which the late form of the tradition of
courtly love produced. The peasant women answer with characteristic coarseness. Such a rustically boorish style had long been em-
ployed in comic literature (although possibly never with the same
balance between moderation and verve), but what had certainly
never happened before was that it should follow directly upon a
speech like Don Quijote's—a speech which, taken by itself, could
never make us suspect that it occurs in a grotesque context. The
motif of a knight begging a peasant woman to hear his love—a
motif which produces a comparable situation—is age old. It is the
motif of the *pastourelle;* it was in favor with the early Provençal
poets, and, as we shall see when we come to Voltaire, it was remarkably long-lived. However, in the *pastourelle* the two partners have
adapted themselves to each other; they understand each other; and
the result is a homogeneous level of style on the borderline between
the idyllic and the everyday. In Cervantes' case, the two realms of
life and style clash by reason of Don Quijote's madness. There is
no possibility of a transition; each is closed in itself; and the only
link that holds them together is the merry neutrality of the playful
scheme of puppet-master Sancho—the awkward bumpkin, who but
a short time before believed almost everything his master said, who
will never get over believing some of it, and who always acts in accordance with the momentary situation. In our passage the dilemma
of the moment has inspired him to deceive his master; and he adapts
himself to the position of puppet-master with as much gusto and
elasticity as he later will to the position of governor of an island. He
starts the play in the elevated style, then switches to the low—not,
however, in the manner of the peasant women. He maintains his
superiority and remains master of the situation which he has himself
created under the pressure of necessity but which he now enjoys to
the full.

What Sancho does in this case—assuming a role, transforming
himself, and playing with his master's madness—other characters in
the book are perpetually doing. Don Quijote's madness gives rise to
an inexhaustible series of disguises and histrionics: Dorotea in the
role of Princess Micomicona, the barber as her page, Sansón Carrasco

as knight-errant, Ginés de Pasamonte as puppet-master—these are but a few examples. Such metamorphoses make reality become a perpetual stage without ever ceasing to be reality. And when the characters do not submit to the metamorphosis of their own free will, Don Quijote's madness forces them into their roles—as happens time and again, beginning with the innkeeper and the whores in the first tavern. Reality willingly cooperates with a play which dresses it up differently every moment. It never spoils the gaiety of the play by bringing in the serious weight of its troubles, cares, and passions. All that is resolved in Don Quijote's madness; it transforms the real everyday world into a gay stage. Here one should recall the various adventures with women which occur in the course of the narrative in addition to the encounter with Dulcinea: Maritornes struggling in Don Quijote's arms, Dorotea as Princess Micomicona, the lovelorn Altisidora's serenade, the nocturnal encounter with Doña Rodríguez (a scene which Cide Hamete Benengeli says that he would have given his best coat to see)—each of these stories is in a different style; each contains a shift in stylistic level; all of them are resolved by Don Quijote's madness, and all of them remain within the realm of gaiety. And yet there are several which need not necessarily have been thus restricted. The description of Maritornes and her muleteer is coarsely realistic; Dorotea is unhappy; and Doña Rodríguez is in great distress of mind because her daughter has been seduced. Don Quijote's intervention changes nothing of this—neither Maritornes' loose life nor the sad plight of Doña Rodríguez' daughter. But what happens is that we are not concerned over these things, that we see the lot and the life of these women through the prism of gaiety, and that our consciences do not feel troubled over them. As God lets the sun shine and the rain fall on the just and the unjust alike, so Don Quijote's madness, in its bright equanimity, illumines everything that crosses his path and leaves it in a state of gay confusion.

The most varied suspense and wisest gaiety of the book are revealed in a relationship which Don Quijote maintains throughout: his relationship with Sancho Panza. It is not at all as easy to describe in unambiguous terms as the relationship between Rocinante and Sancho's donkey or that between the donkey and Sancho himself. They are not always united in unfailing loyalty and love. It frequently happens that Don Quijote becomes so angry with Sancho that he abuses and maltreats him; at times he is ashamed of him; and once—in part 2, chapter 27—he actually deserts him in danger. Sancho, for his part, originally accompanies Don Quijote because he is stupid and for the selfishly materialistic reason that he expects fantastic advantages from the venture, and also because, despite all its hardships, he prefers a vagabond life to the regular working hours and monotony of life at home. Before long he begins to sense that something must be wrong with Don Quijote's mind, and then he sometimes deceives him, makes fun of him, and speaks of him disrespectfully. At times, even in part 2, he is so disgusted and disillusioned that he is all but ready to leave Don Quijote. Again and again the reader is made to see how variable and composite our human relationships are, how capricious and dependent on the moment even the most intimate of them. In the passage which was our point of departure Sancho deceives his master and plays almost cruelly on his madness. But what painstaking humoring of Don Quijote's madness, what sympathetic penetration of his world, must have preceded Sancho's conceiving such a plan and his being able to act his role so well! Only a few months earlier he had not the slightest inkling of all this. Now he lives, after his own fashion, in the world of knightly adventure; he is fascinated by it. He has fallen in love with his master's madness and with his own role. His development is most amazing. Yet withal, he is and remains Sancho, of the Panza family, a Christian of the old stock, well known in his village. He remains all that even in the role of a wise governor and also—and indeed especially—when he insists on Sanchica's marrying nothing less than a count. He remains Sancho; and all that happens to him could happen only to Sancho. But the fact that these things do happen, that his body and his mind are put in such violent commotion and emerge from the ordeal in all their unshakable and idiosyncratic genuineness—this he owes to Don Quijote, *su amo y natural señor*. The experience of Don Quijote's personality is not received by anyone as completely as it is by Sancho; it is not assimilated pure and whole by anyone as it is by him. The others all wonder about him, are amused or angered by him, or try to cure him. Sancho lives himself into Don Quijote, whose madness and wisdom become productive in him. Although he has far too little critical reasoning power to form and express a synthetic judgment upon him, it still is he, in all his reactions, through whom we best understand Don Quijote. And this in turn binds Don Quijote to him. Sancho is his consolation and his direct opposite, his creature and yet an independent fellow being who holds out against him and prevents his madness from locking him up as though in solitary confinement. Two partners who appear together as contrasting comic or semi-comic figures represent a very old motif which has re-

:ained its effectiveness even today in farce, caricature, the circus, and the film: the tall thin man and the short fat one; the clever man and his stupid companion; master and servant; the refined aristocrat and the simple-minded peasants; and whatever other combinations and variants there may be in different countries and under different cultural conditions. What Cervantes made of it is magnificent and unique.

Perhaps it is not quite correct to speak of what Cervantes made of it. It may be more exact to say "what became of the motif in his hands." For centuries—and especially since the romanticists—many things have been read into him which he hardly foreboded, let alone intended. Such transforming and transcendent interpretations are often fertile. A book like *Don Quijote* dissociates itself from its author's intention and leads a life of its own. Don Quijote shows a new face to every age which enjoys him. Yet the historian—whose task it is to define the place of a given work in a historical continuity—must endeavor insofar as that is still possible, to attain a clear understanding of what the work meant to its author and his contemporaries. I have tried to interpret as little as possible. In particular, I have pointed out time and again how little there is in the text which can be called tragic and problematic. I take it as merry play on many levels, including in particular the level of everyday realism. The latter differentiates it from the equally unproblematic gaiety of let us say Ariosto; but even so it remains play. This means that no matter how painstakingly I have tried to do as little interpreting as possible, I yet cannot help feeling that my thoughts about the book often go far beyond Cervantes' aesthetic intention. Whatever that intention may have been (we shall not here take up the problems presented by the aesthetics of his time), it most certainly did not consciously and from the beginning propose to create a relationship like that between Don Quijote and Sancho Panza as we see it after having read the novel. Rather, the two figures were first a single vision, and what finally developed from them—singly and together—arose gradually, as the result of hundreds of individual ideas, as the result of hundreds of situations in which Cervantes puts them and to which they react on the spur of the moment, as the result of the inexhaustible, ever-fresh power of the poetic imagination. Now and again there are actual incongruities and contradictions, not only in matters of fact (which has often been noted) but also in psychology: developments which do not fit into the total picture of the two heroes—which indicates how much Cervantes allowed himself to be guided by the momentary situation, by the demands of the adventure in hand. This is still the case—more frequently even—in part 2. Gradually and without any preconceived plan, the two personages evolve, each in himself and also in their relation to each other. To be sure, this is the very thing which allows what is peculiarly Cervantean, the sum of Cervantes' experience of life and the wealth of his imagination, to enter the episodes and speeches all the more richly and spontaneously. The "peculiarly Cervantean" cannot be described in words. And yet I shall attempt to say something *about* it in order to clarify its power and its limits. First of all it is something spontaneously sensory: a vigorous capacity for the vivid visualization of very different people in very varied situations, for the vivid realization and expression of what thoughts enter their minds, what emotions fill their hearts, and what words come to their lips. This capacity he possesses so directly and strongly, and in a manner so independent of any sort of ulterior motive, that almost everything realistic written before him appears limited, conventional, or propagandistic in comparison. And just as sensory is his capacity to think up or hit upon ever new combinations of people and events. Here, to be sure, we have to consider the older tradition of the romance of adventure and its renewal through Boiardo and Ariosto, but no one before him had infused the element of genuine everyday reality into that brilliant and purposeless play of combinations. And finally he has a "something" which organizes the whole and makes it appear in a definite "Cervantean" light. Here things begin to be very difficult. One might avoid the difficulty and say that this "something" is merely contained in the subject matter, in the idea of the country gentleman who loses his mind and convinces himself that it is his duty to revive knight-errantry, that it is this theme which gives the book its unity and its attitude. But the theme (which Cervantes, by the way, took over from the minor and in itself totally uninteresting contemporary work, the *Entremés de los romances*) could have been treated quite differently too. The hero might have looked very different; it was not necessary that there should be a Dulcinea and particularly a Sancho. But above all, what was it that so attracted Cervantes in the idea? What attracted him was the possibilities it offered for multifariousness and effects of perspective, the mixture of fanciful and everyday elements in the subject, its malleability, elasticity, adaptability. It was ready to absorb all forms of style and art. It permitted the presentation of the most variegated picture of the world in a light congenial to his own nature. And here we have come back to the difficult question we asked before:

what is the "something" which orders the whole and makes it appear in a definite, "Cervantean" light?

It is not a philosophy; it is no didactic purpose; it is not even a being stirred by the uncertainty of human existence or by the power of destiny, as in the case of Montaigne and Shakespeare. It is an attitude—an attitude toward the world, and hence also toward the subject matter of his art—in which bravery and equanimity play a major part. Together with the delight he takes in the multifariousness of his sensory play there is in him a certain Southern reticence and pride. This prevents him from taking the play very seriously. He looks at it; he shapes it; he finds it diverting; it is also intended to afford the reader refined intellectual diversion.

But he does not take sides (except against badly written books); he remains neutral. It is not enough to say that he does not judge and draws no conclusions: the case is not even called, the questions are not even asked. No one and nothing (except bad books and plays) is condemned in the book: neither Ginés de Pasamonte nor Roque Guinart, neither Maritornes nor Zoraida. For us Zoraida's behavior toward her father becomes a moral problem which we cannot help pondering; but Cervantes tells the story without giving a hint of his thoughts on the subject. Or rather, it is not Cervantes himself who tells the story, but the prisoner—who naturally finds Zoraida's behavior commendable. And that settles the matter. There are a few caricatures in the book—the Biscayan, the priest at the duke's castle, Doña Rodríguez; but these raise no ethical problems and imply no basic judgments.

On the other hand no one is praised as exemplary either. Here one might think of the Knight of the Green Caftan, Don Diego de Miranda, who in part 2, chapter 16, gives a description of his temperate style of life and thereby makes such a profound impression upon Sancho. He is temperate and inclined to rational deliberation; in dealing with both Don Quijote and Sancho he finds the right tone of benevolent, modest, and yet self-assured politeness. His attempts to confute or mitigate Don Quijote's madness are friendly and understanding. He must not be put with the narrow-minded and intolerant priest at the duke's court (as has been done by the distinguished Spanish scholar, Américo Castro). Don Diego is a paragon of his class, the Spanish variety of the humanist nobleman: *otium cum dignitate*. But he certainly is no more than that. He is no absolute model. For that, after all, he is too cautious and too mediocre, and it is quite possible (so far Castro may be right) that there is a shade of irony in the manner in which Cervantes describes his style of life, his manner of hunting, and his views on his son's literary inclinations.

Cervantes' attitude is such that his world becomes play in which every participating figure is justified by the simple fact of living in a given place. Only Don Quijote in his madness is not justified, is wrong. He is also wrong, absolutely speaking, as against the temperate and peaceable Don Diego, whom Cervantes—"with inspired perversity," as Castro puts it—makes the witness of the adventure with the lion. It would be forcing things if one sought to see here a glorification of adventurous heroism as against calculating, petty, and mediocre caution. If there is possibly an undertone of irony in the portrait of Don Diego, Don Quijote is not possibly but unqualifiedly conceived not with an undertone of ridicule but as ridiculous through and through. The chapter is introduced by a description of the absurd pride he takes in his victory over Carrasco (disguised as a knight) and a conversation on this theme with Sancho. The passage bears rereading for the sake of the realization it affords that there is hardly another instance in the entire book where Don Quijote is ridiculed—also in ethical terms—as he is here. The description of himself with which he introduces himself to Don Diego is foolish and turgid. It is in this state of mind that he takes on the adventure with the lion. And the lion does nothing but turn its back on Don Quijote! This is pure parody. And the additional details are fit for parody too: Don Quijote's request that the guard should give him a written testimonial to his heroism; the way he receives Sancho; his decision to change his name (henceforth he will be the Knight of the Lion), and many others.

Don Quijote alone is wrong as long as he is mad. He alone is wrong in a well-ordered world in which everybody else has his right place. He himself comes to see this in the end when, dying, he finds his way back into the order of the world. But is it true that the world is well-ordered? The question is not raised. Certain it is that in the light of Don Quijote's madness and confronted with it, the world appears well-ordered and even as merry play. There may be a great deal of wretchedness, injustice, and disorder in it. We meet harlots, criminals as galley slaves, seduced girls, hanged bandits, and much more of the same sort. But all that does not perturb us. Don Quijote's appearance, which corrects nothing and helps no one, changes good and bad fortune into play.

The theme of the mad country gentleman who undertakes to revive knight-errantry gave Cervantes an opportunity to present the world as play in that spirit of multiple, perspective, non-judging, nd even nonquestioning neutrality which is a brave form of wisdom. It could very simply be expressed in the words of Don Quijote which have already been quoted: *allá se lo haya cada uno con su pecado; Dios hay en al cielo que no se descuida de castigar al malo ni de premiar al bueno.* Or else in the words which he addresses to Sancho in part 2, chapter 8, at the end of the conversation about monks and knights: *muchos son los caminos por donde lleva Dios a los suyos al cielo.* This is as much as to say that in the last analysis it is a devout wisdom. It is not unrelated to the neutral attitude which Gustave Flaubert strove so hard to attain, and yet it is very different from it: Flaubert wanted to transform reality through style; transform it so that it would appear as God sees it, so that the divine order—insofar as it concerns the fragment of reality treated in a particular work—would perforce be incarnated in the author's style. For Cervantes, a good novel serves no other purpose than to afford refined recreation, *honesto entretenimiento.* No one has expressed this more convincingly in recent times than W. J. Entwistle in his book on Cervantes (1940) where he speaks of recreation and connects it very beautifully with re-creation. It would never have occurred to Cervantes that the style of a novel—be it the best of novels—could reveal the order of the universe. On the other hand, for him too the phenomena of reality had come to be difficult to survey and no longer possible to arrange in an unambiguous and traditional manner. Elsewhere in Europe men had long since begun to question and to doubt, and even to begin building anew with their own materials. But that was in keeping neither with the spirit of his country nor with his own temperament, nor finally with his conception of the office of a writer. He found the order of reality in play. It is no longer the play of Everyman, which provides fixed norms for the judgment of good and evil. That was still so in *La Celestina.* Now things are no longer so simple. Cervantes undertakes to pass judgment only in matters concerning his profession as a writer. So far as the secular world is concerned, we are all sinners; God will see to it that evil is punished and good rewarded. Here on earth the order of the unsurveyable is to be found in play. However arduous it may be to survey and judge phenomena, before the mad knight of La Mancha they turn into a dance of gay and diverting confusion.

This, it seems to me, is the function of Don Quijote's madness. When the theme—the mad hidalgo who sets forth to realize the ideal of the *caballero andante*—began to kindle Cervantes' imagination, he also perceived a vision of how, confronted with such mad-

ness, contemporary reality might be portrayed. And the vision
pleased him, both by reason of its multifariousness and by reason
of the neutral gaiety which the knight's madness spreads over every
thing which comes in contact with it. That it is a heroic and ideal
ized form of madness, that it leaves room for wisdom and humanity
was no doubt equally pleasing to him. But to conceive of Don Qui
jote's madness in symbolic and tragic terms seems to me forced
That can be read into the text; it is not there of itself. So universal
and multilayered, so noncritical and nonproblematic a gaiety in
the portrayal of everyday reality has not been attempted again in
European letters. I cannot imagine where and when it might have
been attempted.

Literature and Life in *Don Quixote*

by E. C. Riley

> The true hero is a poet, whether he knows it or not; for what
> is heroism if not poetry?
>
> UNAMUNO

The interaction of literature and life is a fundamental theme of
Don Quixote.[1] The subject is not literary theory itself (no one would
be so foolish as to suggest that *Don Quixote* was a sort of dramatized
treatise), but it is useful to approach it from the standpoint of
Cervantes's novelistic theory, with which it is firmly connected.
This may throw more light not only on the theory, but on the
motivation and methods of the author in what looks at times like a
waggish, bewildering, and complicated game or a protracted private joke. We must confine ourselves to the literary and artistic
aspects of matters susceptible of unlimited philosophical extension.
The epistemological questions which the *Quixote* poses are also
literary problems of professional interest to Cervantes as a novelist.

There is a basic preoccupation with literary fiction in the expressed purpose of the book and in the most elemental conception
of the hero. However far the author transcended his purpose, his

"Literature and Life in *Don Quixote*." From *Cervantes's Theory of the Novel*
by E. C. Riley (Oxford: The Clarendon Press, 1962), Part I, Chap. 4, pp. 35–48.
Copyright © 1962 by The Clarendon Press, Oxford. Reprinted by permission of
the publisher.

[1] Ortega first saw its importance, op. cit., "Meditación primera." See also: A.
Castro, "Cervantes y Pirandello," *La Nación* (Buenos Aires, 16 Nov. 1924), *Pen-
samiento*, pp. 30 ff., and many observations in his later essays in *Hacia Cervantes*;
J. Casalduero, *Sentido y forma del "Quijote"* (Madrid, 1949), *passim*; Leo Spitzer,
"Perspectivismo lingüístico en el *Quijote*," *Lingüística e historia literaria*
(Madrid, 1955); M. I. Gerhardt's substantial critical study, *"Don Quijote": la
vie et les livres* (Amsterdam, 1955); R. L. Predmore, *El mundo del "Quijote"*
(Madrid, 1958), ch. 1; and Harry Levin's perceptive essay, "The Example of
Cervantes," *Contexts of Criticism* (London, 1957) [Reprinted above, pp. 34–48].

declared aim was to debunk the novels of chivalry. Whatever else
the hero may be, he is, quite simply, a man who cannot distinguish
between life and literary fiction:

> everything that our adventurer thought, saw or imagined seemed to
> him to be done and to happen in the manner of the things he had
> read. (I, 2)

The discussion of history (matters of fact) and poetry (fiction) in II,
3, as Toffanin first showed, springs therefore, like other such passages, from the very heart of the novel.[2]

The critique of the novels of chivalry is made in two ways: by
more or less direct judgements within the fiction, and also *as* the
fiction. Criticism in fictional form is conventionally parody, and
to some extent the *Quixote* is parody, but it is unusual in containing the object of the parody within itself, as a vital ingredient. The
novels of chivalry exist in the book in just the same way as Rocinante or the barber's basin. They are so palpably present that
some of them can be burnt. Cervantes's originality lies not in parodying them himself (or only incidentally), but in making the mad
Knight parody them involuntarily in his efforts to bring them, by
means of imitation, literally to life.

A more essential characteristic of Don Quixote's delusions than
the fact that they have to do with chivalry is their bookish, fabulous
nature. The golden age of chivalry that he wanted to resurrect had
little to do with the real Middle Ages; it was an age that never was,
the imaginary storybook age of "Once upon a time." History only
inspired him when it merged distantly with fiction as legend. Byron's foolish remark that Cervantes "smiled Spain's chivalry
away" is a confusion of history and literature not far removed from
that of the mad Knight himself. Quixote's Utopian and messianic
ideals may have proved more important in the end, but it was
fabulous romance, Cervantes tells us in the first chapter, that originally captivated his fancy:

> His imagination became filled with everything he had read in his
> books, with enchantments, affrays, battles, challenges, wounds, gal-
> lantries, amours, torments and impossible extravagances [*disparates
> imposibles*]. (I, 1)

In 1752 Mrs. Lennox published her *Female Quixote* about a lady
whose head had been turned by heroic romances, and a modern
Cervantes could as easily create a twentieth-century Quixote ob-

---

[2] Toffanin, *Fine dell'umanesimo*, ch. 15.

sessed, say, with science fiction. Don Quixote the reader of popular romances is the grandfather of Emma Bovary and Joyce's Gertie McDowell. What distinguishes him from them is an obsession with the most impossibly fabulous form of fiction that could be imagined.

His imitation of the heroes of chivalresque novels aims at such completeness that it becomes an attempt to live literature. He is not inspired to a vague sort of emulation, nor does he merely ape the habits, manners, and dress of knights errant; he does not simply adapt chivalresque ideals to some other cause, like St. Ignatius Loyola; he is not even acting a part, in the usual sense. He is content with nothing less than that the whole of the fabulous world —knights, princesses, magicians, giants, and all—should be part of his experience. Once he believes he really is a knight errant, and believes in his world of fiction, he steps off the pinnacle of inspired idealistic emulation into madness. He cannot play his part as he would like except in this fabulous world. In this sense he is trying to live literature.

His choice of literature is a debased and supremely fictitious form of epic; he its idealized and superhuman hero. He has epic aspirations to honour and glory through hardship and danger, the chivalric ideal of service and the hero's urge to shape the world to his pattern. He goes farther than that: in effect he is trying to cast off his earthly, historical existence and live in the rarefied region of poetry. (Since Cervantes's story of this endeavour is itself a poetic fiction—since what is "life" in the story is a literary creation by Cervantes—we begin to see some of the complications of the novel.) Don Quixote is trying to turn life into art while it is yet being lived, which cannot be done because art, and idealistic art more than any, means selection, and it is impossible to select every scrap of one's experience. Life is one thing and art is another, but just what the difference is was the problem that baffled and fascinated Cervantes. If the Knight is like the wise man of Epicurus who would rather "live poems" than write them, his efforts to do this literally are madness. Unamuno identified poetry and heroism in a wide sense, but they cannot be literally identical, if words mean anything at all.

Now the obvious and practicable way for Don Quixote to imitate the books of chivalry would have been through a recognized artistic medium—to have written romances himself, for instance. In fact, he was initially tempted to do so. He many times felt the urge to complete the unfinished novel *Don Belianis de Grecia* and would undoubtedly have done so, and very well too, "if other and continual thoughts of greater moment had not prevented him" (I, 1). The books had too strong a hold on him. He was impelled to take up not the pen but the sword.

Don Quixote is, among a great many other things, an artist in his own peculiar way. His medium is action and, secondarily, words. Consciously living a book and acting for a sage enchanter to record, he is in a sense the author of his own biography. Even when he has abandoned the idea of conventional literary expression he retains many of the writer's characteristics. He composes verse on occasion. He imitates the archaic language of the novels of chivalry. At the start of his venture he anticipates his chronicler by putting the scene of his departure into verbal form—ornate, elevated language which makes a magnificent ironic contrast with the style used by the real author. His fantasies in I, 21 and I, 50 and his description of the battle of the flocks are brilliant pastiches, scarcely more absurd than the sort of writing that inspired them. He is repeatedly stimulated by literature. Cardenio's verses found in the Sierra Morena immediately induce in him thoughts of imitation; Cardenio's reference to *Amadís* occasions his disastrous interruption; the dramatized ballad of Gaiferos and Melisendra provokes him to violence.

His artistic instinct does not desert him in action, though it seldom has a chance to operate fruitfully. He takes much trouble over his preparations. Like a well-instructed writer he thinks long before he chooses names.[3] When conditions are particularly favourable, as on the occasion of the penance in the Sierra Morena, he is most attentive to detail and concerned with effect. This is art in action, if it is also madness. But the idea of bringing art into the business of living was not foreign to Cervantes's contemporaries. The lesson of Castiglione's much-read work was that the life of the perfect courtier should be a veritable work of art. It is perhaps not too fanciful to see the urge to render art in action, which may lie among the motive forces of heroism itself, as one of the distinguishing marks of the Spanish genius. It is realized in two of the most individual forms of Spanish art: the dance and the bullfight, where stylization combines with improvisation and author with actor. In the same way Don Quixote must improvise to meet the situations life offers him, without departing from the conventions laid down by his chivalresque models; and he creates, in part at least, the story of which he is the hero. The difference is that life is long and a

---

[3] M. T. Herrick, "Comic Theory in the Sixteenth Century," *UISLL*, XXXIV (1950), 63, observes that Donatus, Servius, Robortelli, and Castelvetro all attached importance to the choice of appropriate names in the writing of comedy.

dance is short and the world is not contained in a bullring. But the impulse which prompts the Knight to shape his life into an epic and that which puts beauty into the dancer's and the matador's every movement is the same.

Unfortunately he is a bad and a frustrated artist. He overestimates his capacities and underestimates the peculiarly intractable nature of his material, which is life itself. He executes a comic parody. But in so far as he is an artist, certain artistic principles may up to a point be applied to his behaviour. Let me say at once that I have not the least idea whether they were in Cervantes's conscious mind in this strange connexion. Probably not; but it is the privilege of books like the *Quixote* to contain far more than the author could ever have been aware of putting in. He was certainly much concerned with those principles on other occasions. Where literary fiction and "real" experience are so curiously combined it need not surprise us to find unusual applications of literary theory. We shall note them later when they occur.

The *Quixote* is a novel of multiple perspectives. Cervantes observes the world he creates from the viewpoints of characters and reader as well as author. It is as though he were playing a game with mirrors, or prisms. By a kind of process of refraction he adds—or creates the illusion of adding—an extra dimension to the novel. He foreshadows the technique of modern novelists whereby the action is seen through the eyes of one or more of the personages involved, although Cervantes does not identify himself with his own characters in the usual sense.

What is fiction from one standpoint is "historical fact" or "life" from another. Cervantes pretends through his invented chronicler Benengeli that his fiction is history (though dubious history, as we shall see later). Into this history fictions of various kinds are inserted. The *novela* of the *Curioso impertinente* is one example. Another, of a different sort, is the story of Princess Micomicona, a nonsensical tale attached to the "historical" episode of Dorotea, which is part of Benengeli's "history" of Don Quixote, which is Cervantes's novelistic fiction *Don Quixote*. There is no need to make ourselves dizzy with more examples. Tales and histories, of course, are only the more overtly literary parts of an immense spectrum in the novel, that includes hallucinations, dreams, legends, deceptions, and misapprehensions. The presence of chimerical chivalresque figures in the book has the effect of making Quixote and Sancho and the physical world in which these two move seem more real by comparison. At one stroke Cervantes enlarged infinitely the scope of prose fiction by including in it with the world of external appearances the world of the imagination—which exists in books, as well as in minds.

If the reader adopts the point of view of any sane travelling companion of the Knight and Squire, he can see the problem of the unity of the *Quixote* in another light. The literary episodes or "digressions" of Cardenio, Leandra, Claudia Jerónima, and others then appear as true adventures, as opposed to the fantastic ones imagined by the Knight or concocted for him by other people. To the characters they are true; to the reader outside they are things that could have happened; to both they are unusual events, adventures. On examination it becomes clear that Don Quixote's reactions to them and the degree to which he intervenes, if he does, are dictated by the nature of the episode and his state of mind together. A subtle but essential link is apparent between himself and these external events. There is a clear exception to this in the case of the *Curioso,* and another possible one in that of the Captive's tale; about both of these Cervantes himself expressed doubts.[4]

The episodes are complicated by the introduction of pastoral incidents, which, precisely because they are by their nature more bookish than the others, have a special attraction for Don Quixote, although he is never able to enter the pastoral world effectively. Cervantes rings the changes on pastoral in the stories of Grisóstomo and Marcela, the fair Leandra, Camacho's wedding, and the incident of the simulated Arcadia. They have a special place in the life-literature theme, because they represent different levels of an intermediate region which is not impossibly fabulous fiction in the way the novel of chivalry is, or part of the everyday world of innkeepers, barbers, and friars—which is a world that also includes runaway Moorish ladies, seducers, and dukes and duchesses, who are no less real, only less commonly encountered.

Cervantes's ironic vision enables him to put within the pages of *Don Quixote* things that are normally outside books automatically; and also to manipulate the story so that the principal characters are actually conscious of the world outside the covers of the book. He includes within its pages an author (supposedly *the* author), Benengeli. He brings his real self in incidentally as the man who presents Benengeli's fiction to the public. On occasion he mentions himself just as if he were a personage who existed cheek by jowl

[4] See E. C. Riley, "Episodio, novela y aventura en *Don Quijote,*" *ACerv* [*Anales cervantinos*] V (1955–56).

with his characters: as the author of the *Galatea* and friend of the
Priest; as the soldier "something Saavedra" whom the Captive knew
in Algiers; and we are also indirectly reminded of him as the author
of the *Curioso impertinente, Rinconete y Cortadillo,* and the *Numancia.* Not only this, he brings his public into the fiction. Part II
is full of characters who have read Part I and know all about the
earlier adventures of Quixote and Sancho. He even introduces into
Part II the sequel by his rival Avellaneda: the book itself and one
of the characters who belonged to it. He makes Quixote and Sancho
conscious of themselves as the literary heroes of a published work
and therefore conscious of the world outside their story. The
claims to reality of Avellaneda's spurious *Quixote* become in Part
II an issue of some moment to the protagonists. . . .

Cervantes handles his work in such a way as to show his complete
control over the creation he tries so hard to make seem independent.
A curious instance of this occurs at the end of chapter 8 in the
First Part. He abruptly stops the action as one might cut off a
cinematograph projector. Everything is arrested at a dramatic moment when Don Quixote and the Biscayan are engaged in mortal
combat. They are left frozen, with their swords raised, while Cervantes interposes an account, several pages long, of how he discovered Benengeli's manuscript. He often uses the device of interruption as a way of procuring suspense and variety, just as Ercilla
and other writers had done, but nowhere so graphically as here.[5]
This destruction of the illusion is another typical piece of irony.
It is also a piece of artistic exhibitionism displaying the power of
the writer.

Nevertheless, he sometimes has difficulty in containing his novels
and stories within the bounds prescribed by art and the capacities
of his readers. The trouble is the vastness of his imaginative vision
of life. The problem faces every fertile novelist, but life and literature are so intricately geared for Cervantes that sometimes they seem
actually to interfere with each other. A couple of passages are
revealing in this respect. The convict Ginés de Pasamonte has his
picaresque autobiography fully planned, but even he cannot say
how long it is going to be. When asked whether it is finished, he
replies, "How can it be, when my life is not finished yet?" (*DQ* I,
22). The other is from the *Persiles.* When Periandro says to Arnaldo:

---

[5] It will be remembered that this particular scene is also reproduced as a picture, "muy al natural," on the first page of Cide Hamete's manscript (*DQ* [*Don
Quixote*] I, 9; i, 285).

> Do not be concerned for the time being. We arrived in Rome only
> yesterday and it is not possible that in so short a time procedures can
> have been devised, schemes drafted and inventions set up that will
> bring our actions to the happy conclusions we desire. (*Persiles* IV, 4)

it is hard to avoid the suspicion that what he really means is "Give
the author time to work out the plot!" The length of Ginés's book is
adjusted to the length of his life; Periandro leaves it to the author
to bring his travails to their happy conclusion whenever the exigen-
cies of the novel permit. These curious suggestions illustrate the
way in which life and literary composition run *pari passu* in Cervantes.

There is artistic point to the whimsical tricks in *Don Quixote*.
Those alluded to (with the exception of the interrupted combat,
which is the same trick in reverse) all contribute to two major
effects. They give the novel an appearance of receding depths, by
comparison with which most other prose fiction is two-dimensional.
They also give solidity and vividness to the figures of Quixote and
Sancho and make them appear to exist independently of the book
that was written about them. The comments of other characters
sometimes help in this. Cardenio agrees that Don Quixote's madness
is so extraordinary that he doubts whether anyone could have
managed to invent the idea (I, 30). Sansón Carrasco finds Sancho
in the flesh even more amusing than he had suspected from reading
Part I (II, 7).

The author stands well back from his own work, seeming not to
be responsible for his own manipulations. They are conjuring tricks
that enhance the general artistic illusion of reality. One might consider them "improper" aesthetic procedures, if one could possibly
call anything that furthers the end of art unaesthetic. They are
certainly unconventional, but the illusion to which they contribute
is an important constituent of the "poetic truth" of the literary
fiction. The word "contribute" must be stressed: the effect owes
more to art than to artifice in the end. But it is impossible to doubt
Cervantes's single-minded purposefulness behind these tricks. He
practically succeeds in making the reader say of Don Quixote what
Don Quixote said of the hero who was so vividly real to him: "I can
almost say that I have seen Amadís of Gaul with my own two eyes"
(II, 1). And he was successful enough to deceive Unamuno and those
who have judged the creation to be, in some freakish way, bigger
than the mental capacity of the creator. Like conjuring tricks, however, they should not be resorted to too often. As Corneille said in
the *Examen* of his *Illusion comique*: "Les caprices de cette nature

ne se hasardent qu'une fois." Cervantes used similar devices in a few other writings, but he never again attempted feats of literary legerdemain on the same scale in a single work.

Two problems of importance to Cervantes's theory of the novel underlie these intricate manipulations of his invention. The first is the nature and limits of a work of art. The Knight's confusion of fiction and fact is an extreme case, but the author clearly shows that there is some justification for it. Not only the boundaries between what is imaginary and what is real, but those between art and life, are indeterminable. Life and art are continually interfering with each other. Inherent in this problem is that of the nature of artistic truth. What truth is to history, verisimilitude is to fiction. But can you by pretending fiction is history turn verisimilitude into something as potent as historical truth? The question is insistent throughout the *Quixote* and the *Persiles*.

The second problem concerns the effects of imaginative literature on people. Here again Don Quixote is an extreme case. But the matter was one of considerable importance in the Counter-Reformation, especially in Spain. In the century or more since the invention of printing the size of the reading public had enormously increased. The Church was naturally sensitive to the effects of literature on men's minds, and there was a wide awareness, not confined to the Church, of the power of literature and art to influence men's lives. The impact of the printed book in the sixteenth century has some analogy with that of television today, and produced some perhaps not wholly dissimilar reactions.

In Cervantes's novel, imaginative literature has affected the behaviour of many people besides the hero. What sort of a hold, for instance, has fiction on the minds of the Duke and Duchess and all those who concoct for their own amusement fantastic and elaborate situations involving Quixote and Sancho? Or on the Innkeeper, of whom Dorotea, with a significant confusion of ideas, says, "Our host is not far from making a second Don Quixote [or *Don Quixote*]" (I, 32)? Or on the people who devise imitation Arcadias? Books affect people's lives; literature is a part of their experience; Cervantes's novel is, among other things, about books in life.

Precedents of a sort can be found for the way in which Cervantes treats *Don Quixote*.[6] Many of the more obvious forms of critical de-

---

[6] For observations on developments before and after Cervantes, see J. E. Gillet, "The Autonomous Character in Spanish and European Literature," *HR*, XXIV (1956). For later developments, see A. Lebois, "La Révolte des personnages, de Cervantes et Calderón à Raymond Schwab," *RLC*, XXIII (1949).

tachment in writing were formalized early in rhetoric as topics of apology, topics for use in the exordium, the conclusion, and so on.[7] Moral reflections and asides and even the conventional formula "the history relates," common in the novels of chivalry, implied a measure of detachment. In Renaissance prose and poetry comments on the progress of the narrative and announcements of new developments or scenes were common, a relic, probably, of oral poetic techniques. Ariosto and Ercilla regularly remind one of their presence in this way at the end of cantos. Ariosto especially takes up positions alongside his creation from time to time, in the poem yet not of it. This, and his ironical way of suggesting that the story is really controlling him, begin to remind one strongly of Cervantes's methods.[8]

The effect of literary fiction on literary characters makes itself felt in some degree in the *novelle* written after Boccaccio. The influence of the *Decameron* was so powerful that it often occurs to later *novellieri* to make their ladies and gentlemen consciously imitate those in Boccaccio's "framework" by telling tales.[9] A member of the company may even have the *Decameron* with him, when they decide to entertain themselves in this manner.[10] The examples are slight, but to make an invented character aware of literary fiction as such is an advance in sophistication over the mere appropriation of another author's fictional characters for one's own use, as was quite commonly done.

But it was still a long way from making a character aware that he or she had a literary existence. Glimmerings of this Pirandellian idea, however, appear in one of the earliest of all novels, Heliodorus's *Ethiopic History*. "It's just like a play!" exclaim the characters of the events in which they are participating, thus recognizing the resemblance to fiction, if not the identity with it.[11] Heliodorus's little trick of making his figures themselves draw attention to the exceptional nature of the story is strongly reminiscent of Cervantes. Another striking procedure for its time is that used in the remark-

---

[7] E. R. Curtius, *European Literature and the Latin Middle Ages* (London, 1953), pp. 410 ff.; also 85–91.

[8] Ariosto, *Orlando furioso* (ed. Naples–Milan, 1954), e.g. XXXII. ii; XXXV. ii.

[9] E.g. in Firenzuola's *Ragionamenti*. See L. Di Francia, *Novellistica* (Milan, 1924–5), i, 601–602.

[10] Thus in "Il Lasca's" *Cene* (Di Francia, *op. cit.* i, 622).

[11] *Historia etiópica de los amores de Teágenes y Cariclea*, Fernando de Mena's translation of 1587 (ed. Madrid, 1954): cf. pp. 183–184; also pp. 91, 388, 424. Cervantes may have read this translation or the anonymous one of Antwerp, 1554, based on Amyot's French version.

able Renaissance novel *La Lozana andaluza,* by Francisco Delicado. The author introduces himself into the work, not as a character of any importance, nor yet as a mere vehicle for conveying the story, but as a sort of sixteenth-century Isherwood (an exceedingly candid camera), actively engaged in observing and recording everything the prostitute Lozana says and does. He does not exploit the possibilities of this, however, for Lozana's conduct is not influenced by knowing herself (as she does) to be the subject of Delicado's "portrait." [12]

The writer's personal relationship with his narrative was often very complex and its clear expression important to the understanding of the work. The distinction between Dante the author and Dante the pilgrim has been described as "fundamental to the whole structure" of his poem.[13] In the sixteenth century, one may observe a good deal of confusion give way to a clarifying of the author's position *vis-à-vis* his own work. The *Arcadia* suffers from Sannazaro's failure to define his role within the work, and his position outside it as writer, with any clarity. The confusion over who's who in Garcilaso's *Eclogues* arises from the medley made by the poet of personal matters from his own experience, details from the lives and personalities of his intimates, and pure fiction. The chivalresque novelists, feeling the need for some sort of detachment, formally dissociated themselves from the fiction but only confused the issues. Bandello, much more clear-sighted, nevertheless raised other questions when he sought to use detachment as a moral alibi, disclaiming responsibility for the crimes and vices of his characters. A richer and less dubious complication of moral attitudes was contrived by Mateo Alemán, who used the autobiographical form habitual to picaresque novelists. He was remarkably successful in combining objectivity with autobiographical method in *Guzmán de Alfarache.* The picaroon's conversion made this possible: the reformed character could look back and write about himself as "a different man."

Though Alemán's method was not that of Cervantes (who for one thing never presented a prose story as happening to himself), the peculiar achievements of both novelists demanded a highly developed sense of the difference between poetic fiction and historical fact —a development which followed the diffusion of the Aristotelian

---

[12] A. Vilanova, whose edition of the book I have used (Barcelona, 1952), suggests that Delicado's work inspired Cervantes in this respect—"Cervantes y *La Lozana andaluza,*" *Insula,* no. 77 (May, 1952). It is an extremely doubtful supposition.

[13] Francis Fergusson, quoted by R. H. Green, "Dante's 'Allegory of Poets' and the mediaeval theory of Poetic Fiction," *CL,* IX (1957), 124.

poetic doctrines, which justified poetic fiction by the universal truth it contained. A heightened awareness of the relationship between life and literature made possible the unparalleled degree of autonomy enjoyed by Don Quixote and Sancho, and also permitted the author to achieve a simultaneous detachment from and involvement with his work, a highly complex operation but one that no longer brooked confusion. Confident in his freedom and power to control his work completely, he might then, like God, be both in and outside his handiwork. Cervantes, at the very end of his novel, draws away from his creation when he makes Cide Hamete—or rather, makes his pen—say: "For me alone Don Quixote was born, and I for him; he knew how to act, and I how to write . . . ," only to reaffirm their identity with the words "we two are one." [14]

In the critical thought of the sixteenth century, life and literature, though distinguished with a preciseness unknown since Antiquity, came closer together. This is exemplified in Scaliger's doctrines. He ultimately makes the matter of poetry and the matter of reality indistinguishable.[15] The poet imitates nature; Virgil alone did this perfectly; so the modern poet should imitate Virgil (thereby imitating nature) for the edification of his public. If the argument in this simplified form is hardly persuasive, the narrowing of the gap, of which this is but one illustration from the complex corpus of his theory, can be seen in this fusion of nature with a literary model. The levels of fiction were also explored. Piccolomini we find speculating upon imitations of imitations, which recall the stories within stories of *Don Quixote*:

> So being therefore inclined to think that a double imitation of this sort could well be done, I continued to reason how much further one could proceed with this reflection and multiplication [of what is imitated]: that is to say, whether one could not only duplicate, but triplicate and quadruplicate it, and go as far as one liked, finally, as it were one imitator imitating another imitator, and so on and so on. . . .
>
> And in truth, when imitating an imitator, one also in a certain fashion imitates what is true, since it is true that that imitated imitator imitates.[16]

[14] "Para mí sola nació don Quijote, y yo para él: él supo obrar, y yo escribir; solos los dos somos para en uno" (*DQ* II. 74; viii. 267).

[15] See B. Weinberg, "Scaliger versus Aristotle on Poetics," *MPh* [*Modern Philology*], XXXIX (1942), 348–49.

[16] "Inclinando io adunque allora a credere che così fatta doppia imitazione si potesse con ragion fare; andai discorrendo quanto oltra con questa reflessione e moltiplicazione si potesse procedere: cioè se non solo doppia si potesse fare,

By the early 1600's art had become thoroughly introverted. Some curious optical tricks resulted. Artists turned their glass on the working of art and made works of art out of what they saw. Lope de Vega wrote a well-known *Soneto de repente,* the subject of which is simply the writing of that very sonnet. The ironic vision made possible the "play within the play" in *Hamlet,* Corneille's *Illusion comique,* and the incident of the puppet-show in *Don Quixote,* to mention no more. It also produced the possibilities so brilliantly exploited by Calderón in *El gran teatro del mundo* and *No hay más fortuna que Dios.*

Some of the juggling with fiction which is an integral part of *Don Quixote* continued to be popular with authors and readers. Such is the case of all that apparatus of fictitious documents and supposedly second-hand stories dear to European novelists from the seventeenth century on; it owes much to Cervantes although he did not invent it. And some of the more tricksy devices had to wait from the seventeenth century until the nineteenth before becoming again a significant part of works by major writers. In fact, of course, the autonomous characters of Pérez Galdós, Unamuno, and above all Pirandello are anticipated by Quixote and Sancho by some three centuries. So are some of the notions of such disparate writers as André Gide and Lewis Carroll. Long before Édouard in *Les Faux-Monnayeurs,* Cervantes wrote a book about "the struggle between facts as proposed by reality, and the ideal reality." [17] In *Through the Looking-Glass* Alice's distressed and angry reaction to Tweedle-dum's provoking suggestion that she is only one of the things in the Red King's dream recalls that of Quixote and Sancho when their reality is challenged by Avellaneda's rival heroes.

But the closest analogy with the "looking-glass game" Cervantes plays in *Don Quixote* is not in a book at all but a painting. It is roughly contemporary, a masterpiece of comparable magnitude, and the effect is similar. I mean Velasquez's *Las Meninas.* [18] It is full of

---

ma tripla, e quadrupla, e quanto si voglia finalmente com' a dire uno che imiti uno altro imitante, e così di mano in mano . . ." "Ed in vero in imitar un imitante, s'imita ancora in un certo modo il vero; essendo vero che quel tal' imitato imitante imita" (*op cit.,* pp. 37, 39).

[17] Quoted through E. M. Forster's *Aspects of the Novel* (London, 1927). Like so many contemporary writers on the subject, he quite forgets the first modern novel and describes the attempt to combine the two truths as "new" (p. 135).

[18] I believe the analogy extends further and is much more fundamental than is suggested either by Ortega, *op. cit.,* p. 169, or H. Hatzfeld, "Artistic Parallels in Cervantes and Velázquez," *Estudios dedicados a Menéndez Pidal* (Madrid, 1950–57), iii. 289, who touch on the point I am making.

tricks. There in the picture is the painter at work on his own painting, the largest figure in the scene, but dark and unobtrusive. There too is the back of the very canvas we are looking at. Arrested, half in half out of the room, and, as it were, of the picture, is the figure in the doorway. The King and Queen are seen reflected in a mirror on the far wall, which is hung with dim paintings. And the viewer realizes with a shock that he is looking at the picture from the spot, close to the watchful monarch and his wife, from which the picture was painted in effect. One all but glances over one's shoulder. Did a mirror stand there (there is some doubt), or did Velasquez, projecting himself mentally right outside his subject, paint from that spot as though he had been someone else altogether, painting—himself— at work? In either case, he has contrived to be simultaneously outside and inside his subject, and what is more, to draw the outside spectator into it too. "But where is the frame?" exclaimed Gautier when he saw the picture. Picasso's comment was, "There you have the true painter of reality." "His aim," Sir Kenneth Clark has written, "was simply to tell the whole truth about a complete visual impression . . . maintaining, unobserved, a measureless impartiality." [19]

They might all, no less aptly, have been speaking of Cervantes and *Don Quixote*.

[19] Sir Kenneth Clark, *The Sunday Times* (June 2, 1957).

Cervantes and the Picaresque Mode:
Notes on Two Kinds of Realism

by Carlos Blanco Aguinaga

It is quite common nowadays, especially in the Hispanic world, to consider that the modern novel derives its origin from, on the one hand, the picaresque (specifically, *Lazarillo de Tormes*) and, on the other, *Don Quixote,* together with one or two of the *Exemplary Novels.* Indeed, so we are told, *Don Quixote, Rinconete and Cortadillo,* and *The Colloquy of the Dogs,* together with the picaresque novel, spell the destruction of the heroic or bucolic world of the "idealistic" novel; in other words, they resemble each other in function in that they are *not* "idealistic" novels. Hence one should, presumably, conclude that both sorts, in some way, are equally "realistic," indeed the first realistic novels. Such an identification of some of Cervantes' novels with the picaresque at the origin of realism in the modern novel entails, however, an analogy by contraries. Such an analogy, reasonable and satisfying as it may seem, is, strictly speaking, like any other negative identification, elementary and insufficient, because, as I shall try to show, it cannot be raised to a level of positive comparison. To link, as some have attempted, the picaresque with the Cervantine mode is to confuse by vague approximation two kinds of realism which in fact are absolutely opposed: one which we might call dogmatic or disillusionist realism and one which we might call objective realism. These are two diverse ways of conceiving the novel.

To arrive at this conclusion it has been necessary to make a posi-

"Cervantes and the Picaresque Mode: Notes on Two Kinds of Realism" by Carlos Blanco Aguinaga. Translated and abridged by Lowry Nelson, Jr. From *Nueve Revista de Filología Hispánica,* XI (1957), 313-14, 314-16, 328-42. Reprinted by permission of the author and the publisher, *Nueva Revista de Filología Hispánica.* The reader is referred to the Spanish original for elaborate footnotes in which the author expands certain points and takes account of other scholars and critics.

tive comparison between the Cervantine and the picaresque novel, and, in order to achieve the comparison, the point of departure of this analysis has been quite conventional: I have, as is customary, compared the picaresque with those novels of Cervantes in which picaroons or picaresque lives appear, without feeling limited, as most others have, to a consideration of whether the picaroons of Cervantes are happier or neater or pleasanter or nobler than Guzmán or Pablos or Marcos or Lázaro or Justina in their respective novels. My analysis concerns the meaning and form of the novels themselves and the way in which a novelist presents a fictional world. We shall see from the comparison that Cervantes never wrote a picaresque novel—and that his "picaroons" are quite different from the others—because his way of perceiving the world and the writing of fiction, in short his realism, is quite different from that of the most renowned picaresque novelists.

*   *   *

It is well to begin by recalling two of the main traits of the picaresque novel which in *Guzmán de Alfarache*[1] are of crucial importance. (1) In the picaresque novel we always find recounted the story of a vagabond bereft of fortune whose role in life amounts to satisfying, by whatever means, his most basic needs. Hunger is perhaps the chief motivation of the picaroon, and in order to satisfy it while working as little as possible he does anything without achieving any precise identity: he serves several masters, begs, steals, and dupes. In relation to the picaroon all humanity seems to have no higher existential goal than his own, and when it *seems* to have one we are immediately warned that it is mere vanity and gesture. Compared with the heroes of earlier fiction the picaroon is an anti-hero, the lowest embodiment of human reality. In turn, the world in which the picaroon moves is the lowest and most contrary to the ideal, pure, and noble world of the epic, the chivalric novel, and the pastoral. (2) The second trait, which may seem merely formal, though indispensable, is that the adventures of the picaroon are always narrated in autobiographical form.

From the fusion of these two traits we may derive a third in which substance and form are quite the same: the picaroon is always a lone wanderer, a true exile who never achieves authentic dialogue with other men because most of them distrust him and he distrusts

[1] By Mateo Alemán, 1599; translated in 1622 by James Mabbe and most recently reprinted in Tudor Translations, edited by J. Fitzmaurice Kelly (4 vols., 1924).

them all, once he has acquired a little experience. And though he deals with everyone and everyone deals with him, all the diverse attitudes of others are filtered to the reader through his loneness and at the center of his loneness reality, however prismatic, becomes fixed in a single point of view from which, by its very lowness of perspective, the falsity of other points of view is exposed. Because of this single point of view, the loneness of the picaroon results in total isolation from the hostile world and thereby justifies itself: in this isolation the picaroon finds his superiority over the rest of mankind and from this superiority he derives his basis for judging and condemning them. Thus from his isolation spring dogmatic characterizations or distorted accounts of reality through which every deception of the world is laid bare. Besides, just as the picaroon as character is *now* the novelist outside the novel, the judgments and opinions that originated in his life by force of circumstance become transformed into formal and definitive judgments on humanity, which he, now a solitary novelist, no longer pronounces from his lowly origins but rather from a "watchtower" intellectually and morally superior to the world of others. The experience of the picaroon is transformed into the judgment of the novelist: everything that he, throughout his life, has been laying bare serves him now as an example whereby the reader may learn to lay bare reality. Thus, though while he was living his life as a picaroon every adventure helped him to discover *a posteriori* the illusion of the world, the novel about that life is posited *a priori* as an example of disillusion.

*   *   *

In *Guzmán de Alfarache,* the picaresque novel *par excellence,* we are presented with the reality of the world from a single point of view: it is presented in its disillusion and its sinfulness and it is rejected. And since the novel is conceived *a priori,* through the artistic means of the symbols of the "history" itself, of its prehistory, of the preambles, prologues, and the constant and direct intervention of the author, the possibility of incomprehension is minimal, almost nil. The novelist, a god omnipotent and active in his creation, has, by giving it an unequivocal moralizing and juristic form, closed off any possibility of interpretation—indeed might have destroyed the art of writing novels. If Calderón's works were for him "performable concepts," then *Guzmán de Alfarache* is novelized concept, the sum and essence of everything which the picaresque since *Lazarillo de Tormes* implied in its view of the world and in its doctrine.

Guzmán in theme and form is a closed didactic novel, exemplary in its dogmatic realism of disillusion.

Illusion and disillusion, hateful contraries, single viewpoint, thematic and formal closure, naturalism, either/or spoliation of reality, auctorial intervention—nothing could be farther removed from Cervantes' world or from the open tone and form of his novels.

Let us begin our comparative analysis with the *Novel and Colloquy that Took Place Between Cipión and Berganza,* since of those I discuss it is the only one which, with seeming rigor, follows the form of autobiographical narration, the formula of the character who serves many masters, and the habit of moralizing, typical of the most extreme picaresque mode.

At the beginning of the novel, Berganza, the ex-picaroon, undertakes to recount his life and begins, quite conventionally, with the intention of setting forth "from the very start" the names and circumstances of his parents and of his place of origin: "It *seems* to me that the first time I saw the sun was in Seville at the local slaughter house . . . whereby I *would imagine* . . . that my parents *must have been* . . ."

Seems, would imagine, must have been: the reader aware of the conventional method of the picaresque novel cannot help but pause. "Realistic" precision and knowledge of absolute truth appear to have given way to a fictive reality full of imaginative possibilities. Nothing is yet precise. From the very beginning, instead of closing the last door—a closing necessary to avoid being accused of sinfulness—one would say that the narrator, as if braving some dogma, wishes to open up doors and windows for us. We do not know whether any dogma existed that defined the meaning and form of picaresque novels; if it existed in the awareness of novelists, one could say that Berganza had it in mind in beginning his autobiography as much as Cervantes had in mind the dogma of the chivalric novels in beginning *Don Quixote*. The vacillation at the beginning of the *Colloquy* in the face of a reality anterior to the story has no little kinship with that in *Don Quixote*.

> In a village of La Mancha, whose name I do not wish to recall, there lived not long ago one of those gentlemen who keep a lance in the rack, an old buckler, a lean nag, and a swift hound . . . They say that his surname was Quijada or Quesada, for there is some difference of opinion among the authors who deal with this matter, though by likely conjectures we may let it be understood that his name was Quejana.

So far as the place of origin is concerned, there is strictly speaking no real vacillation in *Don Quixote,* but there is explicit imprecision. Besides, it is no longer conscious imprecision, but authentic vacillation, incorporated into the unfolding of the novel, that we encounter in the matter of the surname, that is, in what most importantly concerns a gentleman: his lineage. While Berganza is so bold as to "imagine," the narrator of *Don Quixote* is satisfied with 'likely conjectures." In contrast to the chivalric and the picaresque novels, and in contrast to the confident dogma and mode of defining what is predestined, we have here two fictional principles which, as we shall see, are the essence of Cervantes' mode, because through them all doors are open to unexpected reality which arises within the novel in which characters go about creating their surroundings at the same time that their surroundings create them.

Yet in spite of the lack of precise knowledge of his prehistory, which in itself makes him different from all other picaroons, Berganza, like Guzmán, on contemplating life from the watchtower of a new life, undertakes to moralize and to disabuse us. His account of the *real* and *natural* pastoral life which he has *discovered* through his own experience in the course of his adventures, offers us a fine example:

> All the thoughts I've mentioned, and many more, brought me to see how different the behavior and actions of *my* shepherds and the rest of that crew are from those of the shepherds I had heard and read about from books; because if my kind of shepherd sang, the songs were not harmonious and well composed, but "Look where the wolf is going, Jenny" and others of the same sort—and this not to the accompaniment of flageolets, rebecs, or bagpipes, but to the sound of knocking one stick against another or clacking chips of tile held between fingers; and not with subtle, full-throated, enviable voices, but with hoarse voices which, either singly or together, so it seemed, hardly sang but rather shouted or grunted . . .

And so on, with all that follows about the real names of *his* shepherds and how books are things imagined and well written for the entertainment of the leisured class. Here there is no doubt, as there is none in *Guzmán de Alfarache,* about what is true and what is false: the reality of experience has discovered the illusion of the imagination. That Berganza speaks of "my shepherds" reminds us of the importance that personal experience and the manner of never being ambivalent in autobiographical narrative had for the realism of disillusion in the picaresque novel. To make the parallel complete, we see also the systematic and alternating opposition of contraries whereby an illusionary reality is rejected: "if [they] sang, the songs were not harmonious and well composed;" "not to the accompaniment of flageolets . . . but to the sound of knocking one stick against another;" "not with subtle . . . voices, but with hoarse voices;" "[which] so it seemed, hardly sang, but rather shouted or grunted": reality and deception are divided between the two extremes clearly contrary and irreconcilable. One might say that, in spite of the principle of vacillation, we find ourselves in the picaresque world of disillusion and, at the same time, on a plane of critical reality comparable to that of the most obvious and direct level of *Don Quixote* (windmills: giants), insofar as the reality that dis-covers and destroys itself through experience is a "merely" literary reality. If *Don Quixote* was written to do away with the novels of chivalry, this part of Berganza's autobiography seems most directly to do battle against the pastoral novel.

But just at this point in Berganza's narration, when it seems to conform to the technique and vision of the picaresque novel and when it seems to conform to a single level of realism, we must pause to consider an aspect of the novel under which the autobiographical form becomes pure appearance.

We have seen in the picaresque mode an absolute closed narrative presented by a lone individual from a single point of view, *to a reader* who, naturally, has no power to influence the narrative since it is given *a posteriori* and therefore remains exempt from any possibility of change. Even in the matter of sermonizing or meditating on history, the reader is prevented from taking part, since he is outside the novel. He must deal with them as the picaroon deals with reality; either he accepts them or rejects them. But it happens that, while the picaroon is a loner, Berganza like Cervantes' other characters has a companion. We know of course that Berganza's autobiography, though necessarily narrated after the events, is not addressed to a reader, but rather to a *listener*, Cipión, who is in the process of living his present life in the story itself while at the same time taking part in it as a character constantly injecting himself into Berganza's narration and who, if he cannot change the life already lived of his companion, can still change the way of presenting it through dialogue. He is an interlocutor who can correct, and who corrects constantly—that other key aspect of a picaresque autobiography: present moralizing about past life. Cipión's function in regard to the tale and sermonizing of Berganza (like Don Quixote's in regard to Sancho) is that of the critic of absolute realism and of generalizations. Cipión corrects, modulates, restrains, harmonizes, and more than once casts doubt upon the "truth" of his friend, the ex-picaroon, in order to suggest moderation and the possibility of the ideal. (In turn, he, quite naturally, is corrected by Berganza.) Owing to this method of Cervantes, the alteration no longer occurs between contraries presented dogmatically in opposition, but rather between two points of view, at times contrary, at times not, in which the novelist neither passes judgment nor says the last word. Because this picaroon of Cervantes is not alone (since his autobiographical narration is directed, in vivid dialogue, to another protagonist), the reader, instead of confronting a closed and flat reality which he must accept or reject, perceives a modulated reality, almost parenthetical, a dual reality on which he himself may mediate or even vacillate. In place of a dogmatic monologue that obliterates any dialogue, Cervantes gives us a dialogue in actual process, the possibility of ambivalence. And thereby all absolute truth, all the disillusion which Berganza illustrates in attempting to draw lessons, does not go beyond being just one point of view in the great colloquy of the world. As Américo Castro said many years ago: not a flat mirror but a prism.

Strictly speaking, then, the autobiographical form of the picaresque is merely apparent in this novel, and what we really have—Cervantes' "artfulness"—is an autobiographical narration within a dialogue. The novel is the dialogue, with all its tangents and digressions, and the life of Berganza, though central, is only one of its parts. Once again in Cervantes, then, we find a novel within a novel. The elemental, direct, closed, and absolute plane of the picaresque disappears with it.

But of course the complications do not end here; rather, they open up for the reader even more possibilities in interpreting the fluid reality with which Cervantes presents us. If in response to such considerations we suspend our reading and, drawing back critically, survey the panorama of the *Exemplary Novels* we have been perusing, it is evident that Cervantes has brought us to focus upon the autobiography of Berganza, in which we have become so absorbed as to lose sight of the fact that it is not only a novel within a novel, but also that these two novels in turn are part of another novel, *written* as such, by a character in the more comprehensive novel, *The Deceitful Marriage,* which includes the *Colloquy,* this novel in turn being *read* by another character while its author takes a nap. Joaquín Casalduero is right in reminding us that *The Deceitful Marriage* and the *Colloquy* must be read as a single novel. We would destroy the complexity of Cervantes' world if we did not see as a whole this superimposition and continual interchange—as in *Don Quixote*—between apparent reality and real reality, real reality and critical reality, history and novel, novel and novel, in which everything is continually flowing into its apparent opposite and combining with it, to the point that it is no longer possible to distinguish the opposites and set them at odds—to accept or reject either dogmatically.

But it still remains to take into account the final (really the first) and most important dislocation of perspective from which Cervantine reality acquires its greatest complexity: as we well know, Berganza, the ex-picaroon who tells his life and moralizes, and Cipión, his active critic, are two dogs. Two dogs who by some miracle—like any miracle, quite inexplicable—have acquired the gift of speech. In distinction, then, to the "naturalistic" realism of the picaresque, what takes place in this novel "falls under the category of those things they call miracles." Owing to this, among other things, the picaresque novel is being satirized. It is not difficult to see the jest implied in the fact that the attempts at moralizing are put in the mouth of a dog who, because he can miraculously speak, thinks that he is more intelligent than he is and that he has right to judge. Berganza (a Guzmán on all fours) thinks he possesses the secret of the world. But Cipión is also present, a kind of critical conscience: "Just look at your paws," he says to him, "and you'll stop playing the dandy, Berganza. What I mean is that you should realize that you are an animal lacking in reason, and if for the moment you show some reason, we have already settled between the two of us that it is a supernatural and unprecedented thing." They are words which, if applied to the presumption of absolute wisdom on the part of the protagonist-narrator of the picaresque novel, seem equivalent to Cipión's in his final advice: "You see, Berganza, no one should intrude where he is not invited, nor should he ever undertake anything not within his competence." It would seem, then, that the *Colloquy* is hardly a burlesque of the pastoral novel; it is rather a parody of the picaresque novel as a dogmatic and self-complacent form. In its formal and thematic "realism" the picaresque is as ideal, absolute, and fixed as the chivalric novel is in its: the naturalistic novel and the idealistic novel thus stand in contrast to the objective realism of Cervantes whose spirit does not allow, either in theme or form, any fixity. At the ultimate bottom of the box of several bottoms that is the *Deceitful Marriage* and *Colloquy of the Dogs* (in the Prologue Cervantes himself calls his novels "a game of billiards") ve encounter, among other things, a frontal critique of the way of writing novels which Cervantes *seems* to have followed.

Before going on to *Rinconete and Cortadillo* let us return for a moment to the most external aspect of the *Colloquy* itself, that is, the novel which the Licentiate reads while its author, the Ensign, takes his nap. With no more than the title, without antecedents, without background to give us some notion in advance of the personalities of Cipión and Berganza, the novel begins in dialogue form: action without presentation. The result of this innovation in technique is that the personalities of Cipión and Berganza and the world in which they move come into being before our eyes and ears through the miracle of the word. Nothing proceeds from the definition to the defined. Cipión and Berganza are the two dogs we see and hear now, mutually creating themselves by means of dialogue. In contrast to *Guzmán de Alfarache,* not to mention the chivalric novel, the novel in this instance is what begins here and now through the miracle of the word. It could have begun at some other point. Nothing preceding the story itself interests Cervantes, and thus once again the *Colloquy* resembles *Don Quixote.* Let us again recall the beginning of *Don Quixote:* Cervantes gives the reader a minimum of background, but not only is it, like Berganza's, vague and imprecise, but also he himself immediately undertakes to divest of any importance what happened before the narrative begins in comparison with what will begin happening when he, the novelist outside what he narrates, takes it up. After the vacillation concerning the name of the goodly gentleman, we read the following: "But this has little importance for *our tale;* let it suffice that *the telling of it* not stray one bit from the truth." This declaration concerning the art of narration is as important as its contrary which we find at the beginning of *Guzmán de Alfarache.* In contrast to Mateo Alemán, what Cervantes always does is engulf us in his story without anticipating anything, as in the splendid title of Chapter 2 of the second part of *Don Quixote:* "In which is narrated what will be seen." "Our tale," "the telling of it," what one sees and hears, always in present action, that which is vouchsafed us heading in the direction of the future, the realm of possibilities—this is what absorbs Cervantes. And it is in the direction of the future that the *Colloquy* thrusts itself, without preliminaries or introductions which are now, in the last of the *Exemplary Novels,* dispensed with, though in their typically laconic way they are characteristic of Cervantes' narrative manner.

But not only does the *Colloquy* begin, so to say, at any given moment and at the instance of a miracle, but also, owing to the very miracle, it likewise never ends. The two dogs have been caught unawares by speech: the word itself is the miracle of creation be hind which is the artist, a new and objective god who thrusts it into life and lets it take its course. But everything is imprecise, vacillat ing, insecure, in word and in creation. Cipión and Berganza, full aware of this, in order to take advantage of present time and t enjoy it as one enjoys the unforeseen in life, decide to speak, t speak as much as possible, recounting their lives to each other in the night—without fear of tangents and digressions or what might occur unplanned—so that at daybreak no one could discover thei secret and end the miracle. Up to this point we have considere one side of reality: the life and reflections of Berganza, filtered through the prism of Cipión and the various "bottoms" of th work. The other side is still missing: the life of Cipión. Just as th reader gets set to hear it in further dialogue, the novel ends. We d not know whether the dogs met on the following night or whethe the miracle continued in effect. Cervantes—who himself does no know all—has given us the only fragment of fictional reality within his reach and has given it to us without judging it, with opennes and objectivity. Complete openness, because with the end of th novel nothing is closed: the miracle of creation by the word ca continue operating and in the realm of the possible there is alway hope. Both reader and novelist retire from the scene with the feelin that more life is always possible, though never certain, and by wa of proof, there remains on the page a fragment of it charged with infinite possibilities. The final words which bring us back to th first and encompassing novel, *The Deceitful Marriage,* are typica of Cervantes' art of the novel. The Ensign awakens (he a characte in a "real" novel who has written a "dream" novel) and exchange a few words concerning the merits of the *Colloquy* with the Licen tiate (he a character in a story supposed to be real and who has rea a "dream" novel), and thereupon, since they have refreshed "th eyes of the understanding," they decide to set out for Espolón "t refresh the eyes of the body." " 'Let's be off,' said the Ensign. "And with that, off they went." Thanks to this laconism so pecu liarly Cervantine, everything is still possible in the imagination history and fiction, deeds and fantasy, waking reality and dreamin reality. Reality is all: "eyes of the understanding" and "eyes of th body." Everything fits into Cervantes' reality, because everything i concerned with man. And thus, through his manner of presentation since nothing is ever given *a priori,* Cervantes opens rather than shuts the last door.

Rinconete and Cortadillo is the novel of Cervantes most commonly linked with the picaresque. From our point of view let it suffice to say that, like the *Colloquy,* it is a work thematically and formally open and that its realism also has nothing to do with that of *Guzmán de Alfarache.* In distinction to the *Colloquy,* nonetheless, it seems so clear and obvious at first glance that on occasion it has been considered more a sketch of local color than a novel. But then one of the characteristics of sketches of local color is that, however limited to a concrete time and medium, it is nevertheless totally free and open in that it could be what it is or something quite different. The will of the artist chooses, either arbitrarily or by chance, any sort of reality wherever it may be found and ends his depiction of it at any point at which the characters leave the canvas to carry on their present lives. The sketch of local color has neither beginning nor end. It is independent of background and precise continuation.

The technique is clearly evident in the classic beginning of *Rinconete and Cortadillo:* "At the inn of Molinillo, which lies on the edge of the famous plains of Alcudia as we travel from Castile to Andalusia, on a hot summer day two boys of perhaps fourteen or fifteen met by chance . . ."

In contrast to *Don Quixote* and Berganza's autobiography, we are here given a precise place; but at this place two boys, whose names we will not know till we are inside the story, meet *by chance.* The novel, thus, begins here just as it might have begun at some other point. Determinant background remains, from the first moment, excluded. Here as in *Don Quixote* what matters to Cervantes is the story which will take shape before our eyes and ears from the very moment that he, the novelist outside what is narrated (and therefore unaware of any past), gets around to telling it. Narrative *a posteriori,* though conceived before the story, has no place in Cervantes' art.

After this the two boys (mark that from the beginning of the novel they are not loners) begin to converse, and it is only through their dialogue, which is, for that matter, full of feints and clever word play, that we begin to know who they are. From this it cannot be concluded that their lives are determined into the future; for just as Don Quixote let himself be guided by Rocinante, so they are going to let themselves, from the moment they meet, be guided by chance. Within the novel, after certain evasions and vacillations occurring in the present as they narrate their past lives, they tell each other their names and antecedents. Afterward in concert they deceive the muleteer, rob those who are taking them to Seville, and, after a few more clever thefts, end up in the courtyard of Monipodio. What is said and done in this courtyard constitutes the novel within the novel. It is, most precisely, a sketch of local color within the primary sketch of Rinconete and Cortadillo, which is presented before two spectators who (like Cervantes and like the reader) make no judgment but rather, overawed, see and hear life in process. It turns out that the two spectators decide to leave the "sketch" since, while Monipodio's courtyard may offer an engrossing spectacle, it is also wicked and dangerous. Rinconete waxes moral about this and decides that it is time to leave for other surroundings. *"But in spite of all this,* led by his youth and inexperience, he went on with this life for several months, during which occurred things that call for lengthier exposition, and so it is left for another occasion to recount his life and miracles, along with those of his master Monipodio . . ."* Nothing is concluded, and in this opening toward the future, any moral commentary gets lost. Once again in Cervantes the reader remains with the hope of more life, which is always possible.

I have left *The Illustrious Kitchen Maid* for last because, though it is in no sense a picaresque novel, we encounter in it the best description of what picaresque life meant for Cervantes and also one of the most important clues to his "realism." The novel deals with the adventures of Diego and Tomás, their loves and marriages, and the happy ending in which their lives achieve fulfillment. As in any "idealistic" novel, the story narrated here has its background and its sequel. We are told of the origins of the two boys and how, after what is narrated, they continued outside the novel to live happily. Given the fact that at the very beginning the picaresque life of Diego Carriazo is described for us and judged, the whole technique, foreign to Cervantes' best practice, deserves our attention.

Cervantes first introduces Diego and Tomás; and then before going on to tell their adventures, dwells on those that Diego underwent previous to the narrative—which is what incites Tomás to set out on his own. But even before, the first thing Cervantes tells us is that "in Burgos, a famous and illustrious city, it is not many years ago that two rich and prominent knights lived: one was called Don Diego de Carriazo and the other Don Juan de Avendaño." They are the fathers of Diego and Tomás, thus described laconically, though precisely, in this background account. At once the narrative goes on to relate the picaresque life of Diego. With the exception of the autobiographical form, we ought to have here all the elements to account for Diego's turning into a picaroon. But the striking thing is that we are told explicitly and primarily that Diego was not thrust into the picaresque life, but rather that he has thrust himself into it by choice and for no reason predetermined by his background.

> Carriazo must have been thirteen when, carried away by a roguish inclination, though no ill treatment by his parents impelled him to it, he made a break, as boys say, from the house of his parents out of mere whim and pleasure and went out into the world, and so content was he with the free life that even in the midst of the hardships and discomforts that it entails he scarcely missed the abundance in his father's house, nor did going on foot tire him nor the cold vex him nor the heat bother him . . . In the end he brought off the business of being a picaroon so ably that he could well lecture in the academy to the man from Alfarache.

Lineage and place of origin, the obligatory background of the picaresque mode, are given by Cervantes in this instance with precision; but as if there were not already something intrinsically odd in Diego's being a knight like his father, Cervantes at once declares emphatically that nothing in his background predetermines the personal history of Diego. It is *inclination,* and not hereditary traits or mere surroundings, that brings individuals to act the way they do. The individual rises above the type. It seems to me no accident—nor merely a result of the great renown of *Guzmán de Alfarache*—that what begins by denying one of the basic characteristics of the picaresque should end by saying that Diego "could well lecture in the academy to the man from Alfarache," to whom, doubtless, he could teach the other aspect of the world, both its optimistic and its heroic side, and also its perspectivism. How different the visions of reality are in Diego and Guzmán! Diego knows well enough the evil of the world and of men, their wretchedness, the determinism of hunger, and the jails; but he also knows heroism, liberty, love, and optimism. In his vision of the world, opposites become reconciled: they flow toward each other, encompassed under the sign of total reality. And everything becomes a voluntary joyful acceptance of that reality: nothing is rejected because of its opposite, since there are no absolute opposites. "For him all seasons were a gentle early springtime"—without fear of the yearly Augusts which Guzmán so dreaded. In the *elogium* that follows the life of the picaroon, we encounter a phrase which brings us from formal considerations to the thematic center of Cervantine realism: "There [in picaresque life] you find clean filth." As Ortega y Gasset well said, speaking of *Don Quixote,* the realism of Cervantes is gorged with idealism—and vice versa, one must add. In Cervantes the planes of reality always intersect, so that no one of them seems to represent absolute truth. There is an open presentation of the interplay between matter and spirit, not an opposition between them, that would allow from a spiritual point of view a rejection of matter (as in the picaresque) or from a material point of view the rejection of the spirit (as in the most obvious and false plane of reality in *Don Quixote*). Reality is "clean filth" or "filthy cleanliness," and it is all presented by the novelist (a poet imitating reality) without rejecting any of its parts: a vital acceptance and a presentation, never a rejection if it means *resolving* the "harmony" of contraries which is the world. Not for nothing did the Licentiate Glass say "that good painters imitate nature, but the bad ones spew it forth." Cervantes, a presentational novelist, depicts reality as someone who sees it in all its complexity, from the outside, without aspiring to know it absolutely and from within, like the picaresque character-novelist or the theological playwright or the satirist. In contrast to the premeditated narration of lives *a posteriori,* we encounter a multifaceted presentation of lives coming into being in the present. In contrast to the realism that tells us that all the world is "dump heaps and nasty places," as well as illusion, we have the prismatic realism of "clean filth." In this phrase, as in the word "baciyelmo" (basin-helmet), so well explicated by Américo Castro, the opposites, instead of confronting each other for battle ("militancy is man's life on earth," and militancy alone), coalesce to underscore the ambiguity of reality and show us that "realism" does not necessarily mean absolute disillusion and filth in contrast to the illusion and cleanliness of imaginary or idealistic novels— all of which signifies not a rejection of matter or spirit (that is, of life), but rather a fusion of both in vital enjoyment; not an opposition between Sancho and Don Quixote, but rather Sancho and Don Quixote co-existing, living, becoming, before our eyes and ears within their story. For Cervantes realism does not mean absolute truth versus false illusion, nor does it mean life contemplated under the aspect of death, but rather life itself, which is time, not eternity. It does not mean a single point of view presented in advance with the pretext of *a posteriori* narration, but rather presentation and interchange of all points of view. And finally, the so-called pica-resque novels of Cervantes have nothing in common with the picaresque novel whose formal and thematic culmination is *Guzmán de Alfarache:* they are in opposition to it. For Cervantes, writing novels meant not giving out honors or titles, making decisions or judgments, but rather creating a world in the image of the one we perceive, one which is, from its very creation, independent of its creator, a world always fragmentary, though complete in every fragment: a world which, like our own, is in the process of becoming outside of us, while we are becoming in it and in the interplay between each of us and the rest. Writing novels for Cervantes is, in some sense, letting do and letting live in the created world of half-truths and half-lies which no one has yet known how to demarcate satisfactorily. This is a vision of the world that tells us that the novelist (a most rare inventor) is indeed like a god who by the word casts forth reality, though like a god perhaps a bit skeptical of his ability to judge, however confident of the freedom of his creation and full of love for it. He is like a god who creates and withdraws because his task, in Cipión's words, is not to intrude where he is not invited. He is first a creator and then a spectator who observes benevolently and ironically the progression of what he has created, though no longer able to censure any of its parts or any of its creatures. He is a god who at the most, if he wishes to set things right, casts on the world a new character, endowing him with speech which inevitably implicates him in dialogue in which some point of view, among many others, becomes his. It is a reality, created by the word, which is in the process of becoming a disciplined work, but which is also heading in the direction of a destiny unknown in time, a destiny in which everything is always possible.

It is in this sense that we can speak of Cervantine realism and contrast it with the realism of the picaresque and any other sort of realism of disillusion. It is in this sense of complete openness and prismatic presentation, and only in this sense, that the novels of Cervantes are *exemplary* and totally different from the rest of the "open" literature of the Spanish Baroque.

On the *Interludes* of Cervantes

by Edwin Honig

I

These eight short plays are among the most beguiling things
Cervantes ever wrote. Part of their charm is the appropriateness of
the simple dramatic form to Cervantes' lighthearted, often elusive
treatment of his subjects. This is notable in a writer whose ingenuity in creating character was offset by his casual use of literary
forms. Except for *The Siege of Numantia,* his plays read like episodic narratives, his stories like dialogues and dramatic sketches,
and his best-known novel is a hodge-podge of tall tales and long-
winded colloquies from which his main characters are often excluded. His pastoral novels, *La Galatea* and *Persiles y Sigismunda,*
written according to anachronistic formulas, fail badly; his poetry
is often blank verse or a kind of rhymed prose. And when he hastily
completed Part II of *Don Quixote,* he did so in self-protection because a literary opportunist named Avellaneda, whom nobody has
yet identified, had had the gall to write and publish a fraudulent
sequel to the widely popular Part I.

So the formal and evidently deliberate achievement of these dramatic pieces is something unusual in the Cervantes canon. The interlude *(entremés)* is usually dominated by its farcical tone. It is
made up of a short comic incident and is meant to be performed
between the acts of a full-length play in order to quiet an audience.
It deals with stock characters and a temporarily unhinged situation
reassembled at the end by a token banquet, dance, or marriage.
In these respects little had changed since the days of ancient Plau-
tine comedy, on which were patterned the situations and character
types of the *entremés.* But Cervantes' own account of his indebted-
ness turns blithely on the ironic distortions of personal experience.
He remembers as a boy watching the actor-writer Lope de Rueda

"On the *Interludes* of Cervantes." From Miguel de Cervantes, *Interludes*: A
New Translation and with a Foreword by Edwin Honig (New York: The New
American Library [A Signet Classic], 1964), pp. ix–xxvi. Copyright © 1964 by
Edwin Honig. Reprinted by permission of the publisher.

set up a crude stage in the town square and put on plays "with the greatest imaginable skill and sense of decorum" in front of "an old blanket drawn both ways by cords." What particular plays or how many of them Cervantes saw he does not say. Neither does he mention the earlier Spanish prototypes of the popular theater in the late Middle Ages, when performing troubadours (*juglares*) produced their farces on current subjects in the public squares. Nor does he mention two of his own contemporaries, Juan de Timoneda, who translated Plautus and wrote farces, or Juan de la Cueva, who imitated the classical dramatists and wrote interludes as well. The name of the greatest of his forerunners, Gil Vicente, the Portuguese-Spanish poet-dramatist, is likewise missing from his account. What needs to be added to his statement, then, is that through such sources, enriched by borrowings from the highly popular *commedia dell'arte,* Cervantes wrote the most distinguished pieces in a dramatic genre that has flourished in Spain for centuries under various names—*paso, auto, entremés, sainete, género chico.*

His interludes turn up in the collection *Eight Plays and Eight Interludes: New and Never Performed,* issued in 1615, the year before he died. How they came to be published Cervantes describes in [his] Prologue. [It is thus] we know that the by-then-famous author of *Don Quixote* saw them published by a bookseller eager to make the most he could of a new work by an established writer. Cervantes ruefully summarizes his vain attempts to return to the theater, which he had left in the 1580's:

> . . . thinking the times were still the same as when they sang my praises, I again began to write a few plays. But I found no birds in last year's nests—I mean, I found no managers who wanted them, although they knew I had them. And so, I put them away in a trunk, consecrating and condemning them to eternal silence. In good time a bookseller told me he might buy them from me, although a royally licensed stage manager had told him that a good deal could be expected from my prose, but from my poetry, nothing at all. To tell the truth, I was certainly pained to hear this, and I said to myself, "Either I have changed and become another person or the times have improved immensely—which is generally the other way around, since people always praise the days gone by."

Always on the outside of literary society and lagging behind its fashions, Cervantes did not recoup the slight reputation he may have had as a dramatist thirty years earlier. But with the unexpected success of *Don Quixote,* and just turned sixty-five, he was embarked on a fresh literary career, producing novels, stories, and poems, as well as the book of plays.

The collection of *Eight Plays and Eight Interludes* belongs to this profoundly lighthearted period. Among the full-length plays are three takeoffs on his own traumatic experiences as a slave; a religious romance; one about a wandering actor among the Gypsies; and another about a thief turned holy man. (Yet the best-known of his plays, *The Siege of Numantia* [1585], a national epic of resistance in Roman times, was not included in the collection.) Posterity took his ironic subtitle literally: the plays are still almost "never performed." This is only relatively less true of the interludes, which are written in a condensed version of the episodic form characteristic of all his narratives. They concern the contemporary underworld and the middle- and lower-brow society of small towns and cities—country bumpkins, divorce courts, magicians, impostors, unemployed soldiers, unsheltered students, ineffectual husbands, saucy maids, irritable housewives, fatuous sacristans, garrulous whores. His most frequently revived, if not most intriguing, farce, *The Cave of Salamanca,* brings in the prevalent addiction to necromancy just when the action is about to descend into self-congratulatory adultery. The ingenious student who momentarily rescues middle-class respectability gets a tasty dinner for his trouble —a reward that almost equals the sum Cervantes got for his book of plays.

II

Always wanting to be a dramatist and a poet, Cervantes was destined to become the world's foremost novelist. Still, what he achieves in the interludes is something very close to the concentrative spirit of poetry and something characteristically dramatic as well. They might be called dramatic poems, as Ricardo Rojas has noted—and not merely because two of them are written in blank verse. They are brief, completely rounded-off, self-sufficient pieces, achieving a tightness of form that cannot be found in his work in the other genres. Their modesty of aim and slightness of incident are belied by the full-blooded particularity of their characters. For these are not stock types going through their paces in a well-worn anecdote, but vital individuals with distinct voices. They are dramatic in the way that Don Quixote and Sancho Panza are dramatic: their voices engage each other and depend on each other; they come alive through the irritation of their complementariness, by the mere fact that they are thrown together and must reckon with each other. Finally, they also in some sense absorb each other although their identities remain unchanged.

The situation on each *entremés* is the occasion for the fugal and dialectical encounters of such characters. They are supremely aware of being actors, of drawing on and out of one another the impulse of opposition, which stimulates the sense of their individuality. Like the various musical instruments in a jam session, they are alternately incited by one another to solo performances of unexpected virtuosity, and yet are constantly overtaken, merged, and absorbed by the racy dissonance of the whole ensemble playing together. One remembers the Soldier in *The Hawk-Eyed Sentinel,* more confident of his ability to ward off possible suitors than of the likelihood that he will win the scullery maid, whom he is compelled to resign at the end to the smug Sacristan. One thinks of the bickering councilmen, in *Choosing a Councilman in Daganzo,* heatedly exchanging insults and pedantic quibbles, then giving the rustic candidates for office the occasion to demonstrate similar traits of their own. There is the dialectical interplay between each of the couples in *The Divorce-Court Judge,* mercilessly challenging each other's existence, but only, in effect, reinforcing it by their persistent assertiveness. The couples' incompatibility is amplified by the opportunity they are given to enumerate their grievances publicly in open court. But the fact that they agree to be judged helps to reinstate them in the community, against which individually they would seem to be rebelling. The status quo is thus maintained, and the principle of incompatibility is acknowledged only that it may be transcended by the social injunction: "That any truce, however short,/Beats the best divorce." A truce, not a settlement or resolution, is the note on which all the interludes end. Reality, which includes the incompatibility of individual wills, must be given its due, but the social injunction that checks it also dissolves for the moment all individual differences in the interludes.

The force of reality does not destroy the incompatibility principle, but absorbs it. Its dominance is upheld in the various interludes by an image of authority, which according to a law of comedy must intervene to redress absurdity and restore to the audience the commonsense view of society. And yet one observes several unexpected departures from this formula. In *The Divorce-Court Judge* and *Choosing a Councilman in Daganzo,* the formula is kept intact. In *Divorce* the Judge is the benign authority, and his rule triumphs at the end, as one would expect: even a shabby reconciliation is better than a divorce. In *Daganzo,* similarly, after a comic exposé of rustic follies, pretenses, and ignorance, the rule of the Council, sustained throughout by Cloven Hoof, the college graduate, is finally confirmed by the humanistic Peter Frog just after the intrusive Sacristan has been reproved for his impertinence.

In *Trampagos: the Pimp Who Lost His Moll,* the social norm is that of the underworld, closed in on itself, with its own code of conduct, which seems to ape the behavior of people in respectable society. The one intrusive note, hardly louder than a whisper, occurs when a constable is seen approaching. Then Trampagos is quick to allay the gang's momentary consternation as the law passes by: "The constable's a friend/ Of mine—no reason to be scared of him./ . . . Suppose/ he'd stopped, he couldn't nab us. I'm sure of that./ He'd never squawk, because his palm's been greased." Subsequently, when Trampagos takes the Preener as his new moll, the fortuitous appearance of the semi-legendary master pimp Escarramán puts the authoritative seal on the match, which closes the play.

Another equivocal conclusion occurs in *The Basque Impostor* when the deluded whore Cristina is not only kept from getting her due revenge on the pair who have tricked her but is also forced to give them a good dinner instead. Her vanity and cupidity are presumably more culpable than the deceptiveness of the hoaxers.

In *The Wonder Show, The Cave of Salamanca,* and *The Jealous Old Husband,* the image of authority is actually subverted. Chanfalla, the manager of the show, closes the curtain on a pandemonium of deluded town fathers fighting with an uninitiated quartermaster, and Chanfalla's last speech suggests that the whole town is to be hoodwinked in the same way on the following day. In the *Cave* the equally guilty maid and her mistress—whose assignations are interrupted, first by a poor student, then by the returning husband—are gotten off the hook by the vast credulity of the husband and his appetite for magical hocus-pocus. But the near-adulterers are not punished. In the *Husband* the compulsively watchful old man is similarly betrayed and his wife left unpunished, after her intimacies with the Gallant, because the husband's jealousy is apparently the greater folly. In each instance the society restored at the end of the play looks very much as it was at the start. The basic authority here is not vested in a higher law, an abstract justice. It resides in the particular character of individuals, who despite (or because of) their crumbling follies, their designs on one another, their conflicts and incompatibilities, not only need but also choose to depend on one another.

If such characters are supremely aware of being actors, what keeps them from becoming merely histrionic, flat, and unreal? The answer seems to be that they are all caught up in the illusion that their world is real, that they do not have to quarrel with it, and that they have to demonstrate its actuality by being themselves, the individuals they were meant to be. Anything else—as, for example, the assumption that they are grossly more or less real than themselves—would be inadmissible on such a stage. For to view them as simply inflated or deflated types would give rise to a mistaken identification, the sort of thing Cervantes had already ridiculed in the Maese Pedro [Master Peter] scene of *Don Quixote*. (There the furious Knight mounts the stage to destroy what he imagines are blasphemers of his ideal but who, when he cuts them down, turn out to be sawdust and rag dolls.) The lesson is that as soon as you interfere with the magical distance safeguarding the illusion between audience and actor, the indispensable illusion of reality turns to dust. To discover how such a many-sided illusion comes about, we must look at the sort of characters who are created to embody it in the interludes.

III

To begin with, each character fills a social role that is both typical and functional. In some instances such roles are immediately discernible in the characters' names. On the simplest level we have the identifying noun—the Judge, the Old Man, the Porter, the Constable, and so forth. On another level characters in their social roles are mocked by some distinguishing attribute in their names. A trio of whores are called Preener, Wagtail, and Straybird. A quartet of councilmen are called Cloven Hoof, Sneeze, Hardbread, and String Bean; the rustics, who are candidates for office, are identified as Gassing, Craggy, Hock, and Frog. Occasionally there is a folkloric figure, like Escarramán, the escaped prisoner, after whom a popular dance is named—a character who has only to put in an appearance and recite his history to start the revel that concludes the interlude. Roque Guinarde, a contemporary Robin Hood figure, does not even appear, but is simply alluded to when a metaphor for real benevolence is needed. Then there is the character with a ridiculous name (Trampagos, Chiquiznaque, Chanfalla, Aldonza de Minjaca), who actively takes on something of its absurdity in the part he plays. Servant girls, who are usually named Cristina, are typically lively, curious, young, and mischievous. Young wives with old or gullible husbands will have realistic names—Leonarda or Lorenza—and their husbands, ironically distorted common names, like Pancracio, which suggests something like "all-governing," or Cañizares, which by association with dried grass or reeds suggests "straw-tubes."

As characters, the types they represent are centrally moved by the dialectics of the situation (the thematic matter) and by the need to act in opposition to other characters. So Cañizares, the deceived old husband, with perception whetted by jealousy, rises from dramatic typology to inveigh tellingly against his wife's confidante, Nettlesome, who stands for all neighbors. So, too, the Soldier overreaches his role as "the hawk-eyed sentinel" to show up the loutish Sacristan, who in fact defeats him. Where the folly hinges on flagrant superstition or ignorance, the main instigator (a stage manager or a neighbor) has only to appear and the gullible victims come swarming to him.

Through the interplay of characters in their thematic roles emerges the all-too-human situation in a typical action leading to dramatic revelation. In such an action the characters parody the roles of dupes and gulls, and because they are not seeking fulfillment or trying to achieve a serious purpose but are only pretending to do so, their words and behavior are not strictly ordained, as those of their counterparts in tragedy or romance would have to be. They can be more effectively themselves and freer—which is to say, individual and unique—because they are only going through the motions of being a type, a cog in a machine, a "somebody else." Something similar marks off Don Quixote and Sancho Panza. Each in his mock-serious quest (one to validate an anachronistic chivalric code, the other to leap an implacable class barrier and govern an island) becomes a dramatic character who bursts the typological mold in which he was cast, although in fact he has all along drawn his identity from it as a comic figure.

Nobody in the interludes is punished, nobody is rewarded, and everything turns out as it should be—that is, reconciled at the end, though only momentarily, to the way things are. Although the status quo prevails, something has been altered and revealed. How can this be, and how is it done? One might say that when the characters reveal themselves freely, they thereby reveal something intrinsic to drama: they reveal the fact that in the dramatic moment the artifice of reality does indeed become the desired reality; and so the illusion, with all its creaking machinery, momentarily displaces (i.e., becomes truer than) everyday reality.

The trick hinges on some threat to the established order, something mechanically initiated (the plot), and its consequence (the resolution) involves the restoration of the order. The trick, then, sets up a "well-ordered disorder" (*orden desordenada*), whose ready acceptability is a consequence of the audience's recognition that the art of illusion depends on nature itself being outdone.[1] Such maneu-

---

[1] *Don Quixote,* Part I, Chapter 50, the Knight is explaining the wondrous and irresistible fascinations to be found in books of chivalry: "Over there . . . an

vering with illusion is borne out in the three interludes that would appeal most to a modern audience: *The Wonder Show, The Jealous Old Husband,* and *Trampagos, the Pimp Who Lost His Moll.* It is also basic in two others: *The Divorce-Court Judge* and *The Cave of Salamanca.* In these plays some forbidden but cherished illusion intrudes to blur the circumstantial world of everyday life and momentarily raises it and the characters to a new—an exalted or special—view of themselves. This is traditionally the instigative element in farce, in which men's follies are played on in order to make them appear ridiculous. Yet in the Cervantes interludes the conventionally crude, dehumanizing attitude never creeps in. The kind of trick is sexual or magical or both, but in effect the dupes never really lose face; even their chastisement is minimal. As Cervantes puts it in *The Basque Impostor,* "A joke's not funny if it makes a person look contemptible." Contempt would degrade the character's humanity—an attitude Cervantes was temperamentally incapable of sustaining. Instead of roundly censuring or whipping his characters for their foibles, Cervantes involves them in the spell of an illusion that is larger than themselves. From this inescapable illusion they either emerge unchanged but better informed or, as in *The Wonder Show,* are swallowed at the end by the illusion.

In *The Wonder Show* the illusion is twofold and more intricate than it looks. For vanity's sake and to keep up appearances, the "better people" in town, the officials and their families, are constrained to accept the stage manager's conditions without question. To see the invisible tableau he has prepared, the audience must qualify by being legitimately born (not bastards) and pureblood Christians (not heretics). Anxious to prove themselves qualified, each tries to outdo the other by reacting to what he plainly does

---

artfully wrought fountain of varicolored jasper and smoother marble; and there another of rustic design, with tiny clam shells and the twisted white and yellow houses of the snail arranged in a well-ordered disorder, mingled with bits of gleaming crystal and counterfeit emeralds, the whole forming a work in which art, imitating nature, would seem to have outdone the latter." The factitious and, in every sense of the word, fake paradise that Don Quixote so lovingly details may go a long way toward accounting for the wide appeal of his character —the disarming nature of Cervantes' central achievement in the novel—which, in turn, may fairly be described by the Knight's own words earlier in the chapter, where he alludes to books of chivalry in general: "books . . . which are read with general enjoyment and praised by the young and old alike, by rich and poor, the learned and the ignorant, the gentry and the plain people—in brief, by all sorts of persons of every condition and walk in life—do you mean to tell me that they are but lies?" (Excerpts translated by Samuel Putnam, *The Ingenious Gentleman, Don Quixote de la Mancha* [New York: The Viking Press, Inc., 1949], I, pp. 441–43.)

not see as though he were really experiencing it vividly with all his senses. The illusion here is that the better townspeople, who make up the inner audience, must pretend to see or imagine what is not there in order to be an audience at all. Outdoing the manager's initial deception, the last word in self-delusion comes when the Mayor has his compliant nephew mount the stage and dance with the invisible figure of Herodias—who made John the Baptist lose his head. The nephew, of course, simply gyrates alone, dancing with himself. The other side of the illusion is that when an intruder, the Quartermaster, enters, the audience refuses to return to the reality of their uninitiated lives but incriminates the newcomer as a bastard and a heretic for outrageously saying he cannot "see" the tableau. The illusion has swallowed them and the curtain comes down on the riotous dupes as the stage manager steps forth, promising to take in the whole town in the same way at the next performance. And yet it is not the illusion that has triumphed so much as the folly of those who would deliberately take it as reality in order to preserve the appearance of negative virtues—their not being bastards and their not being heretics.

In *The Jealous Old Husband* there is another remarkable illusion, although it is directed at only one character while the others join together to sustain it, enact it, and to some extent enjoy it. This occurs when the young Gallant is secretly hidden in the house of Lorenza, the lovelorn wife, under the watchful eye of her old husband. A neighbor lugs in a gigantic tapestry; in an appropriate corner there is a full-sized representation of Rodamonte the knight; the Gallant stands behind this and then slips into Lorenza's room. Lorenza joins him there (though presumably offstage) and realistically tells her husband what is going on as she embraces the Gallant. The trick is so bold and the husband so firmly convinced of his own vigilant security that he is compelled to take the reality as a delusion of his wife's, while on his side of the door his young niece is frantically supporting the reality (till it becomes unclear whom she is abetting, the husband or the wife) by urging her uncle to break down the door. When he reluctantly threatens to do so, the wife opens the door, hurls water in his face, and thereby allows the Gallant to slip out unnoticed. Unlike the figure of Herodias, the silent Gallant is visible to everyone except the husband. Conveyed through an illusion (the tapestry), the punishing reality he represents does not touch the husband. The husband is sunk in the illusion that no male can get inside the house. In this he remains deceived; he is simply made to apologize to Mistress Nettlesome, his neighbor. But the audience, knowing that she initiated the trick, can assume that the old man's blind jealousy will be punished again and again. Being what he is, he must continue to be duped by his own jealousy and deluded view of reality.[2]

In the *Trampagos* interlude the central illusion is that a company of pimps and whores share the sentimental virtues of respectable people, especially regarding the fidelity of husband and wife. And just when the point has been grandly secured, we witness a quick turn toward the more familiar underworld expediency of choosing a new moll for the widowed pimp.

In *The Divorce-Court Judge*—the shortest interlude and the only one that dispenses with a plot—the illusion overarching the complaints of the contentious couples is that the public airing of their grievances will bring about the desired divorce. But in actuality they thereby keep intact the legal machinery of the court, whose job is to remind them that all marriages are like pitched battles punctuated by brief truces.

In *The Cave of Salamanca* the husband's undisturbed gullibility fortifies the illusion when his idealized view of his wife's fidelity is shown to be the counterpart of his superstitious belief in magic.

What we get in these last brief products of Cervantes' genius is the extraordinary freedom of the characters to be themselves in a framework of considerable but not unlimited fluidity. There is nothing problematic in their makeup. In fact, because the problematic element is lacking, commentators who search for the means to aggrandize the author continually fill in the picture by suggesting biographical parallels to the plays and to the characters. It is as if the sense of felt life, the spectacle and play of vital existence insisting upon itself, were not enough, when it is, in fact, everything. In this regard, what Américo Castro, in discussing the basic theme of *Don Quixote,* calls "life as a process creative of itself" may also be applied to the eight interludes. For here too the value is existential, and the characters, "instead of being logically arbitrary . . . become vitally valid, and we accept them not as farce or an amusement, but as one accepts all that appears authentic."

---

[2] An odd footnote to this particular form of high jinks is Cervantes' famous derogatory comment on translation in *Don Quixote* (Book II, Chapter 62). There he suggests how little he relishes such delusive operations when he says that reading a translation is "like looking at Flemish tapestries from the wrong side," where "though the figures are visible, they are full of threads that make them indistinct. . . ."

Ocean of Story

El último sueño romántico de Cervantes

by William J. Entwistle

The last phase was a passionate love of story-telling. Cervantes, though he kept enough in hand to promise a new *Decameron* under the title of *Weeks in the Garden,* packed a score of short stories and anecdotes into an envelope of romantic adventure, and thus made his "great *Persiles.*" Few books have ever been announced with more confidence by an author. In the preliminaries of the Second Part of *Don Quixote,* the book being then about four months from completion, he announced that it was to be "either the worst or the best composed in our language, that is, of books of entertainment; and I say I regret having said 'the worst,' because in my friends' opinion it will attain the extreme of possible goodness." Two years earlier he had said that it was a work which "dares to compete with Heliodorus." It was to fulfil a programme announced as early as the first part of *Don Quixote* (I, 47), where the Canon of Toledo describes the perfect novel.

> In spite of all the criticisms levied against such books, he found one good thing in them, namely, the opportunity they offered for a good brain to display itself, with a large and spacious field wherein the pen could run without any sort of hindrance. One could describe shipwrecks, storms, duels and battles, while depicting a valiant captain with all the qualities needed, as he shows foresight in divining his enemy's ruses, and an orator's eloquence when persuading or dissuading his soldiers, being prompt in decision and as courageous in awaiting attack as in making it. The author can paint a lamentable tragedy or some unexpectedly cheerful occurrence; a lovely, honest, discreet, circumspect lady; a valiant and courteous Christian gentleman; a farouche barbarian; a courtly, valiant and tactful prince; forming a

"Ocean of Story." From *Cervantes* by William J. Entwistle (Oxford: The Clarendon Press, 1940), pp. 172–82. Copyright 1940 by The Clarendon Press, Oxford. Reprinted by permission of the publisher.

picture of goodness and loyalty in vassals and of greatness and munificence in lords. He can display his knowledge of astrology, cosmography, music, statecraft, and he might even, if he wished, appear as a necromancer. He can put on view Ulysses' wiles, Aeneas' piety, Achilles' valour, Hector's ill-fortune, Sinon's treason, Euryalus' friendship, Alexander's liberality, Caesar's bravery, Trajan's clemency and truthfulness, Zopyrus' faithfulness, Cato's prudence, and in short all those actions that make perfect a hero, whether he concentrate them in an individual or distribute them among many. If this be carried out in a pleasant style and with ingenious inventiveness, steering as closely as possible to the truth, our author would no doubt compose a cloth woven from various lovely threads. Once completed, it would be so perfectly beautiful as to attain the best end proposed for literature, that is, as I have said, to join doctrine to pleasure. The free style of such books allows the author to exploit the epic, lyric, tragic, and comic veins, with all the qualities included in the sweetly pleasing sciences of poetry and oratory; for the Epos can be written as well in prose as in verse.

It has been pointed out[1] that this description corresponds to the praise Alonso López (called El Pinciano) gave to Heliodorus in his dialogues of *Ancient Poetic Philosophy* in 1596. For that critic Virgil and Homer were two figures in a triad which included the Greek novelist, and he specially praised the incognito of the hero and heroine. It is clear that Cervantes' mind was already eager to rival the unapproachable standard of his art as novelist, though it happens that he succeeded not in the *Persiles* but in the *Quixote*. The elevation and variety which he sought to attain were present in *Don Quixote* in the strictly human measure permitted to the novelist, and the attempt to gild the lily in his later work proved his undoing. It suffers indeed from what might be called the exemplary fallacy. The portrait of the perfect prince fails to excite admiration because it is monotonous. Persiles and Sigismunda arouse no interest in themselves or their adventures, and the parade of a rather transparent incognito is merely irritating. The author himself must have tired of their perfection, since he allows them little space in his best chapters, and botches the end of the book to get them married and put away. Still, no doubt, the experiment had to be made to be believed. The epic poets of the age were striving to express the perfect character, and a novelist who believed in the prose epos was bound to test his theory. Had he lived longer he might have agreed that the novel, like tragedy, needs the saving human touch of imperfection.

[1] A. Castro, *El Pensamiento de Cervantes* (Madrid, 1925), p. 44.

The correspondence between Cervantes and Heliodorus may be worked out to any desired number of decimals. Invention required that the plot should be his own, and the principle of imitation required that it should run parallel with the admired model. The incognito of the hero and heroine in each book has a double source: the desire to avoid unwelcome attentions from corsair princes, and convenience in making together a religious pilgrimage. Each heroine is an example of chastity, sometimes under inconvenient conditions. They are both extremely beautiful, and have no other attributes to interest us. The manly beauty of the hero, and his equivocal status as "brother" of his lady-love, exposes him to the importunities of a princess who goes to extreme limits in her suit. The athletic ability of Theagenes is enhanced for Persiles by the annexation of the sports from *Aeneid* V. Each book starts *in medias res* and goes on to a vast recital of past events. The range of the Greek novel is from the Aegean to the extreme south of the known world, and that of the Spanish work is from the unknown north to Spain and Italy, the heroine being in each case a princess of the remotest regions. The first scene is on a wild sea-shore, among islands and robbers. Capture and massacres and escape follow, and then more capture and separation and reunion. To the barbarized Spaniard Antonio corresponds the barbarized Greek Knemon, both being fugitives as the result of crimes of violence. But this parallel can go on for ever, so continual are the coincidences. Whether Cervantes also consulted Achilles Tatius is the more doubtful because of the complete satisfaction he seemed to find in Heliodorus.

In addition to this supreme source, we have seen that Cervantes had in mind the *Aeneid* and reproduced with a difference the fifth book. He drew his northern geography from the spurious travels of the Zeni brothers, to which the date 1380 was wrongfully attached. He acknowledged the debt (IV, 13) in respect of the island of Frislanda. The notion that the northern seas were wholly occupied with islands came from poring over contemporary maps, such as those in Ramusio's volumes. Olaus Magnus gave him some notion of Vikings and sea monsters. As for the customs of their presumable inhabitants, Cervantes obtained his material not from the north but from the west. His barbarians practise the rites and wear the clothing of Garcilaso de la Vega el Inca's American aborigines in the *Royal Commentaries,* published in 1609.

This date, 1609, is therefore to be attached to the opening chapters of the whole work, and it is valid also for the eleventh chapter of the third book, where the expulsion of the Moriscos is considered to be imminent. It is probable that the book was begun in 1609 and at least roughed out. It was far enough advanced in 1612 to be announced for future publication, and in 1615 it lacked only four months of completion. None the less, death prevented the author from perfecting his work, since his last chapters are hurried and infelicitous in the extreme. But while these dates may be looked upon with some confidence, they do not necessarily apply to other parts of the novel. It would seem that Cervantes swept the contents of his note-books into this compendious frame, with the result that the inset novelettes are of all three exemplary styles. Two of them (*Antonio the Barbarian* and *Renato*) refer to the latter years of Charles V, and the mage Soldino (III, 18) is caused to prophesy the battles of Lepanto and Alcacerquibir (1571 and 1578). Despite that indication we are informed that Tasso's *Gerusalemme* has appeared (1584); in short, there is nothing to be obtained by attempting a chronology of these adventures.

Persiles enjoyed some favour in its time, and has always found admirers. Don Luis Fernández-Guerra held that it was a

> treasure of adventures and dramatic situations, of experience and philosophy, of masterly maxims, finished phrases, brilliant idioms, and of descriptions filled with the clearest and most enticing truth.

Azorín has more recently felt the charm of the misty northern seas and the distant islands; he maintains also that the golden Cervantine prose reached its perfection in this book. These critics are concerned with details. They do not answer Mayans' charge that the principal theme is obscured by the episodes; but they invite us to enjoy the narrative as it comes. It is a bolder stroke to call this work, as Professor Farinelli has done, Cervantes' last romantic dream. The word "romantic" has always had a fascination for this scholar, who thereby thrusts on one side the demand for perspective and proportion. It was Cervantes' intention to write a novel on the classical pattern not only of Heliodorus but, at a second remove, of Virgil; but we may admit that it was his pleasure to pour out on paper the varied content of his fancy, without considering sufficiently the unity and texture of the whole. His description of the northern islands corresponded to the prejudices of his age. Spaniards were prepared to accept many things as probable in distant lands which they would not allow in Spain; and it is in accordance with this prejudice that Cervantes' narrative is so firm and credible in the first half of the third book (in which the pilgrims cross from Lisbon to Valencia) but at once loses outline in Perpignan. In the far north anything might be true; but to consider his islands to be charming or his voyage to be an elegant progress, as Azorín does, is to dilute the author's text with too many of the reader's preferences.

The principal action is thin and is botched at the end. The hero and heroine are present throughout, and parts of the first, second, and fourth books are given to their affairs. But they are figures rendered pallid by their aureoles, and all their evolutions are the tritest commonplaces of romance. It is not so much a matter of proportion between the fable and the episodes, but of the insipidity of the fable itself. It is lost in a dim haze, so that only the interpolated episodes stand clearly before us. A similar affliction besets Cervantes' style. It does reach formal perfection in this novel, but it is so often applied to insignificant matter that the effect is hollow and dull.

It is then the inset stories that make the *Persiles*. These are of the utmost variety of theme and style, and are very variously placed in the common frame. The first book contains a group of four: *Antonio the Spanish Barbarian, Rutilio the Italian Dancer, Manuel de Sousa Coutinho or the enamoured Portuguese,* and the history of *Transila or jus primæ noctis*. The first is, for the most part, a realistic sketch based on pundonor, and it may have some autobiographical interest. There is Italian fantasy in the second, together with a copious injection of witchcraft. The third pokes fun at the Portuguese, who alone are capable of dying of love. The fourth is set in Ireland because its inverisimilitude would not permit a nearer approach to Spain. It introduces the spirited Transila who objects to making her bridal bed common property, and it furnishes Cervantes with his Mauricio, an astrologer. The name is Irish, being that of Desmond Fitzmaurice of Munster, but the custom castigated derives from Garcilaso el Inca. In addition the author asks for our interest in lasciviousness as embodied in Rosamunda (the fair Rosamond of Woodstock), and slander personified in Clodio. They live up to their qualities, and each dies as the result of ingrained vice.

The second book is taken up with the love of King Policarpo for Sigismunda and that of Princess Sinforosa for Persiles, thus giving a typically Cervantine tangle. Then follows an immense recital of Persiles' adventures, with somewhat ironical comments by Mauricio, who finds the story long for an episode in an epic plot. It becomes a series of tableaux, since the author seems already to have lost interest in his hero. We hear of a wedding among fisherfolk, an allegorical boat-race, a dream, an unlucky king, a female pirate, and the taming of a modern Bucephalus. Witchcraft and astrology also thicken the soup, and at the end Cervantes throws in the story of *Renato and Eusebia* to show that a trial by battle may not justify the innocent.

It would seem from a passage in the third book (chapter 19) that Cervantes intended his heroes to move in an atmosphere charged with destiny. Hence the various witches: Rutilio's witch, Zenotia, the Jewess Julia. Mauricio makes prognostications by judicial astrology, and Soldino is a clairvoyant. The book opens with a false prophecy, which induces the barbarians to practise human sacrifice. So Persiles moves like Aeneas amid portents and wonders; but Cervantes employs the squalid machinery of omens and wizardry which may have seemed more plausible than that of Olympus in his age, but now unites improbability to nausea. This tendency towards the loathsome supernatural had been typical of the Spanish outlook from the days of Seneca and Lucan, and it was exemplified in Ercilla's *Araucana*, the greatest of Spanish epics and much admired by Cervantes.

To the third book the hero and heroine contribute only movement. We are on firm Cervantine ground so long as the party travels through the Spanish meseta, and the novelettes are numerous and good. Two are romantic: Feliciana de la Voz runs away from home to avoid an unwelcome suitor and Ambrosia Agustina does the same to recover the affections of her errant husband. From Giraldi Cinzio Cervantes obtained the motif of an enemy's magnanimity, when he shows how a noble Portuguese mother protected a suppliant even when she knew him to be her son's murderer. The story of *The Talaveran Wanton* recurs at intervals through the third and fourth books. She is a lively sinner, and her career might have borne the moral that the wages of sin are death, were it not for the princely intervention of Persiles. There is a brilliant sketch of rustic courtship by the Tagus, and an amusing affair of some students detected in obtaining alms under false pretences. On reaching Valencia Cervantes uses his knowledge of the Moorish descents on the exposed coast, with the connivance of local Moriscos.

Entering France midway in the book, the narrative loses this realism. We hear of a vengeful Scottish heroine, Ruperta, who enters a youth's chamber with intent to kill and remains to marry. Reaching Italy before the book closes, we find a country with recognizable sites and characteristics, but more ingenious and romanesque than Spain. It is the land of cunning intrigue and fit for Isabella Castrucho, who feigns demon-possession in order to baffle her father's favourite and be cured by the student of her own choice.

The last book is the weakest. It is devoted to clearing up the ends of the main action and some minor ones, and develops two new themes: that of the duke who falls in love with a portrait, and that of the Roman courtesan Hipólita. The description of her Renaissance elegance and lack of scruple is much more interesting than the use Cervantes has made of the trite Joseph and Zuleika motif.

This then is the work of which its author entertained such high hopes. Its models were the best that ancient epic or romance could provide, and it gave the writer scope to express all he remembered or imagined. A master's hand shaped the narratives and the prose, and many maxims and reflections serve to show his ripe experience of life. But the spectacle of unrelieved virtue in the main persons proves intolerable, and the work falls into fragments. It is then the exemplary novelist who emerges, in this last book as in his first, putting his hand to plots that are lifelike and some that are arbitrary. To the arbitrary he concedes, perhaps, too great a space, prompted by the tolerant yearnings of a green old age. For bad and good alike he devised happy endings, but the author of the third book has the keen sight and sure hand which fashioned *Rinconete* and *The Dogs' Colloquy.*

Note on Translations

Currently *Don Quixote* is available in three good modern translations. The best are those by J. M. Cohen (Penguin Classics) and Walter Starkie (Signet Classics) because their idiom more nearly reproduces Cervantes' flexible grace and their discovery of equivalents is more resourceful. Still, the translation of Samuel Putnam (originally published complete in 1949 by The Viking Press and then somewhat abbreviated in the Viking Portable Library) is in literal accuracy commendable. Useful notes are provided by both the Starkie and the Putnam versions.

Scholarly translations of Cervantes' lesser works are not always easily available or extant in English. The *Complete Works of Cervantes,* unhappily incomplete, were announced under the authoritative editorship of James Fitzmaurice Kelly at the beginning of the century. Actually published were: the *Galatea,* translated by H. H. Oelsner and A. B. Welford; *Don Quixote,* translated by John Ormsby; and the *Exemplary Novels,* translated by N. Maccoll. More recently two selections, nearly coinciding, of the *Exemplary Novels* have been published: *Six Exemplary Novels* (Barron's Educational Series), translated by Harriet de Onís, and *The Deceitful Marriage and Other Exemplary Novels* (Signet Classics), translated by Walter Starkie. Cervantes' most enduring dramatic works, the *Interludes,* have been translated by Edwin Honig (Signet Classics). No adequate modern translation of *The Travails of Persiles and Sigismunda* exists; for the few earlier versions consult *English Translations from the Spanish* by Remigio Ugo Pane (Rutgers University Press, 1944).

It should be noted that in translation titles and names are subjected to different attempts at normalizing or anglicizing. From earliest times the title and name of Don Quixote have been written thus in English, even though Spanish orthography and pronunciation since the seventeenth century have required Don Quijote. Either spelling should be considered correct in English. The first originally represented a sound, roughly *sh,* that was fast disappearing in Cervantes' day and the second represents the modern Spanish pronunciation, a strongly aspirated *h,* which has by regular phonological change taken its place. Differences in the spelling of names may represent either changing Spanish norms or attempts at anglicizing. In any event knowledge and tolerance in such matters should prevail over ignorant snobbery or decree.

Chronology of Important Dates

1547 Miguel de Cervantes Saavedra born the son of Rodrigo de Cervantes and Leonor de Cortinas, fourth in a family of seven. Baptized October 9.

1568–69 Poems of Cervantes published in commemoration of the death of Isabel de Valois, third wife of Philip II, edited by López de Hoyos, thought to be an Erasmist and teacher of Cervantes, though on flimsy grounds.

1569 In Rome, possibly in the service of Cardinal Giulio Acquaviva.

1570 Heroic service on the *Marquesa* at the battle of Lepanto, October 7, won by Don John of Austria, illegitimate son of Charles the Fifth (the First of Spain), against the Turks. In action lost the use of his left hand.

1575 After continued residence in Italy, set sail on the galley *Sol* with his brother Rodrigo. Captured by Turks and taken to Algiers as slave of his captor Dali-Mami, a Greek renegade.

1575–80 Captive in Algiers where he unsuccessfully, though resourcefully and heroically, organized four attempts to escape with his fellow Christian prisoners (cf. *Don Quixote*, I, 39–41).

1577 Rodrigo, ransomed by his family, left for Spain to arrange rescue which failed.

1580 Cervantes ransomed by a Trinitarian Friar, Juan Gil.

1581–87 After secret service in Portugal and Oran, attempted a literary career in Madrid as a dramatist with little success. Liaison with Ana Franca de Rojas, mother of his illegitimate daughter Isabel de Saavedra.

1584 Publishes pastoral novel *La Galatea*. Marries Catalina de Salazar y Palacios, eighteen years his junior.

1587–95 Minor commissary for the Armada and later itinerant collector of supplies mostly in Andalusia. Implicated in interminable legal and financial difficulties concerning the keeping of accounts.

1597   Jailed in Seville for alleged malfeasance.

1599   Daughter Isabel enters service of his sister Magdalena.

1602   Perhaps in prison again for old accounts.

1604   Word of *Don Quixote* begins to circulate; casually and condescendingly mentioned by Lope de Vega. Privilege for Castile granted in Valladolid, September 26.

1605   *Don Quixote* (part one) issued in January with rights sold to the publisher. Threat of pirated editions in Portugal. Second edition issued in Madrid later in the year. Murky scandal explodes in Valladolid suggesting that his sisters and natural daughter were living loosely or carelessly. Cervantes exonerated.

1608   Isabel married well, though under clouded circumstances of subterfuge and rapacity.

1609   Cervantes joins the lay confraternity of Slaves of the Most Holy Sacrament in Madrid and certain members of his family make similar professions.

1612   *Exemplary Novels* published.

1613   Cervantes becomes a member of the Franciscan Tertiaries at Alcalá de Henares and a pensioner of the Count of Lemos.

1614   *Journey to Parnassus* published. The "false Quixote," a spurious continuation of Cervantes's first part, published at Tarragona by the otherwise unknown and perhaps pseudonymous Alonso Fernández de Avellaneda.

1615   The second part of *Don Quixote* published in December. Also published the same year: *Eight Plays and Eight New Interludes, Never Before Performed.*

1616   Cervantes dies on Saturday, April 23, in Madrid, leaving his widow and a friar as executors.

1617   Posthumous publication of *The Travails of Persiles and Sigismunda.*

Notes on the Editor and Contributors

LOWRY NELSON, JR., editor of this volume, teaches Comparative Literature at Yale University. He is the author of *Baroque Lyric Poetry* (1961) and various essays on English and Romance literatures.

GERALD BRENAN is one of the most distinguished and wide-ranging British interpreters of Spanish culture. Besides *The Literature of the Spanish People* (1951, second edition 1953), he has written a remarkable book on the Spanish Civil War, *The Spanish Labyrinth* (1943, second edition 1950) and two fine autobiographical and interpretative books on his Spanish experience, *The Face of Spain* (1950) and *South from Granada* (1957).

HARRY LEVIN, Irving Babbitt Professor of Comparative Literature at Harvard University, has written previously on "*Don Quixote* and *Moby Dick.*" He is widely known for his books on Joyce, Marlowe, *Hamlet,* the French Realists, and two volumes of collected essays.

THOMAS MANN (1875–1955) needs no identification as a novelist. His many essays on literature appear in *Essays of Three Decades* (Alfred A. Knopf, Inc.) and *Essays by Thomas Mann* (Vintage Books).

WYSTEN HUGH AUDEN, the distinguished Anglo-American poet, has written many essays on literary and other subjects. A full representation may be found in *The Dyer's Hand* (1962).

LEO SPITZER (1887–1960) wrote a vast number of essays mostly on Romance literatures and linguistics. A relatively small though representative collection may be found in his book *Linguistics and Literary History* (1948), which contains the greatly expanded version of the essay published in this anthology.

ERICH AUERBACH (1892–1957), who like Spitzer taught in Germany, Turkey, and the United States, published his major work *Mimesis: The Representation of Reality in Western Literature* in 1946 (English translation, 1953). His other important works concern mainly Dante, Vico, and Romance philology.

EDWARD CLAVERLY RILEY, Fellow of Trinity College and Professor of Spanish in the University of Dublin.

CARLOS BLANCO AGUINAGA, author of books on Unamuno and other studies, teaches Spanish literature at the University of California, San Diego.

EDWIN HONIG, who teaches at Brown University, is the author of a study of García Lorca (1944) and a book called *Dark Conceit: The Making of Allegory* (1959). He is also a well-known poet and translator.

WILLIAM J. ENTWISTLE (1895–1952) was Professor of Spanish at Oxford. His interests encompassed Arthurian literature, the Spanish ballad, Cervantes, and Slavic philology.

Selected Bibliography

Reference

Fitzmaurice Kelly, James, *Miguel de Cervantes Saavedra: A Memoir.* Oxford: The Clarendon Press, 1913.

Ford, J. D. M., and Lansing, Ruth, *Cervantes: A Tentative Bibliography of His Works and of the Biographical and Critical Material Concerning Him.* Cambridge: Harvard University Press, 1931.

Grismer, Raymond L., *Cervantes: A Bibliography.* New York: The H. W. Wilson Company, 1946. Volume II: Minneapolis: Burgess-Beckwith, Inc., 1963.

Publications of the Modern Language Association. Annual Bibliography.

Criticism

Avalle-Arce, Juan B., *Deslindes Cervantinos.* Madrid: Edhigar, 1961.

Castro, Américo, *Hacia Cervantes.* Revised edition. Madrid: Taurus, 1960.

Durán, Manuel, *La Ambigüedad en el Quijote.* Xalapa: Universidad Veracruzana, 1960.

Entwistle, William J., *Cervantes.* Oxford: The Clarendon Press, 1940.

Flores, Ángel, and Benardete, M. J., eds., *Cervantes Across the Centuries.* New York: The Dryden Press, 1947.

Frank, Waldo, *Virgin Spain.* New York: Boni and Liveright, 1926. Chapter IX: "The Will of Don Quixote," 191–226.

Gilman, Stephen, *Cervantes y Avellaneda: Estudio de una Imitación.* Mexico: El Colegio de México, 1951.

Hatzfeld, Helmut, *Don Quijote: Forschung und Kritik*. Darmstadt: Wissenschaftliche Buchgesellschaft, 1968. A collection of scholarly and critical essays in German.

Immerwahr, Raymond, "Structural Symmetry in the Episodic Narratives of *Don Quijote*, Part One." *Comparative Literature*, X (1958), 121–35.

Madariaga, Salvador de, *Don Quixote: An Introductory Essay in Psychology*. Oxford: The Clarendon Press, 1935. Paperback revised edition: London: Oxford University Press, 1961.

Monas, Sidney, "The Lion in the Cage: The Quixote of Reality." *Massachusetts Review*, I (1959), 156–75.

Ortega y Gasset, José, *Meditations on Quixote*, trans. Evelyn Rugg and Diego Marín with introduction and notes by Julián Marías. New York: W. W. Norton & Company, Inc. (The Norton Library), 1963. The original Spanish text, *Meditaciones del Quijote*, was first published in 1914.

Predmore, Richard L., *The World of Don Quixote*. Cambridge: Harvard University Press, 1967.

Riley, E. C., *Cervantes's Theory of the Novel*. Oxford: The Clarendon Press, 1962.

Río, Ángel del, "The 'Equívoco' of *Don Quijote*," in *Varieties of Literary Experience: Eighteen Essays in World Literature*, ed. Stanley Burnshaw. New York: New York University Press, 1962. Pp. 215–40.

Swanson, Roy Arthur, "The Humor of Don Quijote." *Romanic Review*, LIV (1963), 161–70.

Unamuno, Miguel de, *The Life of Don Quixote and Sancho According to Miguel de Cervantes Saavedra*, trans. Homer P. Earle. New York and London: Alfred A. Knopf, Inc., 1927. The original was published in 1905.

TWENTIETH CENTURY VIEWS

European Authors

TWENTIETH CENTURY VIEWS

British Authors

TWENTIETH CENTURY VIEWS

American Authors